THE ENCYCLOPEDIA OF
Inventions

THE ENCYCLOPEDIA OF
Inventions

Author

Jessica Snyder Sachs

Franklin Watts
A Division of Scholastic Inc.
New York Toronto London Auckland Sydney
Mexico City New Delhi Hong Kong
Danbury, Connecticut

Photographs ©: Cover (clockwise), NASA; Peter Millward; Musée de l'Air, Paris; Photo Researchers/Nelson Morris; Courtesy of Winifred Latimer Norman; Picture Quest/Elizabeth Simpson/FPG International. American Heritage Library: 23 (l), 30 (tr), Kennedy Galleries, 112 (tr), Metropolitan Museum of Art, 118, Bruce Wrighton, 97 (b); American Museum of Natural History, 21; Analog Devices, Inc., 67; AP/Wide World Photos: 38 (bl), 105 (l); Aretê Archives, 124 (r); Peter Arnold, Inc.: Jacques Jangoux, 99, David Scharf, 86 (r); Art Resource: 43, Bridgeman, 166 (l), British Museum/Werner Forman Archives, 28, Image Select, 143 (c), Erich Lessing, 10, Newark Museum, 112 (tl); AT&T Photo Archives: 37 (r), 38 (tr); Bethlehem Steel, 149 (r); Bibliothèque Nationale, Paris/Bulloz; British Museum, 170 (r); Brown Brothers: 63 (b), 167 (l); Cameramann International Ltd.: 34 (r), 120 (t); Woodfin Camp & Assoc.: John Murmaras, 151 (r), Chuck O'Rear, 71 (t); Caterpillar Tractor Company, 164 (l); Chrysler Corp., 81 (b); Consolidated Edison Company of N. Y., 113 (b); Corbis: Bettmann, 12 (t), 42 (br), 81 (t), 110 (t), 115 (t), 122 (t), 131 (l), 136 (l), 156 (t), 157, 169 (b), Philip James Corwin, 178, Macduff Everton, (all) 55, Charles E. Rotkin, 64, Joseph Sohm/ChromoSohm, 130 (tl), UPI, 165 (l), 176 (bl); Culver Pictures, 175 (r); From Barry Cunliffe's The Oxford Illustrated Prehistory of Europe, 22 (b); Diderot Encyclopedie, 73; Elgin National Watch Company, 162 (tl); Field Museum of Natural History, 62 (l); FPG International: 174 (r), Arthur Tilley, 141 (l), Grant White, 172; Friday Associates International, 63 (t); Goodyear Tire & Rubber Company, 163 (l); The Granger Collection: 11 (l), 15 (r), 36 (l) 41, 69, 77, 92, 113 (t), 117 (b), 125, 127 (t), 129 (l), 131 (r), 155, 166 (r), 167 (r), 175 (bl); Grant Heilman Photography/Larry Lefever, 90 (l); Grolier Archives: 97 (t), 108 (tl); H. Roger-Viollet, 147 (t); Hagens Clock Manor Museum, 162 (tc), www.hpmuseum.com, 9; IBM, 60 (t); The Image Bank/Terry Madison, 8 (l); Israel Sack, Inc., 162 (tr); J. M. Davis Arms & Historical Museum/Jean Miele, 78 (l); John Deere, Co., 108 (tcr); Liaison Agency/Ed Lallo, 164 (r); Library of Congress, 174 (l); Marine Corps Museum Branch/Jean Miele, 78 (r); Regis McKenna, 179; Medical Images/Howard Sochurek, 170 (l); Medichrome/Stock Shop/Patrick L. Pfister, 18; Methodist Hospital, Texas Medical Center, Houston , 46 (r); Metropolitan Museum of Art, Bashford Dean Memorial Collection, Gift of Helen Fahnestock Hubbard in memory of her father, Harris C. Fahnestock, 1929, 58 (b), Gift of the Estate of James Hayen, 1959, 162 (tlc); Musée de l'Air, Paris, 14 (t), 128; Museum of Modern Art Film Stills Archive, 38 (tl); NASA, 129 (r), 138, 139, 158 (t), 181; National Institute of Health, 171 (l); Natural History Museum, London, 134 (t); NCR Corp. Archives, 31 (b); New York Public Library: 115 (b), 180 (r); NOAA, 132 (t); Novosti/Sovfoto, 173; Parke Davis & Company, Detroit, 83 (l); Susan Peterson, 80; Photo Researchers: Brian Brake, 150, Fritz Henle, 130 (bl), Doug Martin, 177, Nelson Morris, 135 (bl), P. Motta, 132 (b), Porterfield-Chickering, 17 (l), Science Photo Library, 83 (r), Matt Meadows, 84 (t), NCSA University of Illinois, 38 (br), Science Source/Alexander Tsiaras, 85; Photofest, 91 (br); Photographie Giraudon, 37 (l); Picture Quest: Tom Campbell/Photo Network, 109, Elizabeth Simpson/FPG International, 51; Pierpont Morgan Library, 11(l); Private Collection, courtesy, Rosenberg & Stieble, 162 (tcr); Radio Times-Hulton Picture Library, 121 (t); Rainbow/Dan McCoy, 84 (b); Sen'Oku Hakkokan (Sumimoto Collection), Kyoto, 149 (l); Smithsonian Institution, 176 (t); L. S. Starrett Co., 130 (r); The Stock Market: Joe Bator, 114, Peter Beck, 151 (l), Ted Horrowitz, 87, Jean Miele, 149, Peter Saloutos, 79 (l); Superstock/Explorer, 36 (r); Thomas A. Edison, Inc., 65; Tom Stack & Assoc./John Feingersh, 98 (b); Transit America, Inc., 168 (t); Prof. Greenwood, University Hospital, Queen's Medical Center, Nottingham, 16 (l); USIS, 104; Xerox Corp., 98 (t).

Every endeavor has been made to obtain permission to use copyrighted material. The publishers would appreciate errors or omissions being brought to their attention.

Visit Franklin Watts on the Internet at
http://publishing.grolier.com

Library of Congress Cataloging-in-Publication Data

Sachs, Jessica Snyder
   The encyclopedia of inventions / by Jessica Snyder Sachs.
     p. cm.
   Includes bibliographical references and index.
   ISBN 0-531-11711-1
   1. Inventions—History—Encyclopedias—Juvenile literature. [1.
Inventions—History—Encyclopedias.] I. Title.

T15 .S23 2001
603—dc21

00-043780

Contents

Preface

THE BATTLE OF NEW ORLEANS, which pitted American soldiers against British troops in January 1815, was a great victory for the young United States. Led by General Andrew Jackson, the Americans inflicted more than two thousand casualties on the British, while suffering only seventy casualties themselves.

Why is this an appropriate story to tell at the beginning of a book about inventions?

Because the Battle of New Orleans was completely unnecessary. A peace treaty ending the War of 1812 had been signed in Europe two weeks earlier. But there was no way to get the news to New Orleans. There were no telegraph wires or telephones, no airplanes or fast ships, no radio or television, no computers or communication satellites. None of those things had yet been invented!

This book relates how all those inventions, and some two hundred others, came to exist: who invented them and why, how they worked, and how they changed the way people live. Some inventions have made it possible to feed the hungry, cure the sick, and bring knowledge and entertainment to millions. And other inventions pose great dangers, giving mankind new powers of destruction, and even the ability to wipe out life on Earth.

Few ideas strike inventors like lightning bolts. Instead, most come about through trial and error, and are the end result of hard work and experimentation by many men and women over long periods of time.

Thomas Edison and the incandescent lamp, or electric light bulb, is a good example of the process. Edison's achievement was the result of decades of experiments by many others in various countries. Other scientists, not Edison, discovered that an electrically heated filament could give off light. Another inventor created the carbon filament. Somebody else first realized that a glowing filament would last longer in a vacuum, and then another person invented a way to create a vacuum. Edison's contribution was an ordinary cotton sewing thread that had been scorched to deposit carbon on its surface. When sealed in an almost airless glass globe and connected to an electric current, it gave off light for two days. Edison patented the device, and is known as the inventor of the light bulb. But work on the idea didn't stop. Others devised major improvements, such as using tungsten for the filament and filling the bulb with nitrogen instead of removing air from it.

The pace of invention has increased with each new century. People born at the beginning of the twentieth century lived to see the introduction of cars and planes, of radio and television, of nuclear weapons and computers. And they saw the eradication of many diseases, incredible advances in food production, and the almost instantaneous dissemination of knowledge and news. Perhaps most amazingly of all, they also witnessed men land on the Moon and walk in outer space.

What will the twenty-first century bring? We can be sure that there will always be innovative men and women, like those mentioned in this book, who will have brilliant ideas and will succeed in bringing them to reality.

ACKNOWLEDGMENTS

Kenneth W. Leish was the editor of this book. It was designed by Peter Millward of Millward and Millward LLC. Jane Carruth did the picture research, with the help of Vicki Bonono. The text was edited by Lawrence T. Lorimer, and copyedited by David Buskus of Northwind Editorial Services. Fenella Saunders was the fact checker. Pauline Sholtys created the index. Lisa Torchiano was the editorial assistant. Technical support was provided by Linda Dillon and Meghan Fiero.

The author, Jessica Snyder Sachs, wishes to thank her daughter, Eva, for her endless interest in who invented what in this world (and why), and her husband, Gary, for tolerating her daily reports over the dinner table.

ABOUT THIS BOOK

More than two hundred inventions, from Abacus to Zipper, are presented in alphabetical order in this encyclopedia. Many of the articles are accompanied by illustrations or diagrams to help the reader understand how the invention worked and how it was used.

When a word in an entry is printed in small capital letters (SPACE SHUTTLE, for example), that means that there is a separate article on that topic elsewhere in the book.

In addition to the entries on individual inventions, the book contains a number of other features:

Overview Articles

Within the A–Z presentations are a dozen longer articles that give an overview of the technological developments in important fields. The article AGRICULTURE, for example, reviews the history of farming from the first primitive plows to today's diesel-powered combines. Cross-references within the article tell the reader which inventions related to agriculture have separate entries in this encyclopedia.

The twelve overview articles are:

Changing World Sidebars

Scattered throughout the book, in chronological order, are eleven sidebars that focus on individual years throughout human history. These sidebars summarize the events and inventions that changed the way people lived in those years. The sidebar on the year 1460, for example, discusses the effects of the printing press and gunpowder.

The eleven Changing World sidebars are:

Inventor Profiles

Six of history's most important inventors are profiled in the encyclopedia. These profiles appear next to the entry for the invention for which the inventor is best known. The profile on Robert Goddard, for example, is found next to the article on Rockets.

The six inventor profiles and the pages on which they may be found are as follows:

Chronology of Inventions

A time line, relating the dates of inventions to important historical events, begins on page 183.

ABACUS

Mathematicians around the world recognize the abacus as the first calculating machine. Used for thousands of years, the device has appeared in various forms in different countries. The most familiar is the Chinese abacus, in use by 800 B.C. and still used throughout Asia and India. It consists of a rectangular frame with several parallel wires. Beads strung on the wires serve as counters, with separate wires representing different place values (1's, 10's, 100's, and so forth). By moving the beads up and down along the wires, an adept user can quickly perform addition, subtraction, multiplication, and division.

The earliest abacus predated the Chinese form. It appears to have been no more than a board marked with lines over which the user moved counters such as pebbles or shells. Babylonian traders may have used such devices as early as 1000 B.C.

Many Asian children learn to operate an abacus in primary school. The best known of the many forms of this instrument is the Chinese *suan p'an*, which has a dividing bar across the frame. Beads above the bar count 5 and those below it count 1.

In a Chinese abacus, each of the five counters below the horizontal divider bar stands for a single decimal unit. A single counter below the bar on the 1's wire represents 1. A single counter below the bar on the 10's wire represents 10, on the 100's wire 100, and so on.

Each counter above the divider bar equals five single decimal units. Therefore a counter above the bar on the 1's wire stands for 5. A counter above the bar on the 10's wire stands for 50, on the 100's wire 500, and so on.

To operate the abacus, counters are moved toward the divider bar. The number 174 is set out in the second example. Think of the number as 100-70-4. The four counters up against the bar on the 1's wire represent the 4. The 70 is represented by one counter from the top of the 10's wire, which stands for 50, plus two counters from underneath the bar on the 10's wire, which represent 10 apiece. The 50 and the two 10's make a total of 70. The 100 is represented by a single counter from below the bar on the 100's wire.

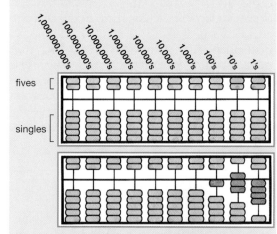

What the Colors Mean

the counters being used

the counters being moved

the counters unused

Simple addition: 823 + 126

First set out 823
3 on the 1's wire
2 on the 10's wire
8 on the 100's wire

Then move in 126
6 on the 1's wire
2 on the 10's wire
1 on the 100's wire

Simple subtraction: 137 − 26

Set up 137
7 on the 1's wire
3 on the 10's wire
1 on the 100's wire

Move away 26
Move away 6 from the 1's wire
Move away 2 from the 10's wire

ADDING MACHINE

The ancestors of the mechanical adding machine were prehistoric counting aids such as the ABACUS. But devices such as the abacus required the user to know how to count. The earliest known machine that added numbers itself was the distance-counting odometer. In the second century A.D., Hero of Alexandria described how such a machine could tick off the distance a carriage traveled by using gears that meshed with one of the vehicle's rotating wheels. The basic principle of this device is still used today in water and gas meters, as well as in bicycle and automobile odometers.

In 1642, the French mathematician Blaise Pascal converted the mechanical gears of the odometer into an adding machine that a clerk could operate. Pascal's invention used a series of interlocking wheels with the numbers 0 to 9 engraved on their rims. In 1671, the German mathematician Gottfried Wilhelm von Leibniz built a similar device that could also multiply by repeat addition.

Such early adding machines were bulky and slow. But for two centuries, their design remained little improved. Then, in 1892, American inventor William Burroughs patented an adding machine more practical for business use. Not only was this new device smaller, quieter, and faster than earlier models, it printed the results of its calculations on a strip of paper. By the dawn of the twentieth century, Burroughs's invention had become a standard office machine. Devices of the same design were popular into the 1960s and 1970s, when they were largely replaced by electronic CALCULATORS.

William Burroughs transformed the awkward adding devices of the 1600s into one of the world's first practical business machines.

ADHESIVES AND ADHESIVE TAPE

Since ancient times, people have been using adhesives to hold materials together. Egyptian carvings dating to 3300 B.C. show workers gluing together wooden planks to make an early form of PLYWOOD. They also used an adhesive of flour paste to make papyrus, an early form of PAPER. Other ancient adhesives included mixtures of egg white, beeswax, and tree resin. In the 1800s, new adhesives were developed. Called cements, they were made of rubber or the chemical mixture pyroxylin. The early 1900s brought synthetic "glues" made of long-chain artificial molecules called polymers.

Among the most familiar adhesives today are pressure-sensitive tapes for masking or mending. An American, Henry Day, patented the first known adhesive tape in 1848, but it never came into common use. The first widely popular use of such tapes began in 1882, with the adhesive bandages invented by German pharmacist Paul Beiersdorf.

So-called Scotch™ tape was invented in 1925 by Richard Drew of the 3M laboratories in St. Paul, Minnesota. The first version of this tape was a strip of mildly sticky, gum-backed paper that painters used to make a sharp edge between different colors. We now know this product as masking tape. In 1930, Drew found a way to apply his colorless, gummy adhesive to the newly invented transparent plastic sheets known as "cellophane." Sales of cellophane tape increased when another 3M employee, John Borden, invented the now-familiar tape dispenser with the built-in roll holder and blade for easy dispensing and cutting.

The next popular advance in adhesive tapes came in 1980 with the introduction of the restickable tapes and papers known as "Post-it™" notes. The weak adhesive used to make these easily removed tapes consists of microscopic bubbles of synthetic resin that burst and glue when pressed. Other modern adhesives include "superglues" made of chemicals called cyanoacrylate esters, which permanently bond a variety of substances (including skin) in seconds.

AEROSOL CONTAINER

Ever wonder how whipped cream gets into its can? In designing the first aerosol containers, inventors asked the reverse question: How can we turn a concentrated liquid into a large spray of mist or foam? U.S. chemist Lyle Goodhue mastered the challenge in 1941 when he designed the aerosol can.

A

Its basic design includes a small valve connected to a strawlike tube that extends down into the can. The can is partly filled with a liquid or powder, then pumped full of a compressed gas. When the valve is opened, pressure moves the mix up the tube. The compressed gas scatters fine particles of the liquid or powder. The gas itself evaporates into the atmosphere.

Most food sprays use carbon dioxide or nitrous oxide as their gas propellants. Nonfood aerosols such as cleaners, pesticides, and hair sprays now employ harmless hydrocarbons. But before 1978, such aerosols commonly used chlorofluorocarbon gas, now known to harm the ozone level of the atmosphere.

AGRICULTURE

The world's first farmers planted their seeds some ten thousand years ago. Their hope was to grow more food than they could gather from the wild. The earliest and simplest farming tools were no more than sticks, used to poke holes or scrape furrows in the earth to prepare it for seeds. Two sticks lashed together at an angle became a hoe. The first PLOW may have been a large, forked branch pulled by two

people while a third person guided its digging end from behind.

But planting, watering, and harvesting by hand was hard, slow work with meager results. Methods had to improve further before farmers could grow more than they needed to feed themselves. An important early advance came some five thousand years ago, when Egyptian farmers fashioned a way to harness their stick plows to oxen. Next, farmers improved their plows with cutting edges made of hardwood, stone, and eventually metal. In the late 1800s, STEAM ENGINES began replacing draft animals as the farmer's main source of power for plowing. Steam engines, in turn, were replaced by the gasoline-powered tractors still used today.

Early farmers planted their fields by simply flinging their seeds across the open ground. This method was wasteful, and farmers had to save too much of their harvest to plant the next year. A tremendous breakthrough came in 1733, when the English inventor Jethro Tull demonstrated an efficient seed-planting machine—a horse-drawn grain drill that plugged seeds into evenly spaced holes in the ground. Since that time, improved seed drills have continued to reduce the amount of seed wasted during planting, enabling farmers to feed still more people.

By harnessing their stick plows to sturdy livestock, the Egyptians became the first farmers to produce more food than they needed to survive.

A

European farming methods of the Middle Ages remained crude and inefficient, with workers performing virtually all work by hand.

To irrigate their crops, early farmers created people-powered WATERWHEELS and bucket PULLEYS to raise water from rivers and lakes and channel it into their fields. Today, many modern farms employ automated water PUMPS connected to miles of pipes and mechanized sprinklers.

Early farmers cut their grains using wooden sickles with sharpened flint edges. Metal blades improved the sickle's efficiency. But harvesting continued to demand legions of seasonal workers. Then, in 1834, the Chicago manufacturer Cyrus McCormick introduced a horse-drawn grain REAPER that would help transform the American prairie into a vast wheat-growing region. McCormick's reaper enabled a small group to harvest acres of wheat quickly and efficiently.

Another piece of farming machinery helped transform the American South before 1800. It was the COTTON GIN, invented by Massachusetts native Eli Whitney in 1793. Whitney's gin mechanized the time-consuming task of removing seeds from cotton by hand. The cotton gin made cotton a profitable crop and encouraged plantation owners to create a vast, slave-based agricultural system.

In the years since, America's farmlands have seen ever larger and faster farming machines. Notable among them was the COMBINE HARVESTER, a machine able to cut, thresh, and bag wheat and other grain crops as it moved across the field. The first combines appeared in the 1880s. Pulled by teams of 24 or more horses and mules, the first practical combines could clear up to 25 acres (10.1 hectares) a day—more acreage than 50 men could cut and thresh by hand. By the early 1900s, combines pulled by steam-powered tractors could clear nearly 35 acres (14 hectares) a day. In the 1930s, gasoline-powered tractors increased the combine's speed to more than 50 acres (20.3 hectares) a day. Today, many American farmers drive enormous diesel-powered combines equipped with lights to work round the clock at a rate of 10 acres (4 hectares) or more an hour.

Even as farming machines were increasing the speed of harvesting, fertilizers were boosting harvest size. Among the first synthetic, or human-made, fertilizers ever developed were the superphosphates invented by English chemist Sir John Bennett Lawes in 1842. Chemical fertilizers such as these, produced cheaply in large quantity, greatly increased yields. Today, the world's farmers use millions of tons of synthetic fertilizer a year, enabling crops to be grown even

McCormick's reaper enabled farmers to harvest an acre of wheat in under an hour—a vast improvement over the twenty hours needed to reap by hand.

A

The horse-drawn combines of the late 1800s weighed up to 15 tons. Such huge machines proved most practical on the wide, flat wheat fields of the Midwest.

on naturally poor or exhausted soil. Unfortunately, excess fertilizer often runs into nearby waterways, polluting drinking water and killing fish.

In 1942, the Swiss chemist Paul Hermann Müller introduced DDT (dichlorodiphenyltrichloroethane), the first widely used synthetic PESTICIDE. DDT killed a variety of crop-destroying insects and helped control such epidemic diseases as malaria. It was followed by other insecticides as well as herbicides and fungicides for killing problem weeds and fungi. The use of pesticides has reduced farm costs and boosted yields in the twentieth century, but many of the chemicals have proven harmful to wildlife and humans. As a result, agricultural scientists continue to look for alternatives that can control crop pests more safely.

In the 1950s and 1960s, plant scientists introduced new strains of wheat and other staple crops that greatly increased crop yields and helped provide for a rapidly growing world population. This "Green Revolution" was only a preview of the genetic engineering that became possible by the turn of the century. New techniques allow plant geneticists to give new plant strains resistance to disease. But there is widespread concern that such genetically altered plants may have unanticipated dangers.

AIR CONDITIONER

Until the mid-1900s, there were few ways to escape the heat and humidity of summer. So hot and sticky was the weather in the nation's capital of Washington, D.C., for example, that Congress was forced to take a long summer recess each year. This all changed with the invention of modern-day air conditioners—machines able to control indoor temperature and humidity.

Modern air-conditioning traces back to ancient times. The ancient Egyptians hung woven mats soaked with water across the entrances to their houses. As the hot desert wind blew through the mats, the water evaporated, cooling the indoor air. Modern devices that use evaporative cooling include cold-water humidifiers, or "swamp coolers." Used for the most part in

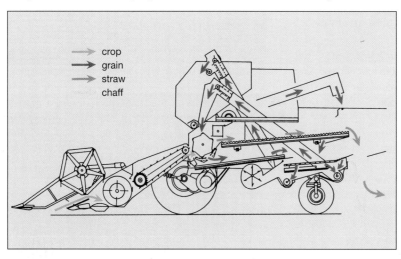

crop
grain
straw
chaff

In a working combine, the crop being harvested travels over a cutter, onto an elevator, and into a threshing cylinder. There, a fan blows away chaff as the grain falls onto a conveyor that carries it to a central tank, from which it is blown into an accompanying truck.

A

How an Air Conditioner Works

This diagram shows how heat and humidity are removed from indoor air by an air conditioner, which then cools the air and blows it back indoors. A simple room air conditioner is shown, but all mechanical air conditioners work the same way.

1. Indoor air is cooled as it passes over an evaporator, a set of coils containing liquid refrigerant. The moisture in the air forms droplets on the coils and trickles outside through a drain hole.

2. Heat from the air causes some of the refrigerant to evaporate, and it passes into the compressor as a vapor.

3. The compressor increases the pressure of the refrigerant vapor, making it hotter. It loses that heat to the outside air, becoming a warm high-pressure liquid in the condenser.

4. The warm liquid refrigerant sprays through the expansion valve back into the evaporator. As it expands, the refrigerant turns into a mixture of cold vapor and cold liquid, and the cycle is ready to begin again.

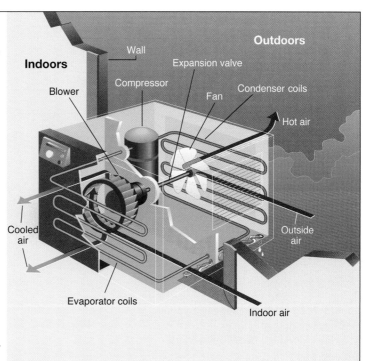

Indoors   Wall   Outdoors

Expansion valve

Compressor   Condenser coils

Blower   Fan

Hot air

Cooled air

Outside air

Evaporator coils   Indoor air

---

arid regions such as the American Southwest, such methods don't work well in humid regions, where both temperature and humidity must be lowered for comfort.

The first effective air-conditioning system for lowering both temperature and humidity was devised in 1902 by the American inventor Willis Carrier. Carrier built his machine for a printing plant that had problems with paper stretching and shrinking whenever humidity levels changed. Carrier's system kept humidity constant by passing the plant's air over a network of small pipes that contained a refrigerated fluid. The cold surface of these pipes cooled the air, and the moisture in the air condensed on the pipes—just as water droplets form on the outside of a glass of ice water.

Carrier's ideas remain the basis of modern air conditioners. A room's warm air is drawn into the air conditioner and passes over a cooling coil that contains a refrigerant fluid with a very low boiling point. The warm air gives up its heat to the refrigerant, and the cool, dehumidified air is blown back into the room. Meanwhile, the refrigerant, vaporized by the hot air, moves to the section of the air conditioner that is outside the house. There the heat is emitted into the air, and the refrigerant is returned to the cooling coil as a liquid.

Carrier began manufacturing his air conditioners in 1915. By the 1930s, they were being installed in public places such as hospitals, movie theaters, offices, and factories. Air conditioners came into widespread home use in the 1950s and 1960s.

AIR PUMP

See PNEUMATIC TOOLS

AIRPLANE

The invention of the airplane has had a greater impact on modern life than has any other twentieth-century invention. It has phenomenally increased the speed of travel, while decreasing the time it takes to receive mail, food, and countless other goods from distant places. It has brought closer contact between the world's peoples, while drastically changing the way they wage war.

At the dawn of the twentieth century, the idea of a practical flying machine remained a dream. Balloons and gliders had proven to be limited, unreliable transports. Then, on December 17, 1903, the American inventors Orville and

A

The Wright brothers made more than 700 successful glider flights over the beach at Kitty Hawk, N.C., before building an engine light enough to power their *Flyer I.* Younger brother Orville was at the controls during the *Flyer's* historic first flight, on December 17, 1903.

Wilbur Wright launched the *Flyer I* at Kitty Hawk, North Carolina, and flew 120 feet (37 meters) in 12 seconds. The Wright brothers' airplane was the world's first powered, controllable, heavier-than-air aircraft. It was powered by a twelve- to sixteen-horsepower engine and propeller designed by the Wrights and Charles Taylor. The craft's structure demonstrated the same basic principles of flight as do today's high-flying jets. Its main wings, or airfoils, the most important lift-providing element of the plane, resembled a box kite, and were located behind a smaller pair of wings, which controlled the plane's climb and descent (the function performed by flaps called elevators on

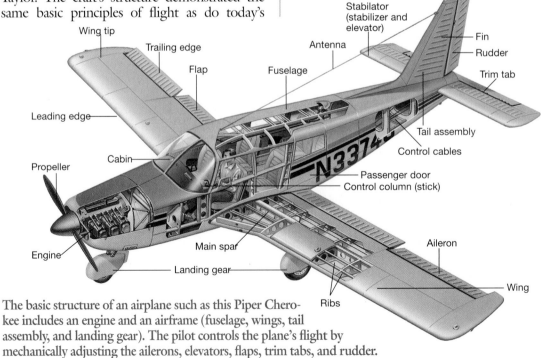

The basic structure of an airplane such as this Piper Cherokee includes an engine and an airframe (fuselage, wings, tail assembly, and landing gear). The pilot controls the plane's flight by mechanically adjusting the ailerons, elevators, flaps, trim tabs, and rudder.

modern-day aircraft tails). With no cockpit, the *Flyer*'s pilot lay in a sort of cradle on the bottom wing.

The first Wright *Flyer* was very tricky to fly. Soon the Wrights and others in America and Europe improved on the design to develop more stable, safer airplanes that were easier to steer and land. Since then, airplane researchers and engineers have made aircraft so reliable that they are the safest way to travel long distances. Most modern airplanes are made of lightweight metal and plastics. They have single rather than double wings, and one to four jet or propeller-type engines. Today's fastest airplanes can attain speeds of more than 4,500 miles (7,242 kilometers) an hour—several times the speed of sound. The highest-flying jets have reached 70 miles (113 kilometers) above Earth.

AIRSHIP

Since ancient times, people have watched smoke waft upward on currents of hot air. But no one thought to harness hot air for transportation until eighteenth-century inventors built the first hot-air balloons. Such balloons weren't really airships, because they couldn't be steered, but only floated along with the wind.

The first inventor to find a way to power and steer a balloon was the Frenchman Henri Giffard. In 1852, he flew over Paris in a hydrogen-filled "dirigible" (meaning "steerable") with a steam-powered propeller and a crude wooden rudder. Later dirigibles had propellers powered by gasoline engines or electric batteries.

The airships of the 1800s looked like fat cigars, beneath which hung a car or gondola for passengers. In 1900, the German inventor Ferdinand von Zeppelin built the first practical rigid airship whose shape was created by an in-

ternal metal frame. More than one hundred such "zeppelins" were built and used for military missions and civilian travel. In 1937, the flammable gas inside the German airship *Hindenburg* caught fire over Lakehurst, New Jersey, killing thirty-six people. The disaster, coupled with advances in airplanes, all but ended the use of dirigibles for air travel.

AMPLIFIER (SOUND)

In a broad sense, an amplifier is a device that increases the power of a force or signal. Levers and gears are examples of mechanical amplifiers. More commonly, an amplifier is an elec-

Lee De Forest (above) invented the triode vacuum tube in 1907. It made it possible to transmit sound over thousands of miles via radio, television, and telephone.

tronic device that magnifies a weak signal into a more powerful one. A familiar example is an audio amplifier that can make a weak radio signal strong enough to rattle windows and to disturb neighbors. Less known but equally important, other amplifiers enable scientists and

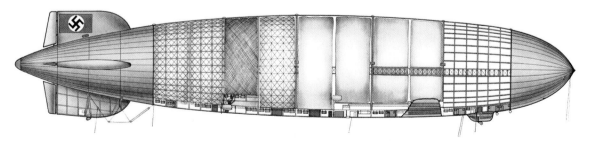

The longest airship ever built, Germany's *Hindenburg* measured 804 feet (245 meters) from nose to tail. Its launch in 1936 marked the climax of travel in lighter-than-air craft. Its fiery destruction a year later signaled their demise.

A

physicians to detect and study small variations in conditions such as temperature, pressure, and chemical concentrations.

All such devices trace back to the work of the American inventor Lee De Forest, who in 1907 invented the audion, or triode, a kind of ELECTRON TUBE. A signal with a small voltage, fed into the tube, emerged with a larger voltage. De Forest's vacuum tube became a key part of early radio, telephone, television, and computer systems.

In 1947, a new kind of amplifier device was discovered—the transistor. Transistors soon replaced vacuum tubes in electronic devices because they required far less power and were much smaller.

ANTIBIOTICS

Technically, most antibiotics are discovered rather than invented. By definition, an antibiotic is a chemical substance produced by one kind of microbe (a minute life form), such as a fungus, to kill another microbe, such as a bacteria. In 1928, the British bacteriologist Sir Alexander Fleming discovered the first antibiotic when he noticed that a spot of mold in a laboratory dish killed surrounding staphylococcus bacteria. The mold was *Penicillium*, from which we get the name penicillin.

The next thirty years witnessed an explosion of new discoveries as researchers began harvesting the microbial world for antibiotic-producing organisms. Only after 1960 did researchers go beyond discovery to improve on nature. They began tinkering with known antibiotics to make them more effective. One early improved antibiotic was ampicillin, which chemists created by attaching hydrogen atoms (acid radicals) to penicillin molecules. More

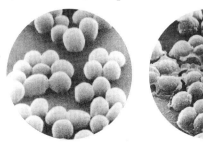

The intact cell walls of *Staphyloccocus* bacteria (left) weaken and collapse (right) after even brief exposure to the antibiotic ampicillin.

than twenty other semisynthetic penicillins have been created. Today, antibiotic discovery and invention continue to proceed hand in hand, as drug researchers scour the natural world for infection-fighting substances and then improve their potency in the laboratory.

AQUA-LUNG

Until the second half of the twentieth century, diving more than a few feet underwater was a complicated, cumbersome, and dangerous affair. Divers needed extensive training to use the deep-sea suits, helmets, and air lines required to breathe below the water's surface.

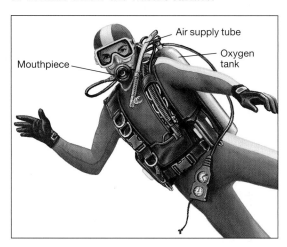

Air supply tube

Oxygen tank

Mouthpiece

When the modern scuba diver inhales, a valve in the mouthpiece opens, allowing air to flow from tanks worn on the diver's back. Exhaled air exits through a separate exhaust valve.

Then, in 1943, the French sea captain Jacques-Yves Cousteau and colleague Émile Gagnan invented the Aqua-Lung, or SCUBA (initials for Self-Contained Underwater Breathing Apparatus). This new piece of equipment freed divers from heavy diving helmets with their air lines connected to air supplies at the surface. For the first time, divers could carry their air supply with them under the sea. They did so with high-pressure air cylinders strapped to their backs.

Breathing with modern scuba gear is as automatic and natural as taking a normal breath. The diver breathes through a special mouthpiece attached to a compressed air tank. An air regulator feeds air to the diver's lungs at ever increasing pressure as his or her depth increases.

Cousteau's Aqua-Lung was first used by Navy divers during World War II. Later, the device created the popular recreational pursuit of scuba diving. Scuba gear is also used by police and fire department diving squads to recover victims of accidents, retrieve submerged evidence, and battle waterfront fires. Scuba is also used in such fields as underwater salvage, mining, construction, and archaeology.

AQUEDUCT

The world's first cities all appeared along rivers and lakes, for then, as now, freshwater was a basic necessity. Only with the building of aqueducts—structures for carrying water over long distances—could large cities grow far from water supplies. Modern aqueducts involve complex systems of canals, tunnels, and pipelines, and typically use pressure to force the water along some or all of the route. Ancient aqueducts were much simpler, relying solely on gravity to move water from source to destination.

The Assyrian king Sennacherib built ingenious aqueducts in the 690s B.C. One gently sloping masonry channel was miles long, using gravity to transport water from a river to the king's distant fields and gardens. Between 300 B.C. and A.D. 100, the Romans built a system of eleven aqueducts to supply Rome with water. They carried 250 million gallons (946.3 million liters) a day.

The Romans built the world's most extensive system of ancient aqueducts, the remnants of which still traverse valleys and gorges in southern Europe. Elevated structures like this used the force of gravity to carry water from the mountains to farms and towns at lower elevations.

ARMOR

At the height of its development in the early 16th century, plate steel armor covered the European warhorse as well as the warrior.

Stone Age warriors used thick hides to protect themselves from the blows of their enemies. By 2000 B.C., Sumerian and Greek warriors had the protection of bronze helmets. Improvements in metal making led to larger pieces of body armor. By the 1300s A.D., European "knights in shining armor" entered battle dressed in full suits of metal armor. Some wore pieces of flexible chain mail, a kind of steel cloth made from linked metal rings. Armor's usefulness in battle came to an end in the 1600s, when guns were invented that could shoot straight through the armor. Today, chain mail is still used in protective gloves worn by butchers. Law-enforcement officers wear "bulletproof vests" made of rugged polymer fibers such as KEVLAR.

ARTIFICIAL ORGANS

Today, thousands of people live active, enriched lives thanks to artificial organs—devices that replace body functions lost through disease or injury to a major organ. Until about 1950, mechanical organ replacements were rather crude and simple—wooden legs, corrective glasses, dentures, and the like. The next decade

A

The air-driven Jarvik-7, originally developed as a permanent heart replacement, is now used as a temporary aid to patients waiting for heart transplants.

brought a burst of creative medical engineering, resulting in the first artificial kidneys, heart-lung machines, cardiac pacemakers and valves, blood-vessel grafts, and artificial joints. Later developments included membrane lungs, implantable eye lenses, artificial tendons and fingers, total joint replacements, and soft-tissue implants for reconstructing faces, ears, and breasts.

The modern era of artificial organs began with the invention of the first artificial kidney, or dialysis machine, in the 1940s by Willem Kolff of the Netherlands. This large, hospital-based device is used to remove poisonous substances from the blood when a patient's own kidneys have failed. Patients with total kidney failure must be connected to a dialysis machine for ten to fifteen hours a week.

Similarly, a heart-lung machine is an outside-of-the-body device used in hospitals. The first practical version was developed in the early 1950s by Philadelphia surgeon John Gibbon. The machine takes over the functions of a patient's heart and lungs—typically during heart surgery.

Next to come were implantable devices such as artificial pacemakers, heart valves, and blood vessels, which a surgeon could place in the body to replace a damaged or diseased part. The biggest challenge in developing such devices has been finding materials that the body will not reject. Great advances came with the invention of human-made materials such as

TEFLON for artificial blood vessels, and polyethylene (*see* POLYESTERS) for artificial joints.

Other artificial organs pioneered during the second half of the twentieth century include an electronically powered artificial larynx, or "voice box" and the cochlear implant—a set of electrodes implanted in the inner ear that can give a sense of hearing to some deaf persons. Burn victims are now being helped with artificial skin made of a mixture of silicon and animal protein fiber. Blood substitutes made of synthetic chemicals have had limited success in patients whose bodies cannot accept natural transfusions.

But even at the end of the twentieth century, medical researchers have yet to achieve what many consider to be the ultimate implantable device—a permanent artificial heart. Designs for such devices exist—most notably the Jarvik-7, a twin-chambered, metal-and-plastic mechanical heart developed by American inventor Robert Jarvik in the 1980s. The first patient to receive a Jarvik heart, in 1982, died after 112 days. Several other patients did little better. After much debate, the U.S. Food and Drug Administration (FDA) in 1990 banned artificial hearts for all but temporary use.

Atom Bomb

See NUCLEAR WEAPONS

Automated Teller Machine

Computer technology revolutionized banking in the second half of the twentieth century. The most visible effect of this revolution was the appearance of automated teller machines (ATMs). Such machines enable customers to withdraw funds or make other transactions at any hour, even when the ATM is far from the bank. The customer uses a magnetized card and a personal identification number (PIN) to access the account. The transaction is instantly logged into the person's account by an electronic connection with the bank's main computers.

Automated tellers are designed to electronically recognize a user by comparing information magnetically stored on the person's bank card with the code number the person enters on the pad. If the card and code match, the information is transmitted to the bank's central computer, which checks the customer's account balance. If sufficient funds are available, an electronic signal activates the ATM's bill-dispensing mechanism, which deals out the correct amount of currency.

Before ATMs, a customer had to visit the bank in person to withdraw money. The first ATMs appeared in Britain in the 1960s, and in the United States and Japan in the 1970s. Customers enjoyed the convenience of quick transactions at odd hours, and banks saved money because they needed fewer tellers. By the late 1990s, ATMs were found worldwide, giving account holders instant access to their cash virtually wherever they traveled.

AUTOMOBILE

An automobile is a vehicle that can move all by itself—it doesn't need an animal or a person to pull or push it.

Nearly three thousand years ago, the Chinese recognized the power of steam, and spec-

ulated about a possible steam-powered vehicle. The first modern example of such a vehicle is a steam-powered gun tractor built by the French military engineer Nicolas-Joseph Cugnot in 1769. Designed to move a large cannon, it traveled very slowly. On a trial run, the tractor crashed, ending its short career.

Then, in 1801, Englishman Richard Trevithick built a steam-powered passenger vehicle, or "horseless carriage." The noisy, smoke-belching machine would go down in history as the first practical use of mechanical power to move a vehicle. But it never proved popular. Soon afterward, American inventor Oliver Evans built a steam-powered dredge (a machine used to clear sediment from waterways). Hoping to generate interest in steam vehicles, Evans drove his invention around Philadelphia for several days. But few people thought his vehicle to be practical.

Still, the work of Trevithick and Evans popularized the idea of steam-powered vehicles in England, and several companies began operating steam-powered passenger coaches. But

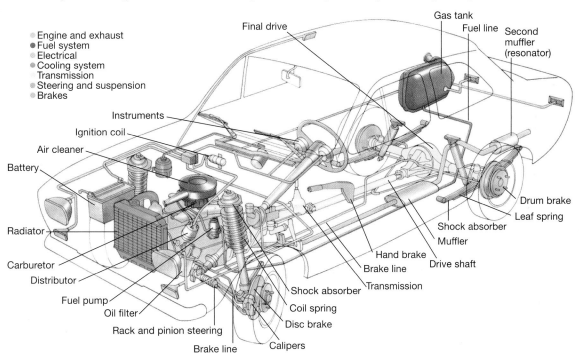

The modern automobile contains seven integrated systems of power and control (see color key above). These basic systems remain much the same no matter the make or model of car. In front-wheel-drive cars, the differential sits on the front-wheel axle and is powered directly by the transmission gears. In rear-drive cars, like that pictured here, a driveshaft transmits power from the front transmission to a differential on the rear-wheel axle.

A

these vehicles were unpopular because they made a lot of noise and damaged roads. The first practical self-propelled steam vehicles were trains, which traveled on tracks built especially for them.

Meanwhile, inventors in the United States and Europe were forging ahead with better designs. A major breakthrough came in 1860 when Belgian-born French inventor Jean-Joseph Étienne Lenoir developed the INTERNAL COMBUSTION ENGINE. Lenoir's simple engine ran on coal gas ignited by an electric spark. It was originally designed to power factory machinery, but a smaller model was used in an experimental road vehicle in 1863.

Advancing on this work in 1876, the German inventor Nikolaus Otto built the direct ancestor of today's car engine. It used the four-stroke principle of operation still found in car engines today: intake, compression, power, and exhaust. Otto's first engine, like Lenoir's, operated on coal gas. But he soon adapted it for use with other fuels, including gasoline. Importantly, Otto's invention was both lighter and more powerful than any previous engines.

Two of the first inventors to exploit this greater power were the Germans Karl Benz and Gottlieb Daimler. Each produced successful motorcars in 1886. Daimler's was noteworthy for its especially light and reliable gas engine. The Benz car was the first to combine motor, body, frame, and wheels into an efficient unit.

In 1895, Charles and Frank Duryea became the first Americans to manufacture and market a successful gasoline-powered car. But it was Henry Ford who made the automobile more than a rich person's toy. In 1914, Ford developed the first assembly line, with workers piecing together cars as the frames moved through the factory on a CONVEYOR. The efficiency of Ford's methods enabled him to reduce the price of his famous Model T, from $850 in 1908 to $290 in 1925, making it affordable for millions.

Since then, many small and large advances have increased the automobile's efficiency and safety. Notable among them was the electric starter, a small electric motor that starts the gasoline engine. Before its invention, a car had to be started with a hand crank. By the 1940s, cars had dramatically changed the way people live. By speeding personal transportation, the automobile has permitted people to live at greater distances from their places of work and has created a new landscape defined by highways. Pollution from car engines remains a major problem at the end of the twentieth century, despite more efficient, less polluting engine designs.

AUTOMOBILE SAFETY RESTRAINTS

A basic law of physics states that a "body," once placed in motion, remains in motion until something stops it. When a car stops suddenly in a collision, drivers and passengers are often thrown forward and then stopped—and badly injured—by the steering wheel or by the windshield. Safety restraints, such as seat belts and air bags, prevent these injuries and have saved many lives.

E.J. Claghorn of the United States patented the first automobile seat belt in 1885, when the auto was still a curiosity. But it wasn't until the 1950s that safety tests with crash dummies convinced major car manufacturers to begin installing lap belts. In 1958, Swedish auto safety engineer Nils Bohlin designed the first combination lap and shoulder belt. Volvo installed Bohlin's "three-point belt" in cars sold in Sweden, and it soon became the industry standard. Today's safety belts feature quick attach-and-release buckles and are made of strong web

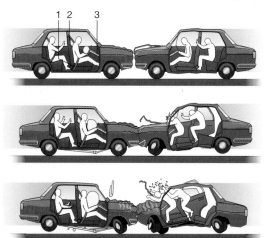

Safety restraints can prevent severe injury and death in a collision. In the car at left, seat belts (1), headrests (2), and air bags (3) check the momentum of driver and passenger, protecting them from the life-threatening injuries suffered by the driver and passenger on the right.

fabric able to withstand six thousand pounds of force. They're bolted directly to a vehicle's underbody and roof rail.

A major drawback of most seat belts is that they don't fit children. In the late 1960s, American carmakers introduced mass-produced child safety seats, and in 1978 Tennessee became the first state to require their use for all small children. By the 1990s, several car manufacturers were offering built-in child seats in family models. The newest versions allow a driver to check at a glance if a child is properly secured: the buckle changes color when it is fastened.

By the 1980s, it became clear that more than half of automobile occupants failed to use safety belts despite their being installed in all cars. This led to the creation of "passive-restraint" systems such as automatic seat belts that closed around passengers when car doors closed. The other major passive-restraint system was the air bag. First introduced in 1972, the front air bag is typically installed in the steering column or the dashboard in front of the driver or passenger. A crash sensor sends an electric signal to an ignition device that triggers an explosion of nitrogen gas within the bag. The bag inflates with great force in less than one-tenth of a second, preventing injury to anyone thrown onto it. The bag collapses again in a little over a second, deflating through small holes in the device's fabric.

By the late 1990s, several carmakers had begun installing these safety features in car doors as well, in order to protect against collisions from the side. But the 1990s also brought the realization that the forceful deployment of an air bag can, in rare instances, seriously injure or even kill a small adult or child. Among the systems under development to solve the problem are electronic sensors to measure each occupant's weight and size and adjust the air bag's force accordingly.

Ax

One of humankind's first tools, the ax remains one of the most important. The earliest axes, crafted half a million years ago, were merely sharpened stones held in the hand. The addition of a handle made of wood or bone, some thirty thousand years ago, made the ax much more powerful.

The stone ax remained the world's primary tool until the first metal blades were forged around 3000 B.C. Iron axes enabled early European peoples to clear vast forests for farming, and remained their chief weapon for battle throughout the Middle Ages (A.D. 500 to 1500). Similarly, in North America, the ax proved to be the European colonists' most valued tool. It reached its pinnacle of power with the forging of all-steel blades in the late 1800s. Today, portable power saws have largely replaced the ax for logging. But it remains among the most important hand tools.

At the end of the Stone Age, early humans transformed the hand ax into an instrument of power with the addition of handles made of bone, horn, or ivory.

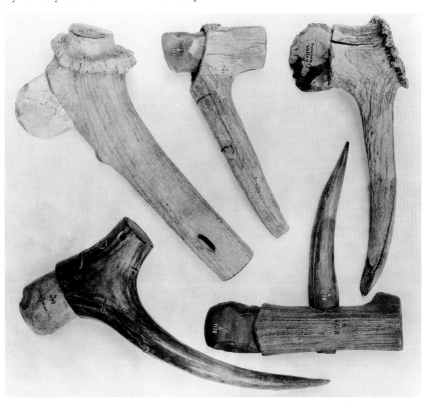

A The Changing World 250,000 B.C.

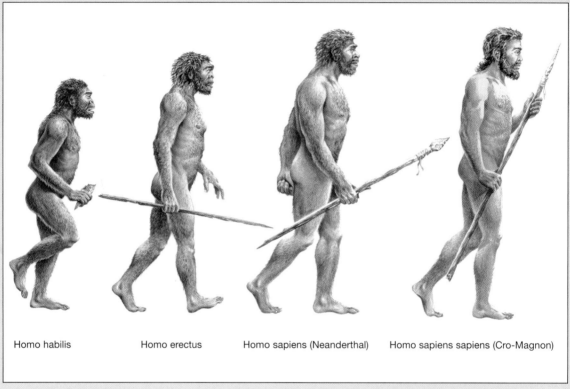

Homo habilis   Homo erectus   Homo sapiens (Neanderthal)   Homo sapiens sapiens (Cro-Magnon)

Benefiting from a larger brain than earlier humans, *Homo habilis* made the first crude tools. With a still-larger brain, *Homo erectus* developed a diversity of tools and used fire. Even more sophisticated toolmaking enabled the Neanderthals and Cro-Magnons to survive the Ice Age.

Early humans have spread throughout Africa, Europe, and Asia, bringing with them simple tools including the hand AX. A remarkably useful, all-purpose device, this sharpened, handheld tool can skin animal hides, cut grain stalks, and, when needed, serve as a deadly weapon.

The river dwellers of the British Isles are showing particular skill in spear manufacturing. Using hand axes, they split hardwood branches into straight shafts, sharpen one end of each shaft to a point, and finally harden the tips with fire. Crude wooden

spears have also been seen in eastern Europe and northern Africa.

Even more advanced in their tool making are the lake dwellers of Bilzingsleben (Germany). They fashion tools from wood, antler, bone, and sharpened stone for piercing and cutting.

Caves remain the shelter of choice throughout Europe. But migrating hunters along the southern European coasts have begun building temporary shelters out of branches and other readily available material. Some are even equipping their hideaways with simple stone hearths for cooking and heat.

A sharpened yew branch served as a multipurpose tool: spear, chisel, drill, and probe.

B

BAKELITE

For many years, the substance known as CELLU-LOID was the only plastic chemists could make. Then, in 1906, the Belgian-American chemist Leo Baekeland produced a new plastic by heating a mixture of two inexpensive chemicals, formaldehyde and phenol. By 1909, he applied for a patent for the new substance under the name Bakelite. Bakelite is a thermosetting plastic—a plastic that hardens when heated. The new substance proved tremendously useful, being resistant to heat, harsh chemicals, and electric current. Bakelite helped establish the early plastics industry and is still used in electrical insulators, adhesives, varnishes, and molding powders.

BARBED WIRE

Illinois farmer Joseph Glidden patented "the wire that fenced the West" in 1874. His inexpensive invention—two strands of wire, twisted together, with sharp metal barbs along their

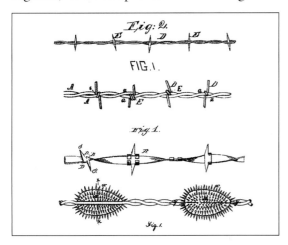

A series of patents chronicled the evolution of barbed wire. They included, from top to bottom: Michael Kelly's "Thorny Fence" (1868), Joseph Glidden's "Winner" (1874), J. Brinkerhoffer's "Ribbon Wire" (1879), and O.O. Phillip's "Solid Cockleburr" (1883).

length—solved the problem of fencing the vast prairies, where lumber for fencing was scarce and expensive. At first, people believed that the flimsy-looking wire would never keep animals from crossing, but, it soon became clear that creatures would avoid its painful barbs. Farmers used the barbed wire to enclose field crops and keep cattle out.

BAROMETER

The single most important weather-forecasting instrument, the barometer measures atmospheric pressure. Its invention in 1643 by the Italian mathematician Evangelista Torricelli stemmed from his realization that air has weight. Torricelli noted that if the open end of

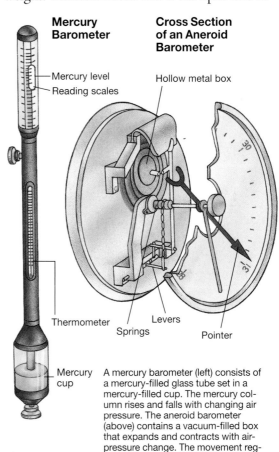

Mercury Barometer

Mercury level
Reading scales

Cross Section of an Aneroid Barometer

Hollow metal box

Thermometer
Springs
Levers
Pointer
Mercury cup

A mercury barometer (left) consists of a mercury-filled glass tube set in a mercury-filled cup. The mercury column rises and falls with changing air pressure. The aneroid barometer (above) contains a vacuum-filled box that expands and contracts with air-pressure change. The movement registers on the rotating pointer.

B

a mercury-filled tube is inverted in a bowl of mercury, the surrounding air pressure will affect the height of the mercury column. Using Torricelli's invention, scientists later learned to predict weather patterns based on changes in local air pressure. A drop in air pressure usually means that bad weather is coming; rising pressure often means clear weather is on the way.

Since air pressure decreases with altitude, barometers called altimeters are used by pilots to tell them how high they are above ground. Altimeters, like most modern barometers, sense air pressure by means of a metallic diaphragm set inside a partial vacuum. This type of "aneroid" barometer was invented by Lucien Vidie of France in 1843. Because of their greater accuracy, mercury barometers similar to Torricelli's are still used in weather stations and scientific laboratories.

BATTERY

When you enjoy music from a portable radio, find your way in the dark with a flashlight, or glance at the time on a digital watch, you're using the most common portable power source known—the battery. Batteries are devices that produce electrical energy, usually by means of a chemical reaction. This reaction takes place in a part of the battery known as the cell, and involves the transfer of electrons (energy-charged particles) between two electrodes in an electrolytic (electron-conducting) material.

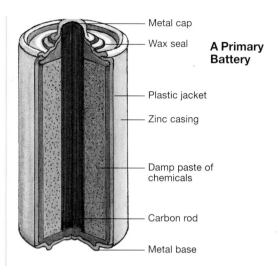

A Primary Battery

- Metal cap
- Wax seal
- Plastic jacket
- Zinc casing
- Damp paste of chemicals
- Carbon rod
- Metal base

Primary batteries such as the common carbon-zinc cell contain ingredients that undergo an irreversible chemical reaction that produces electricity. Such batteries inevitably run down and must be replaced.

When Italian physicist Alessandro Volta invented the battery in 1796, he produced the first nonliving source of continuous electric current. His "voltaic cells" consisted of a stack or pile of electrodes (alternating between one made of tin or zinc and one of copper or silver) separated by a piece of cardboard or leather soaked in a vinegary or salty solution.

Later scientists improved on Volta's design. In 1836, the English chemist John Daniell produced a more reliable, longer-lasting battery using copper and zinc electrodes in sulfuric

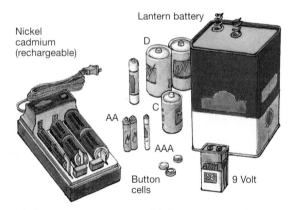

Nickel cadmium (rechargeable)

Lantern battery

D

AA

C

AAA

Button cells

9 Volt

Today, we use a variety of lithium, zinc-carbon, alkaline, and rechargeable nickel-cadmium batteries (above) to power portable devices such as watches, flashlights, toys, and radios. Automobiles get their starting power from so-called "wet" cells such as the lead-acid battery (right).

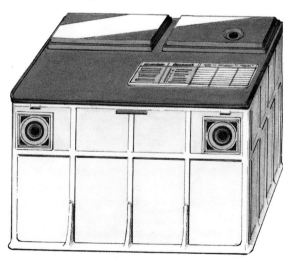

Automobile battery

B

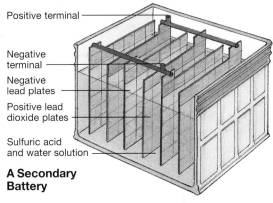

Positive terminal

Negative terminal

Negative lead plates

Positive lead dioxide plates

Sulfuric acid and water solution

A Secondary Battery

Secondary cells such as those in this automobile battery produce electricity via reversible chemical reactions. They can be recharged and used over and over again.

acid. In 1859, the French physicist Gaston Planté invented a practical rechargeable, or storage, battery. It was the forerunner of the modern automobile battery. In 1868, the French engineer Georges Leclanché invented a zinc-carbon battery, using a chemical paste rather than fluids as the electrolyte. It is the ancestor of the dry-cell batteries used today to power flashlights, toys, and small portable machinery. In 1994, Canadian researcher Jeff Dahn used lithium metal to develop a long lasting battery that proved powerful and safe enough to propel electric cars.

BESSEMER CONVERTER

See STEEL

BICYCLE

The first step toward the development of the modern bicycle came in the 1790s, with the French invention *le célerifère*, a rigid wooden two-wheeled contraption that the rider propelled forward by pushing his or her feet against the ground. An important advance came in 1817 when the German baron Karl von Drais devised a steerable front wheel. In 1839, the Scottish blacksmith Kirkpatrick MacMillan added foot pedals. And in 1879, Englishman H. J. Lawson devised a crude version of the chain-and-sprocket driving system used today.

Such early bicycles were often called "bone-shakers" because their iron-rimmed wooden

Built in 1839, the first foot-pedaled bicycle used drive rods to turn the rear wheel (top). The comical-looking pennyfarthing of the 1870s (center) took its name from two British coins—one large and one tiny. By 1900, bicycle makers had developed the basic design still seen in models such as today's mountain bike (bottom).

wheels provided a rough ride. Rubber tires finally arrived in the 1880s, and the first multiple-speed gears soon after. By the 1890s, the demand for bicycles for daily and recreational use had U.S. factories turning out more than a million a year. The years since have seen many style changes. But the bicycle's basic design remains the same; it is still the most efficient means ever invented for harnessing human energy for transportation.

B

BLOOD-PRESSURE GAUGE

See SPHYGMOMANOMETER

BOW AND ARROW

The bow and arrow has long been used as a means of killing animals for food and as a weapon in wartime. When bent, the wooden stave of the bow stores the energy that the archer creates by drawing back its string. Fitted on the string is a long, slender shaft, feathered at one end and pointed at the other. When the string is released, the bow's power propels the

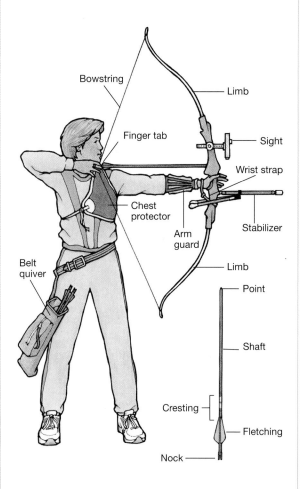

Bowstring
Limb
Finger tab
Sight
Wrist strap
Chest protector
Arm guard
Stabilizer
Belt quiver
Limb
Point
Shaft
Cresting
Fletching
Nock

Today, archery is enjoyed primarily as a sport. New materials have enhanced the accuracy and durability of bows and arrows. For example, the limbs of bows are now made of laminated wood, fiberglass, or a combination of fiberglass and carbon.

arrow through the air, transforming it into a potentially deadly missile.

Early bows were made of wood, and the bowstrings from animal gut or tendons. Arrowheads were made of sharpened stone. By 700 B.C., Assyrian archers were greatly feared for their strong bows and iron-tipped arrows. The bow remained a primary military weapon until the arrival of firearms in the 1400s A.D.

BRAKES

Brakes—devices for slowing and stopping moving objects—were no doubt invented soon after the first vehicles. The earliest known brakes were simple blocks used on horse-drawn wagons. When the driver pushed a lever, the wooden block, or "shoe," pressed against a wheel rim, slowing the wagon.

Then, as today, brakes operated by transforming the energy of motion into another form of energy, usually heat. Typically, they consist of a stationary part (a shoe or pad) that is pressed against a rotating part (a shaft, disk, or drum).

Early automobiles used band brakes, which consisted of a flexible steel band lined with heat-resistant material that pressed against the outside surface of the wheel drums. Until about 1930, all automobile brakes worked mechanically. That is, foot pressure on the brake pedal was directly transferred to the brake shoes by a system of cables. As automobiles became heavier and faster, such mechanical systems required greater and greater effort on the part of the driver. In addition, they produced uneven braking on the wheels.

In 1904, Englishman F.H. Heath invented a hydraulic brake system, in which stepping on the brake pedal activates a series of pistons and cylinders that multiply the force of the driver's foot by forcing hydraulic fluid (usually oil) to exert equal pressure on all four wheels. Hydraulic brakes came into use on cars in the 1930s; they are also used in aircraft.

Even more powerful braking systems were needed to control another important form of modern transportation—the railway train. In 1869, the American manufacturer George Westinghouse patented the automatic air brake. Using compressed air, such brakes press cast-iron shoes directly against the rims of railroad car wheels. Westinghouse's air brakes were among the first power brakes.

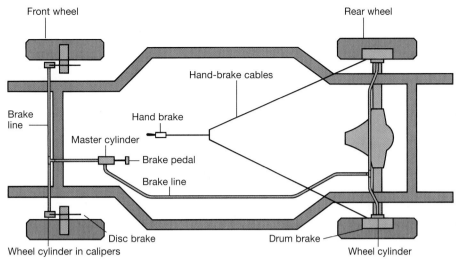

All modern cars have hydraulic brakes that operate on all four wheels. Separate brake lines operate the front and rear brakes so that at least two wheels will have operating brakes if part of the system is damaged. The car shown has disc brakes in front and drum brakes in the rear.

BRIDLE

When humans first rode horses, their one way of controlling the high-spirited beasts was a set of straps attached to a rod of bone or antler inserted into the horse's mouth. This headgear—the bridle—made horses a powerful means of fast travel and of attack in war. Modern-day bridles feature added straps and a metal bit, but they retain their ancient design.

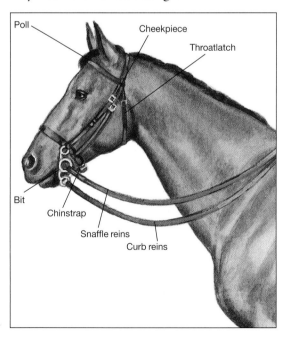

The bridle is the chief means of controlling a horse. It holds the bit, or mouthpiece, in place and allows the rider to direct the animal by turning its head with the reins.

BRONZE

About 3500 B.C., an unknown metalworker in the mountains of southwestern Asia melted a small amount of tin in a larger amount of copper. When the mixture cooled, the result was bronze—an alloy, or metallic mixture. Bronze proved harder and tougher than copper or tin. It could be cast or hammered into complicated shapes. It made stronger and sharper tools and weapons than did stone, wood, or bone. Bronze hoes and spades enabled farmers to grow more food. Bronze weapons enabled Middle Eastern armies to crush their more primitive neighbors and forge the first empires. Bronze making spread from the Middle East to ancient China and later to Europe. It was the most important metal until humans learned to work with iron.

BUTTON

Artisans created button-like disks and knobs as ornaments or jewelry from very early times. At some point, people discovered that buttons could be used as fasteners. The oldest known button that may have been a fastener—a round disk with holes—was found in a peat bog in Denmark and is about three thousand years old. By the 1200s A.D., European nobility were using decorative buttons to fasten their clothes, while common people still used clasps. In the centuries since, buttons have been made from an almost endless variety of materials.

B

The Changing World 3000 B.C.

Civilization is blossoming in Mesopotamia (the river valleys of the Arabian Peninsula), Egypt, and China. Mesopotamians have been using business forms for five hundred years—clay tablets recording trades in the form of slash marks and pictographs. The Egyptians have recently introduced their own methods of record keeping with the invention of the world's first INK (powdered charcoal, water, and vegetable gum) and PAPER (pounded and pressed papyrus reeds).

Such record keeping is becoming increasingly important now that the first strong wooden ships are extending trade across the Mediterranean and beyond. Sea captains from Mesopotamia search for raw materials to supply their

new BRONZE factories. The newly developed metal, made by blending copper with other materials such as tin, has proven far more useful and durable than copper alone. Bronze cutting tools such as axes and knives can be easily sharpened. When dented or bent, they can be reworked into shape without crumbling.

Even outside the cultural centers of Mesopotamia and Egypt, people are using the WHEEL. Both farmers and traders have two-wheeled carts harnessed to oxen. The potter's wheel has made it possible to quickly form large CERAMIC pots—perfect for storing water for drinking and irrigation. With a matching lid, the ceramic pot also makes an ideal food container—impenetrable to pests. Insect-

proof food containers are especially useful for storing the record quantities of grain that farmers are now growing with the help of the newly invented PLOW.

Meanwhile, in other parts of the world, the people of the Americas are producing lots of pottery, though without the help of the pottery wheel. In an important agricultural breakthrough, the cave dwellers of Tehuacán (Mexico) have begun cultivating a large-eared variety of corn that's rapidly becoming a staple of their fast-growing population. To the north, where the dry plains support big game rather than crops, tribes have perfected the art of hunting bison herds using spears and arrows tipped with sharpened flint.

This Sumerian mosaic shows that the wheel was already in wide use by about 2700 B.C. The type of wheel depicted here consists of two wooden planks held together by nailed strips of wood.

CALCULATOR (ELECTRONIC)

The development of the first computers in the 1930s and 1940s hinted at the coming of electronic calculators. But these early computers used bulky vacuum tubes for circuits, making them too large and impractical for office and home use. The first electronic calculators did not appear until the invention of a new kind of electronic switch: the TRANSISTOR. This small but complex semiconductor device could be used to perform many types of computations while storing information in electronic memory. Using transistors made from the semiconducting metal germanium, the French firm Compagnie des Machines Bull produced the first electronic calculator—"Gamma 3"—in 1952. In 1961, the British firm Sunlock Comptometer produced the first model practical enough for office use. And in 1972, Jack Kilby of Texas Instruments developed the first pocket-size calculator using a revolutionary device—the INTEGRATED CIRCUIT—of which he was a coinventor.

CAMERA AND FILM

Centuries before the invention of the first practical camera, artists were using a device called a camera obscura to trace pictures. It was literally a dark room with a tiny hole in one wall. Light coming through the hole produced an upside-down shadow image on the opposite wall.

By the late 1600s, inventors made a smaller camera obscura—a box much like a modern camera. A lens in its hole helped concentrate incoming light. The back of the box was a translucent screen, over which a paper could be placed for tracing images.

In 1727, the German physician Johann Schulze made the discovery that led to photographic film. He found that sunlight would blacken chalk that had been treated with a solution of silver nitrate. (Even today, photographic film is treated with various types of silver compounds.) In 1826, French inventor Joseph Nicéphore Niepce made the first photographs. But instead of film, he used a pewter plate coated with a light-sensitive type of asphalt.

In 1829, Niepce joined forces with the Parisian artist Louis Daguerre to develop the light-sensitive metal plates that became known as daguerreotypes. This early form of photography required an exposure of fifteen minutes or more (this means that the person being photographed had to remain still for fifteen minutes). The resulting image was etched on the metal plate, and no copies could be made.

Then, in 1839, the English scientist William Henry Fox Talbot invented a chemical process that produced a negative image on one piece of paper that could be printed in reverse on a second piece of paper that had been chemically

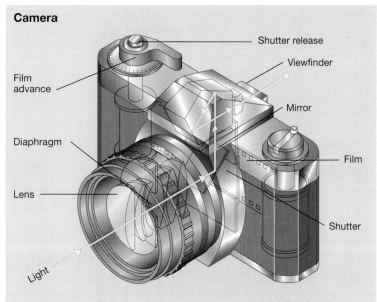

Camera

Shutter release

Viewfinder

Film advance

Mirror

Diaphragm

Film

Lens

Shutter

Light

The modern reflex camera features a hinged mirror that directs light to the viewfinder and away from the film until the photographer presses the shutter release.

C

treated. This negative-positive process became the basis for present-day photographic film.

In the 1880s, American manufacturer George Eastman revolutionized photography by inventing flexible, roll-up film. A few years later, he introduced the first handheld, roll-film camera. Eastman's affordable cameras and their easy-to-develop film popularized photography for both amateur picture takers and professional photographers. Color photography followed in the early 1900s, along with more sensitive films and more sophisticated cameras. In the 1950s, miniaturized electronic parts automated many camera functions, leading to the first fully automatic "point-and-shoot" cameras in the 1970s. Since then, cameras have continued to evolve for special purposes such as X-RAY IMAGING, PHOTOCOPYING, and MOTION PICTURES.

CAN OPENER

Curiously, a span of nearly fifty years separated the invention of the first tin can and the can opener. Not that such a device wasn't needed. The label on a tin of meat taken on an Arctic expedition in 1824 instructed: "Cut round on top near the outer edge with a chisel and hammer." An easier way of opening a can was finally invented in 1858 by American Ezra Warner. Warner patented a device that used a long, can-piercing blade attached to a shorter, rim-clamping blade. Union troops took Warner's can opener into battle during the Civil War, along with their canned rations. Today, similar models are still used in camping kits. The familiar crank-operated can opener, with its cutting wheel, appeared around 1878.

Simple hand-ratchet openers such as this 1874 model made canned food practical for home use.

Electric can openers first became available for use in American homes in 1957.

CANNING

The invention of the vacuum-sealed can around 1800 made it possible to keep many foods for months or years. For the first time, people could enjoy juicy orange slices in winter and unspoiled milk thousands of miles from the nearest cow.

In 1804, French chef Nicolas Appert announced that he could preserve most foods by thoroughly heating them inside airtight glass jars. Six years later, Englishman Peter Durand made the first tin can. His cans were made by hand out of tin-plated iron sheets, which were rolled into cylinders and welded shut with circular top and bottom pieces. Using an improved version of Appert's canning process, Durand showed that the sealed cans could preserve food. His tin cans were used to supply

Canning

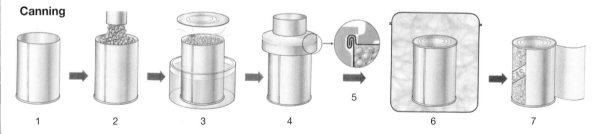

Industrial canning techniques use heat to kill the microorganisms that cause food spoilage. Sterile cans (1) are filled with processed food and liquid (2), then briefly heated in a hot-water bath to drive out remaining air (3) before sealing (4, 5). Large pressure cookers heat the airtight cans to sterilize their contents (6). The nature of the contents (vegetable, fruit, meat, and so forth) determines the temperature and duration of heating needed for full sterilization. Finally, the inspected cans are labeled for sale (7).

food for naval and Arctic expeditions. By the 1830s, canned foods could be bought by ordinary people in Europe.

Most tin cans were made entirely by hand until the invention, in 1866, of a machine for automatically soldering their seams. The early 1900s brought fully automated canning factories with machines that crimped the can parts together with interlocking folds. Manufacturers began using aluminum to make lightweight food and beverage cans in the 1960s.

CARBON PAPER

The boring job of copying documents by hand inspired the invention of carbon paper in 1806. According to patent papers filed by Englishman Ralph Wedgewood on October 7 of that year, the first carbon paper was made by saturating a thin piece of paper in INK, then drying it between sheets of blotting paper. When this "carbon" was placed between two sheets of ordinary paper, the pressure of writing on the top paper caused the ink to transfer from the carbon to the bottom paper. Depending on how hard the writer pressed, he or she could produce several copies by layering the carbons and writing paper. Carbon paper remained an office staple until the 1970s, when the job of copying was taken over by PHOTOCOPIERS and laser printers.

CASH REGISTER

An inescapable fixture of every modern-day store, the cash register traces to the inventiveness of American saloonkeeper James Ritty. In 1879, Ritty left on vacation aboard a transatlantic steamer. Worried that his bartenders were stealing money while he was away, Ritty was inspired by a device in the steamer's engine room. The machine counted the revolutions of the ship's propellers. Ritty wondered if he could design a similar machine to record every cash transaction in his saloon. He did just that when he returned to America.

Ritty's first machine had two rows of numbered keys and a large,

clocklike face with a long hand to track cents and a short hand to record dollars. When keys were pressed to record a sale, a gear turned the "clock" hands to keep a running tally of the day's receipts.

Unable to raise the money needed to manufacture his device, Ritty sold his patent for $1,000 dollars to a businessman who used it to launch the National Cash Register Company (NCR) in 1884. NCR began offering models with electric motors in 1905. Cash registers went electronic with the invention of INTEGRATED CIRCUITS in the 1970s. Today's cash registers feature a range of high-tech functions such as laser-light reading of product bar codes and automatic inventorying of store goods.

CASSETTE (AUDIO)

Sound engineers have been magnetically recording sound and pictures on MAGNETIC TAPE since the 1930s. But recording and replay remained an unwieldy affair for decades, requiring the user to thread tape by hand through the recording or playback machine. The convenient audio- and videotape players we know today came with the development of the cassette. This flattened rectangular case with its prewound tape is designed to be popped into a tape machine without fuss or

Cash-register designs became increasingly elaborate in the first decade of the 20th century.

C

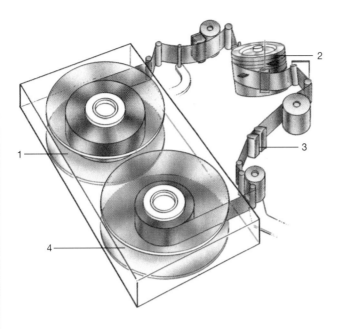

The magnetic tape in a videocassette threads out from the supply reel (1), past the video heads (2) and audio-control heads (3), and onto the take-up reel (4). A variety of shafts and rollers control tension and speed.

tangle. A small opening along the cassette's front edge allows the tape to pass through the machine's record-playback mechanism. Audio-tapes for home use came onto the market in the 1960s, followed by videocassettes in the early 1970s. Today, disc-based recording forms—the audio CD, the video LASER DISC, and others—are reducing the use of cassettes.

CAT SCAN

See X-RAY IMAGING

CATAMARAN

About A.D. 500, Polynesian warriors traveled to the shores of Hawaii aboard amazingly fast, two-hulled ships, each made of two logs connected by a raft of planks. These first catamarans stretched some 70 feet long (about 21 meters) and were powered by many paddlers. Sometime before the year 1000, the Polynesians added sails to their sleek warships and traveled huge distances in the South Pacific. Modern racing catamarans remain among the fastest sailing vessels ever built.

CATAPULT

About 400 B.C., Greek engineers working for the Sicilian tyrant Dionysius invented the world's first artillery weapon—the catapult. The earliest catapults had wooden arms that were drawn back by ropes. Power was generated by twisting the ropes around a winch, and the energy was released by means of a simple trigger. As the wooden arms swung forward, they hurled flaming javelins, rocks, and other large weapons 500 yards (457 meters) or more. Catapults revolutionized warfare by making it possible to break through barricades and once impenetrable walls.

CATHODE TUBE

See ELECTRON TUBE

Catamaran

The catamaran, a twin-hulled sailboat, consists of a central cabin area resting on a pair of stream-lined pontoons. These pleasure craft, among the fastest of sailing vessels, were developed from designs of dugout canoes used by peoples of the Pacific and Indian oceans.

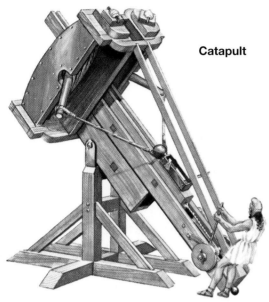

Catapult

The Roman ballista, an early but powerful catapult, was essentially a giant mounted crossbow powered by twin levers held under tension with animal sinew and ropes.

CELLULAR PHONE

In 1983, the Motorola Corporation test-marketed the first cellular mobile telephone service in Chicago. Motorola's wireless "car phones" proved immediately popular with businesspeople eager to make phone calls while driving to and from appointments. Today, small, portable cell phones are used by people in all walks of life.

Conventional phones in homes and businesses are connected to the telephone system by wires and cables. Cell phones use computers and low-power radio transmitters to send and receive calls. To make the system work, areas are divided into geographic "cells," or units, each of which is served by a radio transmitter. As phone users travel from one cell to another, computerized electronic switching systems automatically transfer their calls from transmitter to transmitter. Such a system can serve hundreds of thousands of cell phones. In sparsely populated areas, telephones may connect directly to a satellite.

CELLULOID

A shortage of ivory in the 1860s gave rise to the modern age of plastics. In 1869, while searching for a substitute material for billiard balls, U.S. in-

ventor John Wesley Hyatt combined three parts cellulose nitrate, one part camphor, and a smidgen of dye and alcohol. The result was celluloid—the first plastic to become commercially successful. The most common use of celluloid was for photographic film. For generations, it was the material on which family snapshots and commercial films alike were exposed. Being a close chemical cousin to explosive nitrocellulose, it also proved highly flammable. Indeed, as a photo-film base, it caused several serious fires in movie theaters and hospital X-ray rooms before being replaced by the less flammable cellulose acetate. Today, celluloid is used to make table-tennis balls.

CEMENT AND CONCRETE

The Romans invented cement in the third century B.C. by blending and heating limestone and ash, then grinding the resulting ceramic

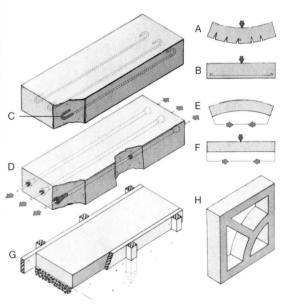

A concrete beam (A) under load pressure (red arrow) may bend and crack. Steel-rod reinforcement (B) takes up the pressure, and hook-bends in the rods (C) provide better bonding between rod and concrete. Prestressed concrete (D) incorporates rods kept under tension (blue arrows) in metal sheathing. A beam held under tension (E) curves slightly until a load (F) is applied. Ordinary concrete (G) is cast over a stone base in a form made of wood planks secured by pegs. Precast concrete blocks (H) are often used as decorative trim.

C

into powder. When this powder is mixed with sand and water, it dries as the strong, stone-like material called concrete. The Romans built some of their most impressive monuments of concrete, including Rome's enormous, domed Pantheon, which is still standing today.

The Romans' method of making cement and concrete was lost for centuries, but was rediscovered in the late 1700s. Today, many large buildings are made of concrete reinforced with metal rods, and there are thousands of miles of concrete highways.

CENTRAL HEATING

Before the 1800s, most buildings were heated by fireplaces and stoves. These room heaters tended to be smoky, inefficient, and uncomfortable. The area near the heat source became overly hot, while distant areas remained cold. A great advance in efficiency and comfort came with the development of central heating. In such a system, warmth from a powerful heat source is transported throughout a building.

The first modern central-heating system used steam to transport warmth. In a basement furnace, a coal fire brought water to a boil in a boiler. The steam that resulted was routed via a system of pipes through the building, bringing warmth to every room. As the steam cooled, it condensed into water and ran back to the boiler to be reheated.

In the 1900s, hot-air central heat became common. In a hot air system, the furnace warms air, which is moved through a series of vents into all the building's rooms.

CERAMICS

Ceramics are useful or ornamental objects made by baking or firing various clay-like minerals at high temperatures. The first ceramics were fired around 10,000 B.C., presumably when Stone Age people discovered, perhaps by accident, that a clay object left in a hot fire became hard.

An engraver cuts an intricate design into a piece of ceramic mounted on a wheel.

For thousands of years, ceramics were made from clay, a natural part of soil in many regions of the world. Over many centuries, people experimented with different mixtures of clay and substances such as carbon, magnesium, and calcium. They also learned to make hotter fires, developing special pottery ovens, or kilns.

In the 600s A.D., Chinese pottery makers began experimenting with a mixture of kaolin

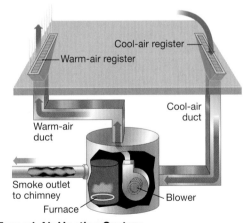

Forced-Air Heating System

Air is heated by a furnace. A blower forces the warm air through a series of ducts into each room. Another set of ducts carries cool air back to the furnace.

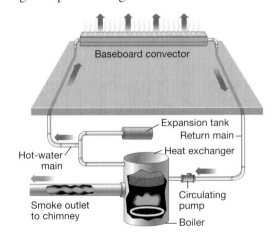

Hot-Water Heating System

Water is heated by a boiler and pumped through pipes to each room, where convectors send out the water's heat. Then the water circulates back to the boiler.

(a white clay) and petuntse (a mineral found in granite). When fired at extreme temperatures of about 2400 degrees Fahrenheit (1300 degrees Celsius), the two compounds fused to produce porcelain, a white, translucent ceramic of great strength and beauty. In the centuries that followed, craftspeople the world over continued to create beautiful new ceramics using new additives including feldspar, bauxite, talc, and silica.

In the twentieth century, chemists began mixing complex chemical compounds and fusing them together at temperatures above 3000 degrees Fahrenheit (1600 degrees Celsius). Combining alumina, silica, and magnesium, for example, produces refractories. These materials are so resistant to high temperatures that they are used to line steelmaking furnaces and to insulate the nose cones of ROCKETS.

CHROMATOGRAPHY

How can chemists find out what chemicals make up a complicated mixture? One of their important tools is chromatography—a method for separating molecules according to their chemical properties by moving them across a special surface.

In 1903, the Russian botanist Mikhail Tswett first discovered the process. Tswett used a device that consisted of an upright tube filled with powdered chalk, through which he poured the juices of green leaves dissolved in alcohol and

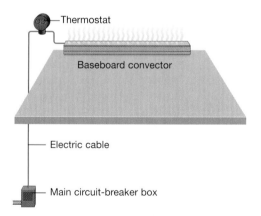

Electric Heating System

Resistance wires radiate heat when electricity is passed through them. The wires can be installed in baseboard convectors, which send out the heat.

In liquid-column chromatography, a glass tube is filled with a specially prepared powdered solid, usually a silica gel or alumina, which is mixed with water or alcohol (called the stationary liquid). The sample to be analyzed is combined with another liquid, one that does not mix with the stationary liquid. When the sample is dropped into the tube, the liquid part of the sample drops to the bottom, but the other components remain near the top and separate into bands, which can be separated and analyzed.

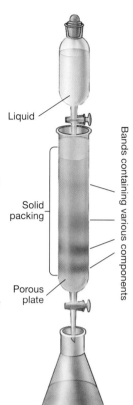

other chemicals. As the dark-green mixture flowed down through the chalk, its components separated into bands of color—orange, green, and yellow—each color representing a different leaf pigment. Tswett called the process chromatography (which means "color writing") because he could see the different bands of color.

Since Tswett's day, scientists have developed many other forms of chromatography, including paper chromatography, invented in 1944; gas chromatography, 1952; and thin-layer chromatography, 1958.

CHRONOMETER

Since ancient times, mariners have known how to determine latitude (north-south position) by the position of the Sun or stars. But determination of longitude (east-west position) remained a problem. In 1714, the British government offered a huge prize to anyone who could solve this problem. British clock maker John Harrison won the award in 1765 after working on the challenge for some thirty-five years. Harrison knew that sailors could determine their longitude if they had a clock that kept highly accurate time despite ship movements and changing weather. They could compare local time (determined by the Sun) to that of the clock, which was set to the time at a known location (Greenwich, England). Harrison called his special clock a chronometer. It was accurate to about one-tenth of a second per day.

The chronometer's great accuracy stemmed from three inventions: a balance that compensated for the effect of temperature changes on the clock spring, a lever that maintained steady power as the clock spring unwound, and a device that kept the clock running even while it was being wound. By the beginning of the 1800s, many ships were equipped with chronometers, allowing them to sail more safely because they knew just where they were.

This early version of John Harrison's chronometer proved accurate enough to enable navigators to determine longitude in the open ocean for the first time.

COMBINE HARVESTER

The combine harvester stands among farming's greatest inventions; it is credited with turning the vast American Great Plains into a sea of amber grain. As its name suggests, this machine combines two complicated tasks—harvesting a grain crop and threshing it (separating the grain from the plant stalk). In a typical modern combine, a cutter bar cuts the grain, and a rotating reel pushes the grain into a threshing system, where the grain is separated from the straw. A large fan blows away the unusable chaff, and a spinning blade scatters the straw back across the field. Meanwhile, sieves separate and clean the grain, and a small elevator lifts it into a hopper.

In the late 1880s, a team of mules pulled the first combine harvester across a California grainfield. The 1920s brought motorized combines pulled by tractors. Self-propelled combines followed in the 1930s.

COMMUNICATION

People have been sharing information by means of pictures, sounds, and symbols for thousands of years. Stone Age wanderers left hunting records drawn on cave walls. Tribal people sent messages from village to village with drumbeats and smoke signals. From these simple beginnings, humans have extended the reach of their ideas with more sophisticated devices and machines. These inventions have shrunk our world into a "global village" that now shares a common culture through mass communication.

Prehistoric wanderers left paintings of horses and cattle in caves near Lascaux, France.

The invention of writing some five thousand years ago began the evolution of writing tools that continues today. The first writing system arose in Mesopotamia, where merchants recorded their business dealings with a series of slash marks and picture words pressed into damp clay tablets. When the tablets were dried in the sun, they provided a permanent record. Five hundred years later, the Egyptians created PAPER and INK. The paper was made out of pounded papyrus reeds; the ink, out of soot and water mixed with vegetable gum. The Egyptians applied their ink to paper using simple brushes and pens made by fraying or sharpening plant stems. About the same time, the Chinese used bamboo, silk, and linen as a writing surface. From powdered charcoal and glue, they also made an indelible ink.

Before 1100 B.C., the Phoenicians, a people living in the eastern Mediterranean, created an early alphabet, in which symbols represented

The early Phoenician alphabet consisted of 22 symbols representing different consonant sounds.

sounds rather than objects. The Greeks adapted the Phoenician script to create the first complete alphabet, which is still in use. Our alphabet comes from the ancient Romans, who refined the Greek writing system.

Books—a collection of flat pages held between covers—were invented in Europe during the first century A.D. But they remained rare until the PRINTING PRESS overcame the need to copy every manuscript by hand. The Chinese created the first presses in the 800s by carving words backward on blocks of wood. They made copies by inking the blocks, covering them with paper, and pressing down.

The German goldsmith Johann Gutenberg revolutionized printing in 1455 with his invention of movable type. Gutenberg made reusable metal letters that could be used to print one page, then rearranged to print another. For the first time, books and flyers could be printed cheaply enough so that individuals could own them. The written word began to spread ideas across Europe and the world.

People have long known that sound travels faster than the speediest messenger. Since prehistoric times, people have blown horns, beat drums, and rung bells to announce important events. With the discovery of electric current in the 1800s, inventors saw that it might be used to send sound messages. The first practical system was developed by Samuel F.B. Morse, who in 1844 used his famous TELEGRAPH code—a series of long and short electrical buzzes—to spell out an electric message along a wire from Baltimore to Washington, D.C. By 1866, underwater telegraph cables linked North America to Europe. Messages now traveled across (actually under) the Atlantic in seconds.

The next step was to make electricity carry the human voice. Alexander Graham Bell did so in 1876 with the TELEPHONE. His invention worked by transforming sound waves into an electrical current that traveled over a wire. On the other end, a receiver transformed the current back into sound. Within ten years, many American cities had telephone service, and long-distance lines were gradually established.

Bell's telephone revolutionized communication, enabling the human voice to travel long distances for the first time.

Meanwhile, the Italian inventor Guglielmo Marconi revolutionized long-distance communication in 1895 with his invention of RADIO transmission. Marconi's "wireless" employed a transmitter that sent electromagnetic waves through the air. A receiver could catch the waves and transform them back into sound. The earliest radios were little more than wireless telegraphs used primarily for ship-to-ship communication. After Lee De Forest developed an ELECTRON TUBE that could amplify radio signals, the radio became a medium for voice and music. By the 1920s, radios were delivering live entertainment and news to millions of homes.

Meanwhile, new technology was creating a new excitement about images. American tourists brought back the first souvenir photographs—called daguerreotypes—from Europe in the 1840s. The technique, invented by Frenchmen Louis Jacques Daguerre and Joseph Niepce, required the subject to remain still for fifteen minutes or longer. But improved processes soon led

The French film pioneer Georges Méliès humorously combined live actors and animation in *A Trip to the Moon* (1902).

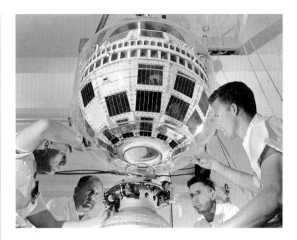

Launched into orbit in 1962, the 170-pound (77.1-kilogram), solar-powered *Telstar 1* satellite relayed television signals beamed into space from Earth.

to more practical CAMERAS, and by the 1890s, photographs were appearing in America's newspapers. On the heels of still photography came Thomas Edison's invention of the first MOTION-PICTURE camera—the Kinetograph—in 1891. By the turn of the century, movie houses were presenting silent newsreels and short-story films.

Then, in the 1930s, the first electronic televisions flickered into action in the laboratories of Britain and the United States. By the 1950s, a majority of households had television, and families were spending hours each day watching it.

New communications revolutionized even world affairs. On January 8, 1815, American troops defeated the British in the bloody Battle of New Orleans. Neither side knew that their countries had signed a peace treaty in Europe two weeks earlier. A hundred years later, news of World War I reached cities all around the world by telegraph in minutes.

In 1962, AT&T Corporation launched *Telstar 1*, the world's first communications SATELLITE. Soon American families could watch live, televised coverage of events in London or Paris. Today's communications satellites receive and transmit signals carrying television and radio broadcasts, telephone conversations, fax transmittals, and computer data to and from more than 130 nations.

Since the early 1990s, the world has also been linked by FIBER OPTIC cables. Within each cable are thousands of hair-thin fibers, and each fiber can carry thousands of telephone conversations and modem transmissions on a single slender beam of laser light.

The most recent leap forward in communications involves COMPUTERS in offices and homes. Now linked in the global computer

By the 1950s, television had become an American family pastime.

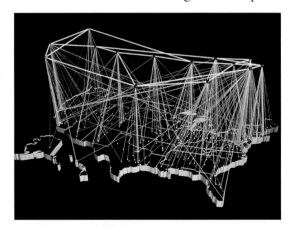

A computer simulation tracks the volume of data traveling over a national computer network.

network known as the INTERNET, people around the world can exchange electronic messages (e-mail), find information, and buy and sell goods in seconds.

COMPACT DISC AND RECORDER

See LASER DISC AND RECORDER

COMPASS

At least three thousand years ago, the Chinese discovered that a magnetized, freely swinging needle aligns itself north to south. At first, this was considered a magical occurrence. But by A.D. 200, the Chinese had devised a magnetic compass to identify north and south. By 1200, sailors in the Mediterranean were using compasses for navigation. The sailors inserted a magnetized needle through a straw, which they floated in a bowl of water. Later compassmakers set the needle on a pivot.

Today, we know that compass needles point to the magnetic poles, which lie near the planet's true, or geographic, poles. Because metal ships and airplanes exert their own magnetism, most modern-day pilots employ a nonmagnetic type of compass: the gyrocompass. (*See* GYROSCOPE.)

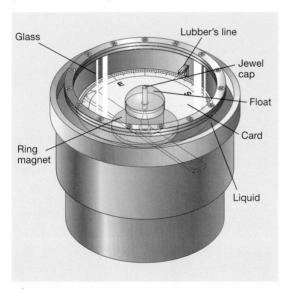

The modern ship's compass consists of a liquid-filled bowl with a floating card marked in degrees and a reference pointer, or "lubber's line," fixed in line with the ship's bow.

COMPUTER

In the 1830s, the English mathematician Charles Babbage became the first person to envision a true computer—a machine that performs calculations and processes information according to a prescribed sequence of operations (now called a program).

Babbage's plans for an "Analytical Engine" described a machine that performed instructions fed to it on punched cards and had a memory unit to store numbers. He began building a working model in 1832, but never finished it. The engineering tools and power sources of Babbage's time were not advanced enough to make the concept work.

Decades later in 1890, American statistician Herman Hollerith built an important ancestor of electronic computers to help tabulate the 1890 U.S. census. Hollerith's invention decoded information about a person's age, occupation, birthplace, and so forth, from holes the census-taker punched in cards. The machine was driven by electricity, and it was used for censuses in many countries.

For forty years after the 1890 census, other tabulating devices were built, but they used mechanical parts. Such machinery was slow and prone to breakdown. Then, in the 1930s, American mathematician Howard Aiken developed a way to use ELECTRON TUBES to perform many of a computer's mechanical functions. His huge computer, completed in 1944, was the first machine able to perform sequences of operations without human intervention.

A demand for higher-speed computers came during World War II, when they were needed to control sophisticated new weapons systems such as guided missiles. In response, American engineers John Eckert and John Mauchly built the first general-purpose, electronic digital computer. Their ENIAC (Electrical Numerical Integrator and Computer) was an 18,000-square foot (1672.3-square meter) giant. It required huge amounts of power and broke down often, but ENIAC was more than a thousand times faster than its electro mechanical predecessors.

The invention of TRANSISTORS in the 1950s revolutionized computer technology. These small devices replaced electron tubes, which required much more energy and burned out quickly. Within a few years, computers went

C

from the size of an entire room to that of a small refrigerator.

In the 1960s, the development of the tiny chips known as INTEGRATED CIRCUITS further shrank computers even as it speeded their function and expanded their memory and power.

Since then, computers have continued to shrink in size, while advancing in memory capacity and speed. In 1998, a U.S. Department of Energy supercomputer named Blue Pacific could calculate at the world-record speed of 3.9 trillion operations per second.

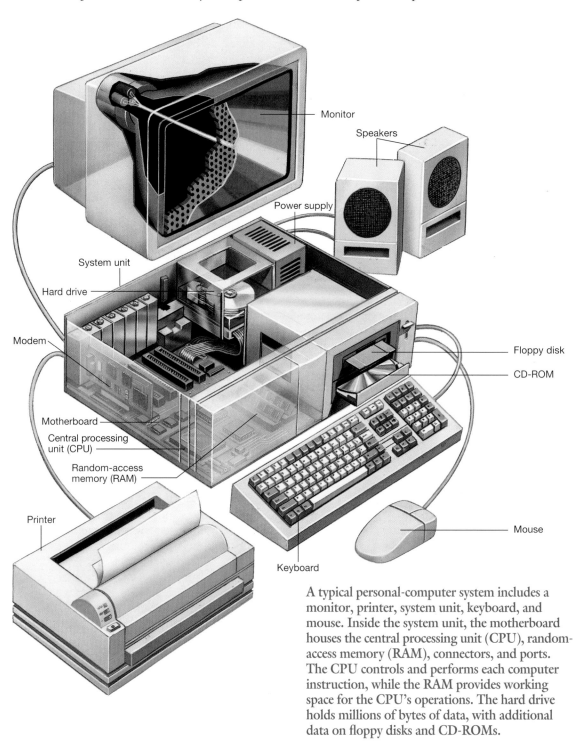

A typical personal-computer system includes a monitor, printer, system unit, keyboard, and mouse. Inside the system unit, the motherboard houses the central processing unit (CPU), random-access memory (RAM), connectors, and ports. The CPU controls and performs each computer instruction, while the RAM provides working space for the CPU's operations. The hard drive holds millions of bytes of data, with additional data on floppy disks and CD-ROMs.

CONVEYOR

The conveyor has become a modern symbol for mass production. Conveyors exist in many forms, depending on their intended use. But in essence, all consist of a mechanized device that moves materials over a fixed path, typically with belts and rollers.

One early automated factory—a 1785 flour mill—employed belt conveyors, bucket conveyors, and screw conveyors to move grain and flour continuously through the manufacturing process. Henry Ford used conveyors to create a moving assembly line in 1913. Today, conveyors are used in nearly every phase of industrial production, greatly reducing the high cost of handling materials. Familiar examples range from automotive assembly lines large enough to hold entire car frames to the small rubber belts used to speed groceries through a supermarket checkout stand.

CORKSCREW

In the 1600s, winemakers in southern Europe began bottling wines in long, thin bottles. To seal the wine in—and to keep out the air—they used the waterproof bark of the Mediterranean cork oak. But it was not until the end of the 1600s that someone invented a device able to neatly and easily remove the cork from the bottle.

No one knows who hammered out the first corkscrew. Like the simplest corkscrews today, it consisted of a pointed metal spiral that was screwed into the cork, and a simple handle for pulling the cork out. In 1795, the Englishman Samuel Henshall invented the popular screw-and-nut corkscrew. Henshall's device greatly eased the job of pulling out the cork with two sets of simple GEARS, one on each side of the screw's handle. Depressing an attached set of levers advances the gears, slipping the cork out of the bottleneck.

COTTON GIN

The cotton gin (short for "engine") is credited with ensuring the growth of both slavery and the American textile industry.

In the late 1700s, the only kind of cotton successfully grown in America was a variety in

The simple design of Eli Whitney's original cotton gin proved so efficient that it remains the basis of modern-day cotton-processing machines.

which the seeds were extremely hard to remove. A picker could clean only about a pound of this short-fiber cotton a day. American cotton growers realized they needed a fast, inexpensive method for cleaning their cotton before they could compete on the world market. The inventor Eli Whitney answered their prayers with his creation of the cotton gin in 1793. The machine featured a revolving cylinder with stiff wire hooks and a slotted metal plate. Turned by a hand crank, the gin cleaned almost ten pounds of cotton a day. Using horse- or waterpower to turn the crank increased production another five times over. Within a few years, cotton plantations were flourishing across the South, creating a demand for slaves to tend ever increasing acreage, as well as supplying the raw material for textile mills in Europe and New England.

Whitney's basic design was so simple and efficient that it is still used in modern-day cotton gins that process 500 pounds (226.8 kilograms) of cotton every 6 to 8 minutes.

CRANE

The crane in its many forms is a hoisting machine that can shift heavy objects horizontally, or side to side, as well as lift them. Modern construction depends greatly on cranes, the largest of which can lift a 3,000-ton load. The essential parts of a crane include a boom, draw works, power unit, wire ropes, sheaves, and hooks. Cranes may be mounted on crawler

C

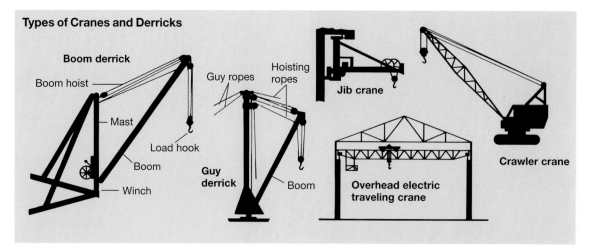

Types of Cranes and Derricks

Boom derrick

Boom hoist

Mast

Load hook

Boom

Winch

Guy ropes

Hoisting ropes

Guy derrick

Boom

Jib crane

Overhead electric traveling crane

Crawler crane

tracks, truck bodies, or self-propelled motor beds.

Some believe that the ancient Egyptians must have used cranes to construct their pyramids four thousand years ago. But the first definite reference to such a machine dates to the 100s B.C., when the Greek historian Polybius wrote of cranes designed by the inventor Archimedes. Ironically, these early cranes were used not for construction, but to drop heavy stones on enemy ships approaching land.

CRANK

One of the earliest machines, the crank is second only to the wheel as the most important motion-transmitting device. The simplest crank is a shaft bent at one end to make a handle, which can turn the shaft.

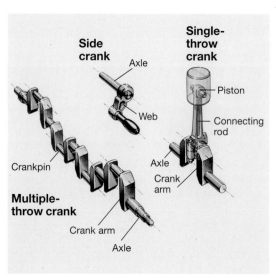

Side crank

Axle

Web

Single-throw crank

Piston

Connecting rod

Axle

Crank arm

Crankpin

Multiple-throw crank

Crank arm

Axle

The crank's importance lies in its ability to convert linear to rotary motion, and vice versa. In a car engine, for example, a single-throw crank changes the up-and-down motion of pistons into the spinning of a wheel.

CROSSBOW

The crossbow was a bow and arrow made more powerful. A heavy bow was mounted on a stock, and the string was drawn back with a crank and hooked in the ready position. The weapon was aimed and fired much like a modern-day rifle, with the squeeze of a trigger. The French were the first to make wide use of the crossbow, about 1050. Improved versions in the 1400s could penetrate a knight's armor. But the weapon was difficult to transport and hard to shoot accurately.

A French soldier of the 1400s readies a crossbow by placing his foot in the stirrup while winding up the strings with a crank and pulleys.

CYCLOTRON

See PARTICLE ACCELERATOR

The Changing World 300 B.C.

C

A mosaic at Pompeii, Italy, depicts Alexander the Great in battle. He carries a spear with a metal point.

War, war, and more war. Since the death of Alexander the Great twenty-three years ago, his vast empire, which reached from Greece to India, has disintegrated. Over half a dozen would-be kings now wage bloody conflict throughout the Mediterranean and Near East, and their armies are wielding ever more terrible weapons.

No fortress can withstand the mighty CATAPULTS with their ammunition of flaming javelins and wall-crushing boulders. Even hand-to-hand combat is undergoing a revolution with STEEL swords. In the hands of a good soldier, a steel blade can literally shatter an iron weapon.

But even relentless warfare cannot stop the advance of civilization. Among the most impressive of technical achievements has been the completion of the Appian Way. The enterprising Romans have built this vast highway between Rome and Capua—a distance of 132 miles (212 kilometers)—in only ten years. Laid on a hard, smooth bed of stone and rubble, the surface is concrete, an artificial stone made from CEMENT.

Meanwhile, the Phoenicians, the great merchant-sailors of the eastern Mediterranean, have expanded the range of their large ocean-worthy vessels. Venturing out into the Atlantic Ocean, they are exploring the west coast of Africa in search of gold and silver. Their travels remain unmatched, except by a Greek geographer-astronomer named Pytheas, who claims to have sailed so far into the frigid northern Atlantic that he encountered islands made of ice.

In Asia, the Chinese have become adept iron-workers. Among their most important inventions is the STOVE, which they use for heating their homes and for firing many new kinds of CERAMICS. In the western hemisphere, the Zapotec people of Monte Albán (in southern Mexico) have invented a writing system and a calendar.

DISHWASHER

In 1886, Josephine Cochrane, a wealthy woman in Illinois, developed the first practical dishwasher. Cochrane's motivation, surprisingly enough, was not convenience. She had servants to do her housework. Rather, she was unhappy because her valuable dishes got broken or chipped when servants washed them.

Cochrane measured her dishes and drew up plans for a large metal rack with wire compartments for securely holding glasses, saucers, and plates. The rack fit around a wheel, which rested over a large copper boiler. When the wheel was turned by hand, hot, soapy water squirted up from the boiler, cascading down over the dishes.

Word of Cochrane's dishwashing machine quickly spread, and she began receiving orders from restaurants and hotels as well as from wealthy friends who had similar problems with dish breakage. Cochrane patented her invention in 1886, and set up a company to manufacture the industrial-size machines. Later, the dishwasher was fitted with an ELECTRIC MOTOR, and in 1914, her company began marketing smaller models for use in homes.

Cochrane's company, later renamed Kitchen-Aid, finally entered the home market in a big way in the 1950s, a decade when American women began spending more time outside the home. Today, many homes have automatic dishwashers. Some have electronic sensors that can tell when dishes are clean.

DNA FINGERPRINTING

See POLYMERASE CHAIN REACTION

DYNAMITE

In 1846, the Italian chemist Ascanio Sobrero created the first modern explosive, nitroglycerin. Unfortunately, nitroglycerin proved as hazardous as it was powerful—anything bumping against it could trigger an explosion. Then, in 1867, the Swedish chemist Alfred Nobel patented a way to pack nitroglycerin into sticks made of absorbent material that cushioned the explosive from shocks. Nobel called his invention dynamite. Safe to handle and easily detonated with a fuse, dynamite was safer and more powerful than the blasting powders then used in mining and construction.

Nobel hoped that the power of dynamite as a weapon would discourage nations from going to war. But he was horrified when his invention was used to make war more terrible. He established a series of international prizes to reward achievements in science and literature and for promoting peace in the world. The Nobel prizes are still awarded each year.

ELECTRIC EYE

See PHOTOELECTRIC CELL

ELECTRIC GENERATOR

In 1831, English chemist and physicist Michael Faraday showed that magnets could be used to produce electricity. In his classic experiment, Faraday wrapped copper wire around a cylinder. When he passed a magnet in and out of the cylinder, an electric current flowed through the wire.

Faraday's laboratory model was the first "dynamo," or electric generator. By showing

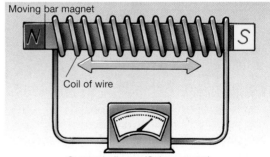

The electricity produced by a magnet moving through a wire coil registers on the galvanometer of a simple laboratory generator.

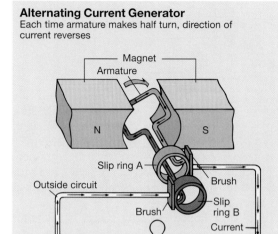

Alternating Current Generator
Each time armature makes half turn, direction of current reverses

- Magnet
- Armature
- N
- S
- Slip ring A
- Outside circuit
- Brush
- Brush
- Slip ring B
- Current

Direct Current Generator
Current always flows in same direction

- Magnet
- Armature
- N
- S
- Commutator
- Brush
- Outside circuit
- Brush
- Current

Generators in use today generally fall into two main types: Alternating-current (AC) generators produce electric current that constantly reverses its direction as it travels through a conductor. By contrast, direct current (DC) always flows in one direction.

the important relationship between magnetism and electricity, it established the working principle for all electric generators to come. Within a few years of Faraday's famous experiment, small electric generators were being built in several countries. But these early generators were little more than curiosities—they could not be used to accomplish tasks.

The advent of practical generators came with the development of strong ELECTROMAGNETS. Using iron-core electromagnets, the Belgian engineer Zénobe Gramme created the first practical commercial generator in 1867. It provided electricity for arc lamps in lighthouses and factories. Many other inventors made further improvements in the 1870s.

In the late 1870s, Thomas Edison invented a practical INCANDESCENT LAMP, and soon there was a great demand for electric generators. The Edison company built the first large-scale generating stations (using a coal-fired steam generator as the energy source). The company was soon supplying electric lighting in New York City, London, and Milan. The first hydroelectric station was opened at Appleton, Wisconsin, in 1882, and by 1895, a hydroelectric generator at Niagara Falls, New York, produced enough electricity to supply the city of Buffalo. Today, the mechanical energy needed to create electricity also comes from the burning of coal, oil, or gas, or from the heat produced by NUCLEAR-POWER REACTORS.

ELECTRIC LIGHT

See INCANDESCENT LAMP

ELECTRIC MOTOR

In the 1830s, American inventor Joseph Henry and English scientist Michael Faraday were experimenting with electricity. They both showed that mechanical energy can be converted into electricity (*see* ELECTRIC GENERATOR). In creating the first electric motors, Henry and Faraday also demonstrated that electricity could be transferred back into mechanical energy.

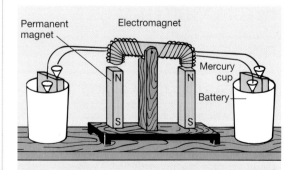

- Permanent magnet
- Electromagnet
- N
- N
- Mercury cup
- Battery
- S
- S

Joseph Henry's 1831 electric motor featured an electromagnet that moved like a seesaw when current traveled back and forth across its length.

D
E

Improving on Henry's design, Vermont blacksmith Thomas Davenport built several battery-powered electric motors in the 1830s, using them to power small lathes, drills, and a variety of other light equipment. But as long as batteries were the only source of current, electric motors remained little more than clever gadgets.

In the 1880s, large-scale generating stations made electric motors a practical source of power for factories and for transportation. The electrical current traveled through wires to the motors, which were used in textile factories, steel mills, and other manufacturing ventures. They also provided power for electric streetcars and subways. By the early 1900s, small electric motors appeared in home appliances such as refrigerators, vacuum cleaners, and washing machines.

Some Parts of a DC Motor

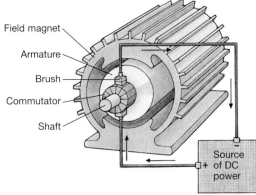

The first electric motors ran on DC current and employed a device called a commutator to continually reverse the current's flow to generate motion.

ELECTRONIC TIMEPIECE

See QUARTZ-CRYSTAL TIMEPIECE

ELECTROCARDIOGRAPH

In 1900 the Dutch physiologist Willem Einthoven built a device that could measure and record the very small electrical impulses generated by the beating heart. After studying the electric patterns produced by healthy hearts, Einthoven showed that certain changes in this pattern indicated various kinds of heart disease.

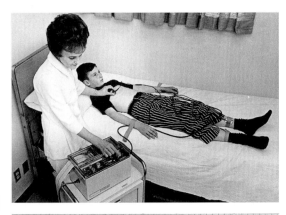

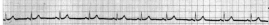

The electrocardiograph records the nerve impulses that cause the heart to contract. It produces a readout called an electrocardiogram, or EKG. The EKG shown here is that of a healthy heart.

By the 1920s, an improved version of Einthoven's device was used regularly to monitor patients. Called the electrocardiograph, it could produce a graph of the heart's activity. Einthoven won the 1924 Nobel Prize in physiology or medicine for his contribution.

Today, electrocardiographs can display information on a computer monitor and save the information in electronic form. The device has extended the lives of millions by enabling doctors to diagnose heart disease in its early, treatable stages.

ELECTROMAGNET

In 1820, the Danish physicist and chemist Hans Christian Oersted showed that electricity has magnetic effects. When he put a compass near a wire carrying an electric current, the needle of the compass swung at right angles to the wire.

Oersted's discovery fascinated electrical engineer William Sturgeon, an Englishman, and the American physicist Joseph Henry. About 1828, Sturgeon devised the first electromagnet by wrapping a copper wire around a U-shaped iron bar. When he sent electricity through the wire (from a battery), the bar became a magnet able to lift twenty times its own weight in iron. As soon as the current was switched off, the bar ceased being a magnet, and the iron weight fell. Soon afterward in the United States, Henry created an electromagnet able to lift more than a ton.

Henry's magnet was soon used in mining to attract iron pieces from crushed ore. More important, electromagnets became an important element in electric motors, helping convert electrical current into mechanical energy to power everything from vacuum cleaners to giant industrial machines.

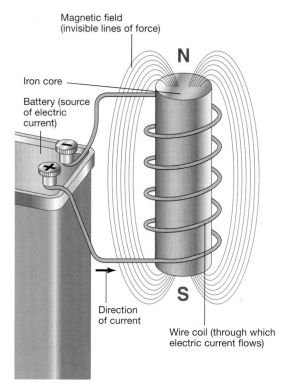

Magnetic field
(invisible lines of force)

N

Iron core

Battery (source
of electric
current)

S

Direction
of current

Wire coil (through which
electric current flows)

A simple electromagnet consists of a source of electricity such as a battery, some insulated wire, and an iron core. When electricity moves through the wire, the iron core becomes magnetic.

ELECTRON TUBE

In the 1870s, the English physicist and chemist Sir William Crookes discovered an interesting property of electricity. He sealed a small metal plate into each end of a glass tube. After pumping air out of the tube, he connected the end plates to a source of electricity, giving one plate a negative charge and the other a positive charge. Crookes found that when the electric current was strong enough, energetic particles began streaming through the vacuum from the negatively charged plate to the positively charged plate. We now know these particles as electrons, a steady flow of which produces electric current.

Crookes's invention—known today as the electron tube, or vacuum tube—ushered in the age of electronics during the first half of the twentieth century. In 1904, building on Crookes's work, the English engineer John Ambrose Fleming designed an electron tube called a diode, which converted alternating electric current (AC) into direct current (DC). In 1907, the American engineer Lee De Forest invented the triode tube, which could strengthen, or amplify, the electrical signal.

Using a combination of these electronic tubes, inventors began developing systems for sending signals through the air, using electron-tube devices both to send and receive. The first of these "wireless" devices could send only simple codes. But soon they were improved to transmit voices and music—today's radio.

By the 1930s, further research had produced a practical television system. In such a system, a special kind of electron tube in the video camera encodes patterns of light into electronic signals. A cathode-ray tube, the television's "picture tube," decodes the signal. The bombardment of electrons against the inside surface of the television tube produces a glow, whose patterns we see as a picture (*see* OSCILLOSCOPE).

In the 1940s, electron tubes led to the development of the first electronic computers. Such early computers used thousands of electron tubes as circuits, and so filled entire rooms. Special fans and other cooling equipment were needed just to dissipate the tremendous heat the tubes emitted. Even more problematic, electron tubes weakened and burned out over time,

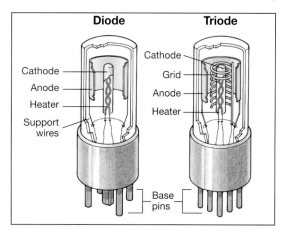

Diode

Triode

Cathode

Anode

Heater

Support
wires

Cathode

Grid

Anode

Heater

Base
pins

As its name suggests, the diode electron tube consists of two electrodes: the inner cathode and the encircling anode plate. Adding a third electrode—the control grid—produces the more powerful triode electron tube.

D E

requiring their constant replacement. They became obsolete in the 1950s with the invention of TRANSISTORS and later INTEGRATED CIRCUITS.

ELEVATOR

Throughout history, people have used various kinds of platforms, ropes, and counterweights to raise and lower heavy loads. In the early 1800s, steam engines powered many such hoists. But these devices were used almost exclusively for freight, rather than for people. The ride on these early elevators was jerky, and the lifting rope or cable could break at any time, sending the elevated platform crashing to the ground. Then, in 1852, the American mechanic Elisha Otis built the first practical safety elevator, or passenger lift. In Otis's device, the lifting cable was attached to a heavy spring on top of the elevator shaft. The pull of the rope bent the spring, which pulled back sliding clamps on either side of the shaft. If the cable broke, the spring straightened out, and the clamps slid into guide rails, stopping the elevator car from falling. This basic design can still be found in most passenger elevators today.

With the coming of electric motors to power these lifts, Otis's safety elevator became an essential part of new skyscrapers, transporting people safely to and from high floors.

ENDOSCOPE

The physician's oath of "first, do no harm" long kept doctors from opening up their patients to see what was ailing them. Then, in 1819, a French physician named Arnaud designed the first endoscope, an open tube with a small light (in this case a candle) that could be inserted inside body openings. For the first time, physicians could literally peer into their patients without cutting them.

After Thomas Edison's invention of electric lightbulbs in 1878, endoscopes were much improved. German physician Max Nitze invented an electric endoscope small enough to be inserted into the tubes leading to the bladder. A few years later, another German, Gustav Killian, invented the bronchoscope, a lighted tube that could be pushed down the trachea to see inside the lungs. All these early endoscopes were rigid tubes, and so could not be inserted into more-difficult-to-reach parts of the body.

Elevator

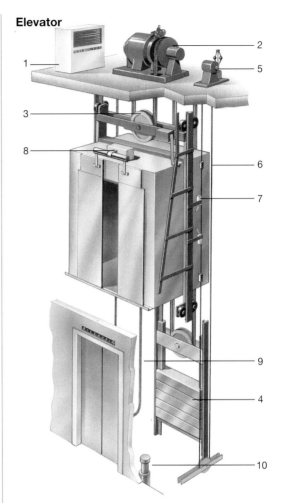

A computer-controlled elevator is activated by push buttons that feed passenger call signals into the computer (1). The computer controls a hoisting motor (2) that winds a loop of steel cable (3), attached by pulleys to the car and to a set of counterweights (4). If the car should fall too fast, a governor (5), connected to a safety rope (6), activates a braking system. The car runs between guide rails, which carry limit switches (7) that stop the car at each floor level. A small motor on top of the car (8) opens and shuts the doors. Power is supplied by means of a flexible cable (9). Should the car descend below ground-floor level, an oil buffer (10) absorbs the impact shock.

A great advance came in the 1960s with the development of FIBER OPTICS—hair-like glass fibers able to transmit intense beams of light. In 1962, Japanese physicians used the first flexible fiber-optic endoscope to see inside hollow organs and body cavities. Its pliable rods and bright lights enabled them to literally see around corners.

Then as today, fiber-optic endoscopes were generally inserted through a small incision.

In the 1970s, small instruments were added to the endoscope, enabling surgeons to perform what has been called "keyhole surgery." This new, less invasive approach to surgery enabled patients to recover much more quickly—in many cases, going home from the hospital the same day as the surgery.

Endoscopy continued to advance with the addition of miniature cameras that transmit pictures of the patient's organs and other internal tissues to a video terminal in the operating room. Today, endoscopes make possible millions of procedures in doctors' offices that once would have required major surgery and long hospital stays. Among the endoscopic operations now common are the examination and surgical repair of joints, sinuses, gallbladder, appendix, reproductive tract, and spine.

ERASER

The eraser has been called the invention that allows us to "try, try again." The first mention of such a device is in a 1752 issue of the *Proceedings* of the French Academy of Sciences. The editors suggested that the gum of the South American caoutchouc tree could be used to erase graphite PENCIL marks. Caoutchouc erasers quickly became so popular that, in 1770, the English chemist Joseph Priestley renamed the gum "rubber," because it could "rub out" mistakes. Disagreement remains as to who first attached the eraser to a writing instrument. By U.S. accounts, the first patents for an eraser-tipped pencil were issued in 1858.

The wide use of typewriters brought the need for a new kind of eraser in the twentieth century. After years of tinkering with paints, secretary Bette Nesmith Graham invented the first correction fluid—"Liquid Paper"—in 1957. Applied with a tiny brush from a tiny bottle, correction fluid enabled typists to correct "typos" in seconds, thus avoiding the frustration of having to retype an entire document.

The 1960s brought electric typewriters equipped with correction tapes that enabled typists to cover mistakes with a "backstroke" key. The ultimate eraser came with the first true word processor, introduced by the International Business Machines Corporation (IBM) in

1964. The machine's magnetic-tape data-storage unit allowed typists to proofread and correct their mistakes before printing. Today, all computer word-processing programs take advantage of the keyboard "delete" key for instant electronic erasing.

ESCALATOR

Like the passenger elevator, an escalator moves people from one level of a building or subway to another—with little to no physical effort on their part. In essence, the modern escalator is a motorized stairway, with all steps connected together by two parallel loops of what looks like heavy bicycle chain. The steps sit on wheels or rollers, which in turn rest on two parallel metal tracks extending from one level to the next. As the steps approach the end of the ride, they flatten, pivot under a comb-like safety plate, and disappear. Only half of the escalator's steps are visible at any one time. The hidden steps are traveling back to their starting position.

The first successful escalator was patented in 1892 by the American engineer Jesse Reno. A rider on Reno's escalator needed to lean forward like a skier facing uphill, because its flat, stepless platform transported people upward at a thirty degree angle. In 1899, an inventor who worked for the Otis Elevator Company

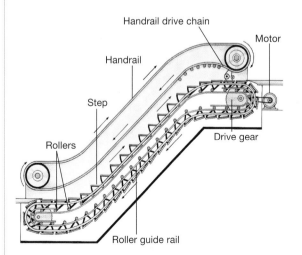

At any moment, about half an escalator's steps can be seen. The invisible half are underneath, moving in the opposite direction.

D
E

built a step-type escalator, later installed in a Chicago department store. Today's escalators can carry from five thousand to ten thousand people an hour at speeds of 90 to 120 feet (27.4 to 36.6 meters) per minute.

ESCAPEMENT

While the history of time-telling devices stretches back some thirty-five hundred years, (*see* TIMEKEEPING), the history of mechanical clocks begins during the 1300s, with the invention of a small device called the escapement. In mechanical clocks and watches, the escapement consists of a toothed wheel and a set of prongs. The wheel is driven forward by

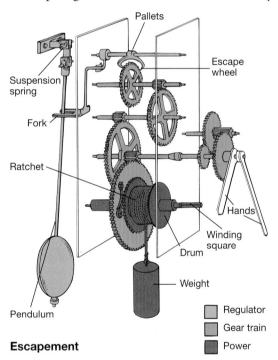

Escapement

■	Regulator
■	Gear train
■	Power

The weight, pulled down by gravity, turns the drum, which turns the gears. To prevent the drum from unwinding all at once, the pendulum, pallets, and escape wheel regulate the power. The pendulum rocks the pallets. The pallets catch and then release the escape wheel, one tooth at a time. This alternately stops and frees the movement of the gears. The rocking of the pallets moves the fork, which, helped by the suspension spring and gravity, propels the pendulum through its arc. A key fits on the winding square to turn the drum and rewind the cord. The ratchet frees the drum to turn in the winding direction without moving the gears.

a source of energy such as a weight or spring, and arrested in rhythmic steps by the prong, which alternately catches and releases the wheel's teeth. In this way, the escapement controls the clock's flow of energy, ensuring that the main cogwheel (which moves the hands) turns with a regular, timekeeping movement.

EYEGLASSES

The ancient Greeks and Chinese knew about the magnifying power of glass beads and crystals. In 1268, the English scientist Roger Bacon observed that such lenses could be used to improve vision. A few years later, the first practical eyeglasses were created in Italy, though their inventor remains unknown. Made with convex lenses, early glasses helped only the farsighted. In 1451, the German scholar Nicholas of Cusa introduced the idea of using concave, or inward-curving, lenses to correct nearsightedness. About 1780, Benjamin Franklin invented the first bifocals, with convex lenses on the lower part of the glasses to focus on near work, and plain glass or concave lenses on top for long-distance sight. In the late 1900s, many people switched from eyeglasses to contact lenses, which adhere to the eyeball.

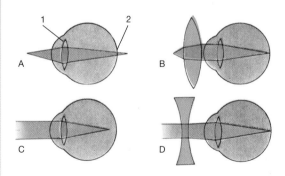

The human eye contains a lens (1) that normally focuses light from an object directly on the retina (2) to produce a sharp image. If the eye lens converges the light rays to a focus behind the retina (A), the eye is said to be farsighted. This defect is corrected by the use of a convex lens (B) that combines with the eye lens to focus the image onto the retina. If the eye lens focuses the light in front of the retina (C), the eye is nearsighted and is corrected with use of a concave lens (D) that decreases the refraction of the eye lens.

F-G

FACSIMILE (FAX) MACHINE

Most people are surprised to learn that the facsimile machine, or "fax," is older than the telephone. In 1843, the Scottish inventor Alexander Bain patented a system for transmitting pictures as electrical signals over telegraph wires. Bain's crude picture transmitter used a swinging PENDULUM tipped with a metal point to "scan" images of letters on a metal sheet. On the receiving end, the electric pulses made contact with a second pendulum, which swung over a piece of chemically treated paper to reproduce the letters. The process was improved in 1847 by Frederick Bakewell, but these early machines were never widely used. The French inventor Giovanni Caselli improved the process in the 1860s and established the first commercial fax line, between Paris and Lyon, from 1865 to 1870.

In 1902, the German physicist Arthur Korn developed the first commercially practical system for transmitting photographs. It used a rotating drum and a PHOTOELECTRIC CELL. Newspapers around the world gradually adopted this system for transmitting news photos. Finally, in 1924, the American Telephone and Telegraph Company (AT&T) introduced a machine able to send pictures over telephone lines. This forerunner to the modern fax used a light-sensitive ELECTRON TUBE to scan images placed on a transparent, spinning drum. The signal sent over the telephone line activated a finely focused light beam that shone on a sheet of unexposed film wrapped around a second spinning drum. Decades of further improvements brought the small desktop fax machine we know today.

FIBER OPTICS

A relatively new technology with vast potential, fiber optics involves the transmission of light through hair-thin glass or plastic fibers. Made of ultrapure silica glass or special plastics, modern optic fibers can carry light signals much farther than metal cables can transmit

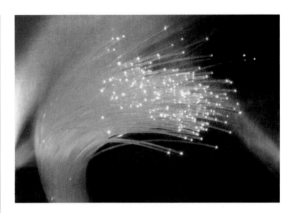

Light speeds through flexible threads of glass called optical fibers. A bundle of fibers can relay an image from one end to the other if the fibers remain arranged in the same pattern.

electrical signals. Their coded light pulses can also carry vastly more information than can electrical signals, and at lower cost. These advantages have brought fiber optics into use in telephone, computer, and cable-television networks, making it the backbone of modern global telecommunications.

Another important use of fiber optics is in medicine, where bundled fibers allow physicians to look inside human organs and deliver laser energy to treat internal disease without major surgery.

Although the possibility of communicating with light pulses occurred to Alexander Graham Bell, inventor of the telephone, the creation of a working system awaited the invention of the LASER in 1960. The key to fiber optics then lay in preventing the laser light from escaping the fiber. Scientists already knew of an effect called total internal reflection, which occurs when light tries to pass from one transparent material into another. In 1970, engineers at Corning Glass Works in New York succeeded in making the first fibers that were able to exploit this effect. The engineers devised ultrapure silica glass fibers in which all light beamed through the fiber's core was mirrored back by an outer reflecting layer.

By 1977, optic fibers were being used for communication (over distances of less than a

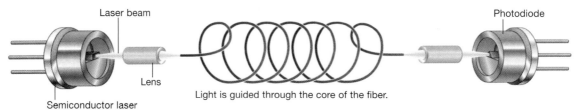

Laser beam
Photodiode
Lens
Semiconductor laser
Light is guided through the core of the fiber.

In many telecommunications networks, optical fibers are used to transmit information over long distances. At one end of the process, for example, digital electronic telephone signals can be converted by a tiny laser into light pulses that can travel for miles through a fiber-optic cable. A photodiode at the receiving end of the cable can convert these optical signals back into electronic signals that can be deciphered and sent on to their destination.

mile). By 1985, optical-fiber communications networks had been established between many cities. Transatlantic optic-fiber cables followed in 1988, with a complete global network completed in 1997. Remarkably, most fiber-optic systems today produce their light waves with lasers the size of a grain of salt.

FILM

See CAMERA AND FILM

FIRE EXTINGUISHER

Before the invention of modern fire extinguishers, a bucket of water was a person's best hope of putting out a small fire. The extinguisher, invented in the early 1800s, consists of a portable, pressurized tank filled with water or fire-smothering chemicals discharged through a nozzle or hose. The first extinguishers were filled with a solution of bicarbonate of soda and water and held a small container of sulfuric acid. Turning the extinguisher upside down mixed the acid and soda to form carbon dioxide gas. The gas, in turn, expelled the liquid through a handheld hose, extinguishing the fire.

Since the 1960s, soda-acid extinguishers have been gradually replaced by dry-chemical extinguishers that can be safely used on electrical and chemical fires as well as on the conventional kind. Today, safety experts urge all home-owners and building managers to keep fire extinguishers within easy reach.

FLUORESCENT LAMP

For hundreds of years, people have known that certain minerals and other substances glow when exposed to forms of energy such as ultraviolet light. Scientists first put this phenomenon to practical use in the twentieth century, with the invention of fluorescent lights.

The French physicist Alexandre Becquerel built the first crude fluorescent lamp around 1859, while experimenting with gas-filled tubes. His laboratory model was inefficient and short-lived. But it demonstrated that suitable gases would fluoresce, or glow, when energized with electricity. Many other inventors experimented with fluorescent lights, including Thomas Edison. In 1910, another French scientist, Georges Claude, found that passing electricity through a tube of neon gas produced a red glow (the neon lamp).

In the 1930s, a team of American physicists at the General Electric Company (GE) built upon Claude's work. They developed phosphors, fluorescent chemicals that glow with a strong white light when exposed to ultraviolet light. They painted these chemicals on the inside of long glass tubes, then filled the tubes with a mixture of gases such as argon and mercury, which emit ultraviolet radiation when excited by electricity. The result

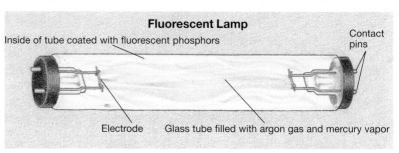

Fluorescent Lamp
Inside of tube coated with fluorescent phosphors
Contact pins
Electrode   Glass tube filled with argon gas and mercury vapor

was the first successful fluorescent lamp, introduced in the United States in 1938. Such lamps proved to be longer-lasting, cooler, and more energy-efficient than ordinary lightbulbs known as INCANDESCENT LAMPS. They soon replaced incandescent lighting in most factories, offices, schools, and other public places.

FLYING SHUTTLE

The clever invention known as the flying shuttle is credited with transforming cloth making from a handicraft to an industry. Before Englishman John Kay invented the device in 1733, the making of woven fabrics required two weavers to sit side by side, passing a shuttle of yarn to each other between the lengthwise threads of a loom. Kay's invention was a hollow wooden device pointed at each end and enclosing a spool of yarn. Attached to the loom by a spring, this shuttle could be shot back and forth across the lengthwise threads with the jerk of a cord. In this way, the flying shuttle both greatly speeded weaving and made it possible to weave much wider pieces of fabric. Most important, the device lent itself to automation, leading to the day when electrically powered equipment replaced the weaver altogether.

Kay's flying shuttle held a spool of yarn that unwound as the shuttle "flew" along a wire from one side of the loom to the other.

FORK

Few things in Western culture are more commonplace than the table fork. Yet this eating utensil did not appear in Europe until about 1100. Historians trace its origins to Byzantium, an ancient city on the site of present-day Istanbul, Turkey, where metalworkers made small, two-pronged forks for spearing sticky foods such as syrupy fruit. By the 1500s, steel and tin forks were being made in Italy, and their use spread through the rest of Europe in the 1600s.

FREEZER

See REFRIGERATOR

GEARS

The simple machines we know as gears have been in use for thousands of years. In essence, they are toothed wheels or shafts. When the teeth of two gears mesh together, they can transfer motion from one to the other, as well as change the direction or magnitude of the force.

The first known use of gears was in a water clock built by the Greek mathematician Ctesibius in the first century B.C. Around 1492, Leonardo da Vinci designed several types of gears, classifying them by the shape of their teeth as helical, conical, and trapezoidal.

For centuries, people fashioned gears of wood or wood inset with stone teeth. They used them in clocks, waterwheels, windmills, and machines of war. Metal gears came into widespread use with the invention of precision gear-cutting machines in 1855. Since then, gears have been used in countless devices.

The most familiar everyday use of gears occurs in automobiles. A gear connected to the drive shaft meshes with other gears in order to transfer the shaft's side-to-side motion to the forward-rotating wheels. The driver can shift from one set of gears to another, determining whether

Helical Gears

Spur Gears

Herringbone Gears

Worm Gears

Bevel Gears

F
G

the car will move forward or in reverse. Gears also determine how the engine's power will be used. In "low gear," a small gear drives a larger one to increase power and decrease speed. In "high gear," a larger gear drives a smaller one to increase speed at the expense of power.

GEIGER COUNTER

In 1911, the physicists Hans Geiger and Ernest Rutherford invented a device for detecting and measuring radioactivity—invisible energy given

How a Geiger Counter Works

Radiation enters a Geiger counter's cylinder and creates an electrical signal that can produce a "click" in a loudspeaker and move the needle on a meter.

Positively charged wire

Electric pulse

Radiation

Negatively charged cylinder wall

Positive ions

Negative electrons

Measuring unit with meter and loudspeaker

off by certain radioactive substances such as the element radium. The device proved extremely useful to scientists studying radioactive substances, and was later used to monitor dangerous levels of radiation, and to prospect for valuable radioactive elements such as uranium.

A Geiger counter consists of a gas-filled cylinder containing a wire that serves as one electrode for an electronic circuit. When radioactive particles pass through the cylinder, they cause its gaseous elements to break into electrically charged particles, or ions. When these particles strike the wire, they produce pulses of electricity that can be transmitted to a counter or a loudspeaker. The higher the count or the more rapid the clicks from the loudspeaker, the more radioactive energy is present.

GENETICALLY ENGINEERED DRUGS

In 1973, American scientists Herbert Boyer and Stanley Cohen devised a way to chemically snip fragments of genetic material (DNA) from one organism and insert the fragments into the cells of another. The second organism then incorporated the new genetic material in its own cell activities.

Medical researchers immediately saw the great potential of what Boyer and Cohen had done. In many serious diseases, a person's body fails to produce enough of a hormone, enzyme, or other vital substance. Often, the needed substance is difficult or impossible to obtain from human donors or animals. If human genes containing the directions for making the substance could be inserted into bacteria or yeasts, perhaps these simple organisms would become living "drug factories."

In 1978, the American biotechnology company Genentech developed *Escherichia coli* bacteria that produced a genetically engineered substance—insulin, for the treatment of diabetes. Soon after came bacteria able to produce human growth hormone for the treatment of growth disorders in children. Other microorganisms have been transformed to produce safe vaccines for a number of harmful viruses, including some strains of herpes, influenza, and hepatitis.

In the 1990s, genetic engineering took a new turn, when "bioengineers" created farm animals that produced human enzymes and other drugs in their milk. In this way, emphysema patients can now obtain the healing drug alpha-1 antitrypsin from the milk of genetically engineered sheep. Special herds of "transgenic" goats, in turn, produce tissue plasminogen activator (TPA), an enzyme that dissolves blood clots.

GLASS

The story of glass begins with the discovery of obsidian, the glassy black volcanic stone used by primitive peoples to make arrowheads, cutting tools, and ornaments. About 3000 B.C., they

F
G

A glassblower begins by dipping a "core" of sand attached to the end of a hollow rod into a well of molten glass.

The artisans shape and trim the hot, softened glass using tools first developed by the ancient Egyptians.

Finally, the glassblower must continually turn the glass as he blows to produce an evenly shaped object.

learned to make a very similar substance—glass—by melting silica sand with ash and other substances. As the centuries passed, people learned to shape glass before it cooled, and later, how to blow glass, creating a hollow container.

Then, in the Middle Ages glassmakers of Venice (now part of Italy) found a way to make clear glass. They used the element selenium to remove silica's natural greenish cast. In the late 1600s, the French developed a process for casting glass plates for windows and mirrors. In 1790, the Swiss glassmaker Pierre-Louis Guinand developed a way of producing the high-quality glass needed to make optical lenses.

GUIDED MISSILE

Guided missiles are the most recent generation of weapons designed to hit a target from a safe distance. In the history of war, they represent the logical next step from the thrown stone, the arrow, the bullet, and the free-flight rocket. Before the invention of missile guidance systems, rockets were simply pointed and launched, with no controls to correct their course en route.

In the 1930s, rocket engineers in the United States and Germany designed several "aerial torpedoes" equipped with GYROSCOPES to guide their course in a preset direction, and with BAROMETERS to maintain preset altitudes. These guidance devices could change the position of fins and flaps that affected the missiles' flight through the air. The most successful of these designs were the V series of rockets developed by German engineer Wernher von Braun and used against British cities during World War II.

F
G

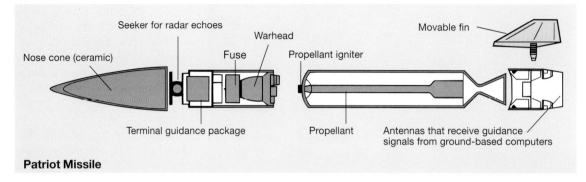

Patriot Missile

- Nose cone (ceramic)
- Seeker for radar echoes
- Fuse
- Warhead
- Propellant igniter
- Movable fin
- Terminal guidance package
- Propellant
- Antennas that receive guidance signals from ground-based computers

The Patriot is a surface-to-air missile that was used by the United States in 1991 in the Persian Gulf war. A terminal near the front of the missile searches for radar echoes coming from its target. Information about the target's position is transmitted to a powerful computer and radar system on the ground. This system then sends signals to an antenna at the back of the missile to guide it to the target.

Immediately after the war, rocket engineers in the United States and the Soviet Union began designing long-range missiles with "inertial guidance systems." These systems used electronic sensors and computers to continuously monitor a missile's position and speed. A short-range, or tactical, missile might not use complicated guidance systems, but would depend on an infrared sensor or radiation sensor to lock onto either the heat of an enemy plane's exhaust or the signals from its radar.

In the 1960s, 1970s, and 1980s, the United States and the Soviet Union developed more sophisticated guidance systems for the long-distance weapons known as ballistic and cruise missiles. The ballistic missile's high, arching flight was guided by the many gyroscopes and accelerometers (acceleration meters) in its guidance system. Far more accurate was the low-flying, ground-hugging cruise missile, programmed to follow a computerized contour map of the terrain (mountains, ravines, and so forth) over which it flew.

GUNPOWDER

Gunpowder, the first true explosive, is a mixture of sulfur, charcoal, and potassium nitrate (or saltpeter). It originated in China, where soldiers used the blend to make explosive grenades and bombs around A.D. 1000. By the early 1300s, Europeans had learned the recipe and were manufacturing their own gunpowder and guns. By harnessing the energy of a chemical reaction, gunpowder created the first weapons that did not depend on the users' muscular strength.

GUNS AND CANNONS

Guns and cannons have done as much to change history as any invention. Cannons spelled the end of feudalism by making it possible to destroy the stone walls of castles. Guns made food more available to hunters, and gave new power to explorers and pioneers facing dangerous animals and hostile native peoples.

Guns have been made in many sizes, from the short-barreled pistol to the long-barreled rifle. The very large gun we know as the cannon has often been mounted on wheels.

The earliest known guns date to the early 1300s. They were clumsy cannons used for battering down enemy fortresses. Around 1350, blacksmiths made the first handguns. Each was little more than a metal tube on the end of a wooden handle. The tube held a metal ball and an explosive that was ignited by a glowing coal or red-hot iron. Often these early guns failed to

A soldier ignites a medieval cannon that is almost as likely to blow up as it is to fire.

The Brown Bess musket, with its flintlock firing mechanism and bayonet, remained the British army's principal firearm from 1690 to 1830.

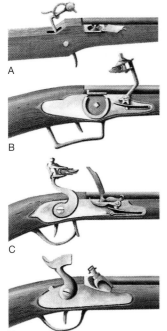

From its invention in the mid-1500s, the musket evolved in safety and reliability with a succession of firing mechanisms. During its 300-year history, they included the matchlock (A), wheel lock (B), flintlock (C), and percussion cap (D).

go off. Sometimes they blew up in the face of the shooter.

Guns have progressed tremendously since those crude and unreliable weapons. But their basic design remains the same. A gun is a machine for shooting bullets—metal balls or cylinders propelled by the force of an explosion. The bullet is directed by the gun's barrel, a tube that also contains the gun's explosive material. All guns have some kind of device for setting off the explosive. The first such devices were slow-burning wicks, followed by triggers and percussion caps. As early guns improved in accuracy, gun makers added sights to help the shooter take aim.

For hundreds of years, all guns used the explosive known as "black powder," a mixture of saltpeter, sulfur, and charcoal invented by the Chinese about A.D. 1000. A great advance came with smokeless powder, perfected by the French in 1884. In addition to being a more powerful explosive, smokeless powder avoided the sometimes-blinding smoke produced by black powder. The 1800s also brought precision-made rifles, which gave a spin to the bullet and greatly improved the firearm's accuracy. Late in the century, efficient repeating arms appeared—the REVOLVER and the MACHINE GUN. These were followed by continuous-firing "automatic" guns in World War II.

GYROSCOPE

In 1852, the French physicist Jean Foucault built the gyroscope, a simple instrument made up of a spinning wheel and axle mounted in a frame that permits free movement in any direction. Scientists were fascinated by the fact that as long as the gyro wheel kept spinning, it remained oriented in the same position, never

The U.S. Army's standard infantry rifle is the automatic M16. The firing of its bullet produces a blast of gas (1) that follows the bullet down the barrel. The gas port (2) traps some of this gas and channels it through a steel tube (3) back to the bolt carrier (4), which contains the firing pin (5). This forces back the bolt, and a new cartridge is pushed into the breech (6) from the magazine (7). An extractor (8) ejects the spent cartridge (9) through the dust cover (10).

F
G

tilting in any direction. From this special quality would come a number of valuable inventions.

Foucault predicted that his gyroscope would one day be used as a compass. This came about in 1908 after the invention of the electric motor provided a way to keep the gyro wheel spinning (and so pointing in one direction) for long periods of time. Gyrocompasses became important on twentieth-century ships, because the ships' steel hulls interfered with the traditional magnetic COMPASS. The spinning gyroscope's resistance to direction change likewise made possible the invention of automatic pilots for guiding ships, airplanes, rockets, and spacecraft.

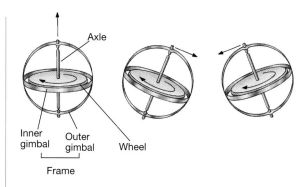

The Properties of a Gyroscope

When a gyroscope is spinning, it always points in the direction it is set (above left). If you push forward on the frame of a gyroscope spinning straight up and down, the axle will tilt to the right or left (middle and far right), not in the direction you pushed it.

The Changing World A.D. 1100

The iron AX is transforming the landscape of Europe, allowing farmers to clear vast forests for cropland. A single farmer can also cultivate larger fields, thanks to several innovations. Among the most important are improved PLOWS, mounted on WHEELS and featuring a new device called a moldboard. Fitted behind the plowshare, the moldboard flips the soil over as the plow passes to create a furrow. Before this, farmers had to turn the soil by tipping the plow every few feet.

European farmers have also devised a new way to put animals to work. A horse-collar HARNESS has made it possible to use horses for plowing and hauling.

Harvesting has been made easier with the use of iron scythes. Some farming communities have begun building WINDMILLS for grinding their grain. Much of the benefit of the new productivity fills the coffers of powerful feudal lords. They control Europe with armies led by knights clad in ARMOR. Thanks to

Hand-forged suits of armor protected medieval knights in battle until the invention of firearms in the 1600s.

new designs for effective metal STIRRUPS, these fearsome soldiers ride securely atop powerful horses, and so tower above the defenseless peasantry.

Europe's feudal lords also employ a workforce of highly skilled craftspeople. Using a new type of hanging LOOM, weavers can produce exquisitely beautiful rugs and tapestries to warm the stone floors and walls of their rulers' drafty castles. Blacksmiths beat out iron lanterns and torch holders to light the castles' cavernous halls and forge ornate iron gates to protect the castles' entrances.

Half a world away in China, the master printers of the Sung dynasty are filling the Szechwan emperor's library with books. A special Court for Printing has been built just to house 130,000 wood blocks used to produce the Tripitaka, the complete Buddhist scripture. Other printing projects include a variety of dictionaries, encyclopedias, and literary works.

HARNESS

In prehistoric times, people learned to employ oxen to pull a cart or PLOW, using a wooden yoke that fit across the animals' chest and shoulders. But the big yoke would not work efficiently on a horse. The horse's more-slender shoulders meant that the yoke fell across its neck, severely restricting the animal's breathing and circulation.

The solution was the modern harness, or horse collar, invented in China around A.D. 500. Such a harness consists of a padded leather collar fitted over the lower neck and chest and attached to pulling straps. Harnesses appeared in Europe in the 900s, and soon the horse was an important source of power, allowing farmers to increase food production. Horses also gradually replaced oxen for pulling carts and wagons.

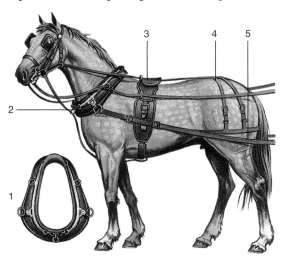

The modern harness includes a padded collar (1), traces (2), saddle pad (3), hip straps (4), and breeching (5). The driver uses an attached bridle to direct the horse.

HEARING AID

A cupped hand behind the ear was the earliest form of hearing aid. It increased the perceived loudness of a faint sound by directing sound

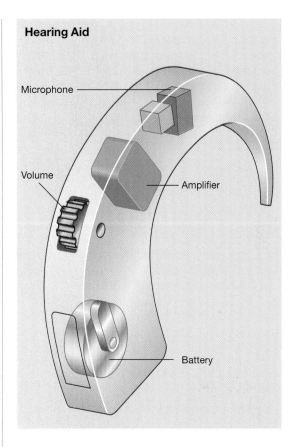

Hearing Aid

Microphone

Volume

Amplifier

Battery

waves into the ear. The first mechanical hearing aids worked in much the same way. The ear trumpet was an early example. Invented between 1650 and 1700, it consisted of a long horn with a wide mouth tapering to a narrow opening placed in the ear. The trumpet's tapered shape condensed sound waves, increasing their pressure as they entered the ear and struck the eardrum.

In the 1870s, Alexander Graham Bell worked on new electrically driven hearing aids. Although he did not create a practical device for the hard-of-hearing, Bell's work contributed to the invention of the TELEPHONE.

In 1901, American inventor Miller Reese Hutchison patented the first practical telephone-type hearing aid. In 1920, American inventor Earl Charles Hanson devised the first hearing aid that used a small electron tube to amplify sound. It and similar designs consisted of an

H I

earpiece connected by wire to an amplifier and battery pack, which were worn on the body.

The invention of the transistor in 1948 made it possible to greatly reduce the size of hearing aids. They became small enough to fit entirely behind the ear. Miniaturization continued, and in the 1970s, one-piece hearing aids became small enough to fit within the ear canal. Some hearing aids today have digital controls that allow the device to adjust for different situations. Millions of people with partial deafness are aided by such devices.

HELICOPTER

A helicopter is a flying machine with rotating blades that serve both as propeller and wings. A helicopter can fly straight up and down and hover in one place, as well as move forward, backward, and sideways.

Toys that worked like helicopters were made in China in the 1300s. It may have been one of these Chinese "flying tops" that inspired inventor Leonardo da Vinci to sketch a flying machine he called the helixpteron, from the Greek

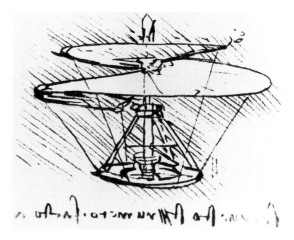

Leonardo da Vinci sketched this *helixpteron* hundreds of years before the first helicopter took flight.

words for "spiral" and "wing." Leonardo's machine, sketched in 1483, was topped by a large spiral screw, the turning of which was designed to pull the machine up into the air.

People began dreaming about helicopters again in 1784, when the French scientists Launoy and Bienvenu showed the French

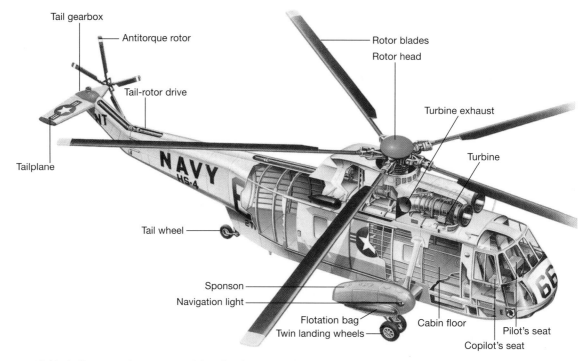

In 1959, helicopter pioneer Igor Sikorsky designed the Sea King for the U.S. Navy's antisubmarine and mine-disposal missions. Twin turboshaft engines enable the Sea King to reach speeds of up to 165 miles (265.7 kilometers) per hour while carrying 840 pounds (381 kilograms) of armament, including homing torpedoes. Since its creation, the craft has been customized to suit the military needs of several nations.

Academy of Sciences a model based on the old Chinese toy. It was little more than a flying top made of feathers stuck in corks at each end of a stick. Spinning the stick briskly caused the top to lift into the air.

Over the next century, many attempted to build a helicopter powerful enough to lift a person. But the helicopter, like the airplane, required a lightweight power source. So its development awaited the invention of the INTERNAL-COMBUSTION ENGINE in the late 1800s. Even then, experimenters found that helicopters were difficult to control and dangerous to fly—if they lost power, they plunged to the ground, unlike airplanes, which could glide to a crash landing.

The first practical helicopters were not developed until the 1930s. The first successful flight was made by pilot Hanna Reitsch in 1937 in a helicopter with two three-bladed rotors, built by the German engineer Heinrich Focke. Two years later, the Russian-born American airplane manufacturer Igor Sikorsky built a single-rotor helicopter that remains in common use throughout the world today.

Just how does a helicopter fly? As the engine-powered blades slice through the air, the shape of those blades creates greater air pressure beneath them than above them. This causes an upward push called lift. The pilot changes the direction of flight through controls that change the angle, or pitch, of the blades.

Helicopters cannot be made as large or as fast as airplanes, but they can land and take off from a small, level spot. They are used for relief and rescue, for observing traffic, and for transporting cargo and people to otherwise inaccessible locations.

HOLOGRAPHY

Holography is the process of creating a three-dimensional (3-D) image of a physical object. Today, virtually all holograms are created with laser beams. But the technique behind these lifelike 3-D images preceded the invention of the laser by more than a decade. In 1947, the Hungarian-British scientist Dennis Gabor developed a technique for creating holograms to enhance images from an electron microscope. But he did not have a source of light powerful enough to make his idea a reality.

Following the invention of the LASER in 1960, the American scientist Emmett Leith de-veloped the first clear hologram image. To create the hologram, a laser beam is split in two. Half of the beam is directed straight at a photographic plate. The other half reflects off the object being photographed. When the two laser signals fall onto the photographic plate, they interfere with each other, creating a pattern that, when lighted by another laser beam, projects a three-dimensional image—the hologram.

A hologram can be eerily realistic. Today, holograms are used for both amusement and scientific study. Holography has also become an important high-tech method for testing materials without touching them. A hologram, for example, can reveal very small changes in size and shape when an object is subjected to pressure, heat, or other forces. Most recently, physicists have developed methods for using sound to create "acoustic holograms" of body parts and underwater objects.

HOUSEHOLD COMFORTS AND CONVENIENCES

For most of human history, housing consisted of no more than a cave, tent, or simple hut. Shelters were heated, if at all, by a fire, and cleaned, if at all, by a crude broom of twigs or straw. Household items, at most, consisted of a handful of clay pots and dishes, perhaps a woven mat or rug for the floor. Such simplicity can still be found in many undeveloped parts of the world.

By contrast, the typical modern home is full of appliances and products designed to ensure the comfort and ease of its occupants. How far back can we trace the invention of such household conveniences? At least seven thousand years, to the first tool made solely for eating—the SPOON. The knife goes back much further. But it doubled as a hunting and digging instrument. The FORK came later, about twenty-five hundred years ago, but didn't become common until the 1300s.

Cooking, heating, and lighting were obviously among the earliest domestic concerns. An open fire outdoors provided all these things for hundreds of thousands of years. Then people began bringing fire indoors, into a central pit located below an opening in the tent or hut roof. By the 1200s, Europeans were building stone chimneys to vent the smoke from their homes.

H I

The Chinese forged stoves of cast iron as early as A.D. 25.

The Chinese invented the first metal STOVES for heating more than two thousand years ago, and their use spread gradually westward through Russia, reaching Europe in the 1400s. Benjamin Franklin greatly improved stove design about 1740 with a cast-iron model that burned wood on a grate. Later models controlled airflow with a set of sliding doors. A much more efficient heating system than the fireplace, Franklin-type stoves would warm America's frontier cabins, farmhouses, and city dwellings for 150 years. In the 1800s, coal replaced wood as stove fuel in towns and cities.

In the 1830s, the invention of the coal-fired steam boiler provided a means of central heating—hot steam traveled through a system of pipes from a central boiler to steam radiators in every room of the house. Then the steam returned as water through other pipes. When homes were heated by radiators, the stove's importance shifted from heating to cooking. Gas-burning cookstoves were first used in the 1840s, and the first electric stoves appeared in 1914. Another advance was the MICROWAVE OVEN, invented by Percy Spencer in 1945 and refined into a popular home appliance in the 1960s.

Home lighting likewise traces back to the open fire. A Stone Age cave dweller who wanted light away from the fire could carry a burning stick. Torches were used for lighting into the Middle Ages (A.D. 500 to 1500), with animal fat, tar, or pitch used to create long-lasting light. Early oil lamps were made from

shells or small animal skulls and filled with animal or vegetable oil, absorbed by a burning wick. The Mesopotamians used beeswax candles around 3000 B.C.

Over the next two thousand years, torches, candles, and oil lamps would move from caves and tents to wood huts and brick houses. Not

Pre-electric household lighting included the Roman lamp (top left), medieval lantern (top right), and 19th-century kerosene and oil lamps (above).

until the discovery of large deposits of petroleum and coal in the 1800s would people fundamentally change the way they lighted their homes. From petroleum came kerosene and the kerosene lamp, introduced in the United States and Britain in the 1850s. They permitted all but the very poor to have enough light to read, write, or sew through dim winter days and into the night.

Another petroleum product—natural gas—was used for street lighting in the early 1800s and began to appear in homes in the 1860s. The electric lighting industry began in 1879,

The salesman in a 1928 advertisement praises the efficiency of General Electric's newest refrigerator: "It never needs oiling."

Despite their bulkiness, the first electric vacuum cleaners helped revolutionize housekeeping at the dawn of the 20th century.

with Thomas Edison's invention of the first practical electric light. Later variations on Edison's INCANDESCENT LAMP would include fluorescent and halogen lamps. But his lightbulb would remain the standard in home lighting throughout the twentieth century.

Another household convenience with a long, inventive history is that of refrigeration, both for food preservation and human comfort. For thousand of years, people stored perishable foods in cool caves and underground storehouses. In the 1800s, natural ice was "harvested" in winter and used for refrigeration. Efforts to create mechanical refrigeration for home use had to wait for the development of safe refrigerants and improved electric motors. Not until the 1930s were RE-FRIGERATORS widely used in U.S. households.

In 1910, American inventor Willis Carrier built the first effective AIR CONDITIONER. Soon mechanical cooling was installed in factories and public places. But home air-conditioning was not widespread until the 1950s and 1960s.

Water supply was a major concern in cities. From early times, AQUEDUCTS were built to assure a supply of clean water. In the 1800s, metal piping made it possible to provide indoor plumbing to town dwellers. Hot water was made by piping water to a tank heated by a steam boiler. Indoor plumbing also made practical the widespread use of the flush TOILET, as well as the first WASHING MACHINES.

Second only to the washing machine in popularity is the home appliance we know as the VACUUM CLEANER. The washer and vacuum were but the first in a flood of electric gadgetry that would ease the modern homemaker's job. In the years following World War II (1939-45), American homes would fill with electric appliances—freezers, clothes dryers, DISHWASHERS, food mixers, blenders, coffeemakers, toasters, and trash compactors, to name a few.

HOVERCRAFT

A hovercraft, or air-cushion vehicle, rides above water, dry land, or swamp on top of a cushion of air. Fans and blowers on the ship's bottom blow air into an area enclosed by a flexible rubber "skirt" and gently lift the craft off the surface. Propellers on top of the hovercraft move the craft along on its constant air cushion.

The basic idea of an air-cushion vehicle traces back to the 1870s, when the British engineer John Thornycroft proposed reducing the drag on a ship's hull by creating an air pocket under the vessel's hull. In the 1950s, several engineers in the United States, Britain, and Europe tried to develop Thornycroft's ideas using a variety of pumps to blow air beneath ships with indented hulls.

In the 1950s, British engineer Sir Christopher Cockerell constructed a working model for the first successful hovercraft. It consisted of two coffee cans and a hair dryer. He obtained a patent in 1955, and in 1959 successfully tested a full-scale hovercraft at Cowes, England.

One of today's largest hovercraft, directly descended from Cockerell's first vessel, provides ferry service across the English Channel. Powered by four 3,800-horsepower gas-turbine engines that drive four lift fans and four swiveling air propellers, it can smoothly transport 60 cars and 416 passengers. In calm conditions, hover-craft can travel at speeds over 90 miles (144.9 kilometers) an hour, making them the fastest large sea vessels in the world.

The hovercraft has found only limited uses because it requires a tremendous amount of energy to keep its air cushion and move forward. Yet it remains unsurpassed in versatility—able to travel over not only water but ice, mud, quicksand, and many other surfaces impossible to cross in traditional vehicles and vessels.

INCANDESCENT LAMP

The incandescent lamp, or "lightbulb," was the first widely used electric light. Its invention is generally credited to Thomas Edison. But Edison's 1879 brainchild was built on the earlier work of others, and later inventors improved upon his design to give us the incandescent lights we use today.

In 1808, the British scientist Sir Humphry Davy became the first to harness electricity to create light. Using a battery, he got an electric current to jump a short distance between a positive and a negative electrode, creating a continuous arc that glowed brightly.

Scientists began using the new arc lamp for laboratory experiments. But the best batteries of that day were short-lived. After the invention of practical electric generators in the 1870s, arc lamps were widely used, primarily as street

A hovercraft ferry departs from the port in Bridgeport, Conn. Such commercial hovercraft can carry up to 60 cars and more than 400 passengers.

As was common in his day, Edison left his schooling to take a job at age twelve. He sold newspapers and candy on the railroad and even printed his own small but popular newspaper, *Paul Pry*. He also found time to continue experiments in a chemical lab he'd set up in the baggage car. Edison later learned to operate the telegraph, an experience that convinced him he could improve the device.

In the 1860s, Edison began his career as a professional inventor in Boston, where the latest work in electricity was being carried out by Samuel Morse, Alexander Graham Bell, and others. There, Edison introduced his first important inventions—a vote-recording machine and an improved stock ticker, used to telegraph information about transactions on the stock exchange.

Thomas Alva Edison received 1,093 U.S. patents in his lifetime—more than anyone before or since. Indeed, few people in the developed world go through the day without using at least one Edison invention. He lit our houses by inventing the first practical INCANDESCENT LAMP, or "lightbulb," and by supplying the first public power from large-scale ELECTRIC GENERATORS. He brought music into our homes with the invention of the PHONOGRAPH, and he helped us communicate by improving the TELEGRAPH, the TELEPHONE, and the MOTION-PICTURE camera and projector. Edison helped develop electric streetcars and automobiles and invented the electric-storage car BATTERY. He invented the first effective MICROPHONE. He even devised waxed paper, for wrapping food to preserve its freshness.

Edison was born in 1847, in Milan, Ohio, the youngest of seven children. A sickly child, he developed frequent ear infections that often kept him from school and eventually left him partially deaf. In school, he did not do well. He was too independent to follow the rules, leading his teachers to label him as a "problem." But Edison loved to read and tinker with machinery. He even set up a chemical laboratory in his cellar.

But Edison's most productive years would begin in the next decade, when he set up his "invention factory," a research laboratory in Menlo Park, New Jersey. Edison was the first to make invention a full-time business. In his laboratory, he brought together a group of engineers and scientists who worked together as a team to produce many important inventions. At Menlo Park, Edison not only invented the incandescent lamp, he also developed the first electric-lighting system for the home, complete with sockets, switches, and insulated wiring. He also was deeply involved in building the first public power stations, in major cities around the world.

Edison continued working in his laboratory until he died at age eighty-four, in 1931. He is remembered not only for his many inventions, but also for his philosophy of solving problems through careful study and determined experimentation. "There is no such thing as genius," he once said. "What people choose to call genius is simply hard work."

Parts of the Incandescent Lamp

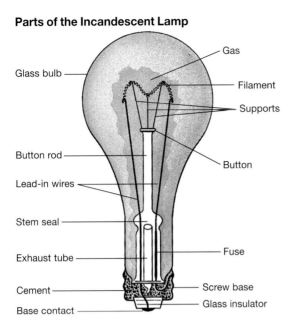

In the typical modern incandescent lamp, a glass bulb encloses a tungsten filament that glows almost white when heated by an electric current passing through it. High-wattage bulbs may be filled with an inert gas that slows down the filament's disintegration.

lamps. They were too bright, noisy, and hazardous to use in homes. Meanwhile, many scientists were experimenting with the idea of creating a lamp by heating a fine wire, or filament, with an electric current. These were the first true incandescent lamps: lamps that produce light by heating a material to such a high temperature that it glows.

In 1845, American inventor J.W. Starr patented an electric lamp that used an electrically heated carbon filament in an airless tube. Starr died the next year. But his work was noted by English scientist Sir Joseph Swan, who in 1860 developed a similar lamp, using a strip of carbon in a glass bottle from which he'd pumped most of the air. Swan's carbon filament burned up very quickly because the glass bottle still contained too much air. When a stronger air pump was invented in 1865, Swan returned to his work, patenting a carbon-filament incandescent lamp in 1878.

Meanwhile, in the United States, Edison was experimenting with hundreds of different materials for making a long-lasting lamp filament. On October 21, 1879, he found a winner: an ordinary cotton sewing thread that had been

scorched to deposit carbon on its surface. He sealed this carbonized thread in an almost airless glass globe. Connected to an electric current, it gave off a steady light for nearly two days. In 1881, Lewis Latimer, an African-American inventor, made incandescent lamps last much longer by using inexpensive carbon filaments; he also developed a threaded wooden socket for his improved bulb.

The next great advance in incandescent lighting came in 1904, when Austrians Alexander Just and Franz Homamen developed a bulb that used tungsten (a metal) instead of carbonized thread. Another important advance was made by American scientist Irving Langmuir, who filled his lightbulb with an inert gas, nitrogen, rather than pumping the air from it.

By the dawn of the twentieth century, affordable incandescent lighting allowed households and workplaces to remain active well into night.

INK

The invention of ink is generally credited to the Egyptians, who in 3000 B.C. mixed carbon (from the soot left when reeds were burned), water, and vegetable gum to make a paint-like fluid for writing on papyrus PAPER. About the same time, the Chinese mixed carbon and glue to create an indelible ink—one that could not be erased. As writing on paper became common, many other inks were made from plant pigments such as indigo, from the dark-stained galls of oak and nut trees, and from the blackish fluids secreted by octopuses and cuttlefish.

INTEGRATED CIRCUIT

From desktop computers to programmable watches, today's numerous electronic devices are made possible by the integrated circuit. This invention is the end result of a series of remarkable advances in electronic miniaturization.

Bulky electron tubes were the first electronic circuits, used in COMPUTERS in the 1940s and 1950s. They were followed by TRANSISTORS, which first made computers practical for many business and government applications. Since each transistor made up just one component of the computer's circuitry, hundreds or even thousands were connected together with metal wires to make a unit. Transistors were far more reliable than electron tubes, but they were still bulky, and wiring them together was a difficult, error-prone job.

Then, in 1959, two American engineers independently found an innovation that ushered in the age of miniature electronics. It was the integrated circuit, developed by Jack Kilby of Texas Instruments and Robert Noyce of Fairchild Semiconductor. What Kilby and Noyce had invented was a way to imprint hundreds of tiny transistors and their connections on a single surface, or "board," made of a semiconducting material such as silicon or germanium. (For more on the manufacture of integrated circuits, *see* SEMICONDUCTORS.) This integration dramatically reduced both the size and cost of electronic circuitry, and it also greatly increased the reliability of electronic components.

By 1971, further miniaturization made it possible to imprint the circuitry for a computer's central processing unit on a single small board. Today, literally millions of microscopic components can be placed on a microchip, an integrated circuit less than a half inch wide. Operating at high speeds, such microprocessors can handle huge amounts of information at one time. They not only provide the brains of home computers, but they control a wide variety of systems in automobiles, home appliances, and heating and cooling systems.

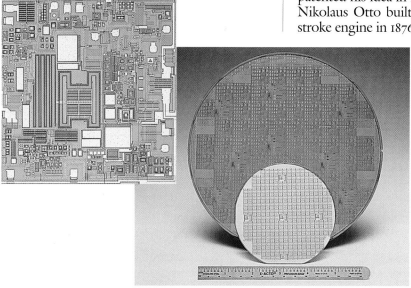

Manufacturers imprint thin silicon wafers with hundreds of identical integrated circuits (right), then cut the "ICs" into separate chips (left) ready for use.

INTERNAL-COMBUSTION ENGINE

An internal-combustion engine transforms the heat energy of burning fuel into power and motion. As its name implies, this type of engine burns its fuel internally, driving a moving piston or rotor that can be connected to a variety of machines that do work. In the early twentieth century, internal-combustion engines revolutionized transportation, making possible the first practical automobiles and airplanes. They did so by providing a more compact, lightweight, and powerful energy source than that of the bulky steam engines that came before.

Scientists tinkered with the idea of an internal-combustion engine as far back as the 1600s. But it was not until 1859 that the French engineer Jean-Joseph Étienne Lenoir produced a practical working model. Reliable but not very powerful, Lenoir's engine ran on natural gas ignited by an electric spark.

The internal-combustion engine's power got a dramatic boost when another French engineer, Alphonse Beau de Rochas, devised a way to compress the fuel-air mixture that the engine burns to create energy. He did so with the "four-stroke cycle" still used today—intake, compression, ignition, and exhaust. De Rochas patented his idea in 1862, and German engineer Nikolaus Otto built the first operational four-stroke engine in 1876.

Today, internal-combustion engines rank among the world's most widely used sources of power. They come in two basic classes. In reciprocating engines, combustion drives a piston back and forth in a cylinder. In rotary engines, combustion drives a turning rotor. Gasoline and diesel engines are examples of reciprocating engines. Gas turbines are rotary engines. The main difference between diesel and gasoline engines is how they ignite their fuels. In the diesel engine, the fuel

Internal-Combustion Engine

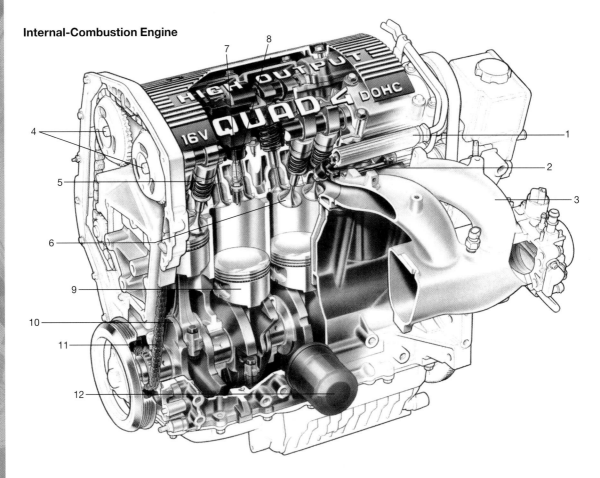

The Quad 4, a four-cylinder, 16-valve automobile engine made by General Motors, illustrates many of the advances in modern, fuel-injected engines. Fuel under pressure enters the engine through the fuel rail (1). Injector valves (2) spray the mixture into each of the four cylinders, which also receive measured amounts of air from the intake manifold (3). Two camshafts (4) rotate the cams (5) that lower the intake and exhaust valves (6). The spark plugs (7) are fired by coils in caps above the plugs (8). The burning gases expand and force each piston (9) downward in turn, rotating the crankshaft (10). The crankshaft also spins the camshaft via a timing chain (11), drives an oil pump that circulates oil through a filter (12), and charges the battery through the alternator. A sensor in the fuel rail monitors the temperature in the exhaust as it is shunted from the cylinders to the exhaust manifold and sends signals to the electronic control module (ECM) under the dashboard. Among its many functions, the ECM controls the air-fuel mixture, sends sparking signals to the coils, and activates the electric fan and water pump.

is ignited directly by the heat of the air compressed in the cylinder. In the gasoline engine, ignition requires an electrical system to provide a spark.

Most recently, computerization has transformed how internal-combustion engines work. In many modern automobiles, for example, a small computer automatically controls speed, choke settings, fuel-air mixture, and antipollution devices. The computer likewise monitors the engine's performance, readjusting settings for maximum efficiency.

INTERNET

In the fall of 1969, a group of computer scientists at the University of California at Los Angeles (UCLA) achieved the unprecedented: They logged onto a computer some 400 miles (644.1 kilometers) away, at the Stanford Research Institute. Their connection, over ordinary telephone lines, used a little known device called a modem to translate computer code into electrical impulses. The scientists' connection lasted only a few seconds. But it marked the first baby step toward the global computer network we now know as the Internet.

Many of the world's great inventions were created, step-by-step, by numerous people. The Internet was invented by hundreds of computer engineers and users, each helping to refine and expand its capabilities. It had its foundations in the Advanced Research Projects Agency Network (ARPANET), a pioneering computer network created for the U.S. Department of Defense in 1968. A major aim was to set up systems and procedures so that every computer on this national network could communicate with every other computer. If one part of the network was damaged or destroyed, the system could automatically reroute communications through different pathways.

In the following years, more and more computers at universities and government agencies were added to the system. Soon scientists and others wanted to use the system to communicate with colleagues around the nation and the world. In 1972, ARPANET introduced electronic mail, or e-mail. Then, in 1974, American computer experts Robert Kahn and V.G. Cerf designed a set of computer programs and procedures that could assure uniform communication between all computers on the system.

In 1985, the National Science Foundation (NSF) took over management of the Internet and developed new ways for researchers to use distant super computers in their research projects.

In 1991, the European Organization for Nuclear Research developed the World Wide Web, an easy-to-use information-retrieval service that allows computer users to travel an "information highway" of documents and pictures. Within a few years, the Web had become the most popular part of the Internet. By 1994, browsers—programs for "surfing the Web"—were being offered to home-computer users.

In the remainder of the 1990s, millions of people discovered the Internet. Some used it for business comuunication, some bought and sold products, and others found entertainment and conversation. By 2000, as many as 100 million people were connected.

IRONCLAD WARSHIP

The idea of armor-plating ships dates to the eleventh century, when Scandinavians reinforced their vessels with iron. In the 1590s, the Korean admiral Visunsin built the first entirely ironclad warships, using them to destroy a Japanese fleet. Still, ironclads remained little used until the advent of steam power in the early 1800s.

In the U.S. Civil War, the Confederate ironclad *Merrimack* easily destroyed a fleet of wooden Union ships. Soon afterward, on March 8, 1862, the *Merrimack* met its match—the armored gunboat USS *Monitor*. The two warships blasted each other for hours until the *Merrimack* finally withdrew, never to fight again. This historic battle is said to have made all the wooden navies of the world obsolete. By 1890, steel was replacing iron, and the world's leading navies were competing to create strong, sleek metal fighting ships. A new era in naval warfare was beginning.

A Currier and Ives lithograph depicts the historic 1862 battle of the Union *Monitor* (foreground) and Confederate *Merrimack*. Jokesters of the day dubbed the *Merrimack* a "floating barn roof," and the *Monitor* a "cheese box on a raft."

JET ENGINE

The first airplanes were made possible by internal-combustion engines that drove propellers. Then, in the 1940s and 1950s, jet engines brought about faster planes than anyone had ever imagined. Thanks to this invention passenger airlines were soon able to fly millions of travelers from city to city throughout the world.

All jet engines work, wholly or in part, in this manner: A jet nozzle at the rear of the engine spurts out streams of hot gases. The backward thrust of these gases produces an equal and opposite thrust that rapidly drives the engine—and the attached plane or rocket—in a forward direction.

Practical work on jet engines for aircraft began in the late 1920s when British scientist A.A. Griffith conducted experiments with gas turbines for turning ordinary airplane propellers. In the mid-1930s, British pilot and inventor Sir Frank Whittle began developing a gas-turbine engine for powering an aircraft without propellers.

About the same time in Germany, Hans von Ohain started working on a similar jet engine. Both Whittle and von Ohain bench-tested their engines successfully in 1937. But von Ohain got his into the air first. On August 27, 1939, von Ohain's engine successfully propelled a Heinkel 178 aircraft on the first jet-powered flight in history. The engine generated less than 1,000 pounds (453.5 kilograms) of thrust but effectively propelled the plane. Whittle, meanwhile, completed his jet engine, which powered a British aircraft in 1941. The first U.S. jet plane flew the next year.

Jet rockets played a significant role in World War II, but piloted jet aircraft did not. After the war, researchers rapidly improved both the engines and the design of the planes, making them a force in both military and commercial aviation.

Today, jet engines generate between twenty thousand and seventy thousand pounds of thrust, and rate among the most-compact sources of power ever developed.

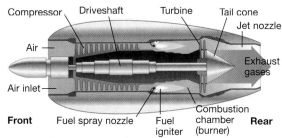

In a turbojet engine, the aircraft is driven forward by hot exhaust gases, produced by burning fuel with compressed air. The burning gases also power the turbine that drives the compressor.

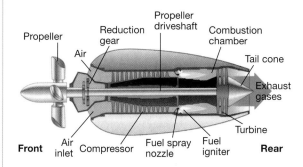

A turboprop engine operates on the same principle as a turbojet, but the turbine also powers a propeller, which provides most of the force that drives the aircraft forward.

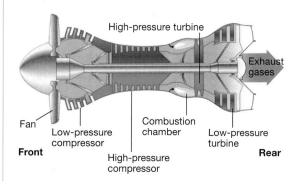

In a turbofan engine, a second turbine runs a fan, which draws most of the incoming air around the engine, providing additional force to drive the aircraft. The rest of the air enters the engine.

The most popular type of jet engine for commercial use is the turbofan, a relatively quiet and fuel-efficient engine.

The simplest and fastest jet engine is the ramjet. Used primarily for rockets, it travels so fast that air is "rammed" into its engine without the need for a compressor. To operate efficiently, ramjets must travel at speeds above Mach 2 (twice the speed of sound).

KEVLAR

In the late 1960s, Stephanie Kwolek, a research chemist at the DuPont Company, developed a new synthetic fiber, which received the trademark name Kevlar. In 1971, DuPont began offering this superstrong fiber for many uses.

Kwolek created Kevlar from a class of materials called liquid crystals, which flow like plastic during molding, but contain molecules that arrange themselves in crystal-like structures.

Kevlar has since been woven into bulletproof body armor and superstrong ropes able to anchor supertankers at sea. It is also used in building canoes and kayaks and in some ultralight aircraft. Its resistance to heat also makes Kevlar valuable as an insulator.

LAPAROSCOPE

See ENDOSCOPE

LASER

In 1960, the American physicist Theodore Maiman flashed an intensely bright light onto a polished rod of ruby crystal. The crystal responded by emitting the world's first laser beam.

Early reports suggest that the device might be used as a terrible "death ray." But although lasers can slice through steel or vaporize human tissue, they have never been used directly as weapons. Instead, lasers have revolutionized global communication. Laser beams now carry telephone conversa-

Ordinary light from a flashlight spreads out in many different colors and directions.

A laser produces an intense beam of light in one color that does not spread out from its source.

A laser beam can heat a spot to several thousand degrees, making it an ideal tool for cutting sheet metal into saw blades.

tions, television signals, and computer data around the world through glass strands called optical fibers. Lasers record and play music discs and videodiscs. Clerks use them to scan bar-coded prices at the checkout stand. Doctors use laser scalpels to perform operations too delicate for the sharpest blades.

The word laser stands for "Light Amplification by Stimulated Emission of Radiation." In stimulated emission, an energy source such as a flash of bright light is used to pump energy into the atoms of a material such as crystal or gas contained within a small tube. The excited atoms then emit their own light energy, or photons, which strike other atoms and produce a chain reaction of photon emission, or laser light.

Ordinary light consists of different wavelengths traveling in different directions. Rays of

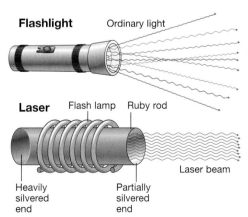

Flashlight — Ordinary light

Laser — Flash lamp — Ruby rod — Laser beam

Heavily silvered end — Partially silvered end

J K L

laser light have the same wavelength and travel in the same direction. The result is a light beam so intense it can drill a hole through a diamond, so powerful it can travel far into space. Indeed, astronomers bounce laser beams off reflectors on the Moon to accurately chart changes in its distance from Earth. Lasers can likewise be bounced off moving objects such as cars and baseballs to gauge their speed.

The principles behind the laser were accurately described in 1916 by the great physicist Albert Einstein. In 1954, a group of scientists led by Charles Townes created the laser's forerunner—the maser, or Microwave Amplification by Stimulated Emission of Radiation. Masers amplify radio waves, a less intense form of energy than light.

LASER DISC AND RECORDER

In 1972, the Philips Company of the Netherlands developed the first experimental laser discs. The technology behind the discs involved using LASER beams and electronic code to record and replay music, words, or computer data.

The audio compact disc, or CD, was first released for sale in 1980. By the end of the 1980s, CDs had made PHONOGRAPH records all but obsolete. Videodiscs likewise became available in 1980, but were slower to catch on. In 1984, along with Japanese partners, Philips introduced the first CD-ROM, or read-only-memory, computer disc. Designed to hold computer programs and large amounts of data, the first CD-ROMs could store and play back the equivalent of more than 250,000 pages of text.

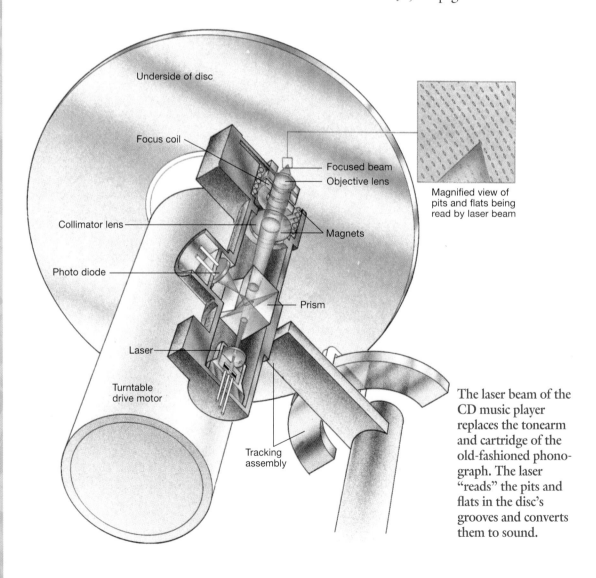

Underside of disc

Focus coil

Focused beam

Objective lens

Magnified view of pits and flats being read by laser beam

Collimator lens

Magnets

Photo diode

Prism

Laser

Turntable drive motor

Tracking assembly

The laser beam of the CD music player replaces the tonearm and cartridge of the old-fashioned phonograph. The laser "reads" the pits and flats in the disc's grooves and converts them to sound.

All three types of laser disc share the same basic technology for digitally recording and re-playing information. First, electric signals from a microphone, camera, or text scanner are converted electronically into binary code (a series of zeros and ones). A laser beam is used to etch this binary code into a plastic disc as a series of microscopic pits. A metal master is made from this disc, and thousands of plastic copies can be pressed from the master.

A disc player is used to reproduce the plastic disc's stored information. Inside the player, a laser converts the pattern of the pits into electric pulses, or binary code. Instantly, an electronic converter transforms the binary code into the desired information—whether music, a movie, or computer data.

LATHE

A lathe is a machine tool that trims irregularly shaped materials into precisely shaped, rounded forms. A piece of wood or metal, secured at both ends, is rotated rapidly while a suitable cutting tool is applied.

The lathe is also among the oldest of machine tools. One early example was used by the Etruscans of present-day Italy in the 700s B.C. Later,

the Romans used lathes to shape wood and soft stone and metal. By the Middle Ages, Europeans used lathes powered by cranks or foot treadles.

Around 1800, lathes were adopted to cut spiral grooves into screws, creating a powerful new fastener. Soon afterward, steam power greatly increased the power of the lathe. It could produce machine parts of precise specifications, contributing to the manufacture of firearms, early railroad cars, and a variety of other industrial products.

LEVER

Among the simplest yet most important of machines, the lever makes work easier by magnifying the force that can be exerted on an object. In its most basic form, a lever consists of a bar pivoted at some point (called the fulcrum) along its length. Weight or force applied at one end of the bar lifts up the other end and its load. The position of the fulcrum in relation to the point where the load sits and the point where the force is applied determines the capacity of the lever. The Greek scientist Archimedes is reported to have said that with a sufficiently long lever and a fulcrum strong enough, he could lift the world.

An 18th-century lathe operator (right foreground) uses a foot treadle to turn a wooden beam while cutting a spiral groove in the beam's rounded surface.

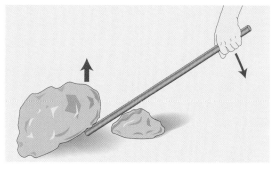

In the lever's simplest form, a pushing force applied to one end of a bar efficiently lifts a load at the bar's opposite end, thanks to a supporting fulcrum (small rock).

No one knows who invented the first lever. Among the earliest forms was the Egyptian shadoof (1550 B.C.), a device that enabled workers to lift buckets of water many times their own weight. Later, the Greeks used levers in war machines such as CATAPULTS. Crowbars, pliers, nutcrackers, wheelbarrows, and playground seesaws are all forms of levers.

LIGHTBULB

See INCANDESCENT LAMP

LITHOGRAPHIC PRINTING

In 1798, the German printer Aloys Senefelder developed a practical way to print images—before this, nearly all printing had been confined to the letters of the alphabet. Senefelder used a greasy crayon to draw a picture on a flat stone. When he treated the stone with an acid, the greasy lines of the picture repelled the liquid, but the rest of the stone remained wet. Senefelder then spread an oil-based ink across the stone. It stuck to the greasy drawing, but not to the wet areas. When he pressed a piece of paper against the surface, Senefelder created a copy of the picture. He called the process lithography, from the Greek words for "stone" and "writing." Senefelder's invention was the first significant printing development since Gutenberg invented the PRINTING PRESS, more than 350 years earlier.

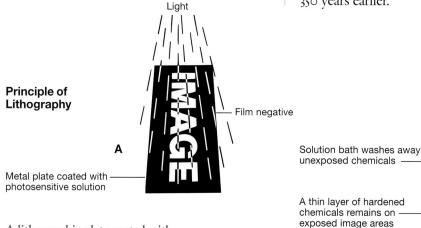

Principle of Lithography

Light

Film negative

A

Metal plate coated with photosensitive solution

Solution bath

Solution bath washes away unexposed chemicals

A thin layer of hardened chemicals remains on exposed image areas

B

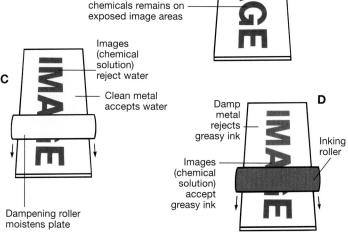

Images (chemical solution) reject water

C

Clean metal accepts water

Dampening roller moistens plate

Damp metal rejects greasy ink

D

Inking roller

Images (chemical solution) accept greasy ink

A lithographic plate coated with photosensitive chemicals is exposed to light through a cutout film negative (A). Then a solution bath washes away the chemicals except from the area that was exposed to light (B). A wet roller then moistens the plate (C), but the water is rejected by the exposed area. Finally (D), the exposed area accepts greasy ink from a roller, while the damp metal rejects it. Only the inked area will be replicated during the printing process.

Then, just over one hundred years later, in 1906, came a major improvement in the process. Early lithography was limited because the stone image began to wear out after a few hundred copies were made. The new process, called offset printing, put the original image on a metal cylinder. The image was transferred (or "offset") to a rubber blanket, which then rolled against the paper to make a copy. Soon afterward, printers developed ways to print in four or more colors on the same sheet, making it possible to reproduce full-color images.

Today, offset lithography is the predominant printing method. Some offset presses print on continuous rolls of paper, creating full-color images at lightning speed.

LOCK AND KEY

The oldest known lock was an Egyptian door fastener used about 2000 B.C. It consisted of a large wooden bolt pierced with holes that slid into a lock housing whose pins dropped into the holes for locking. The lock could be opened only with a key with pegs in the same pattern. Years later, the Greeks devised keyholes, enabling a person outside to use a key to move an inside bolt. These early locks were easy to "pick"—to open without the intended key.

A thousand years later, during the Renaissance, doors could be secured with a lever-tumbler lock. Securer locks were made in England by Robert Barron in 1778 and Jeremiah Chubb in 1818.

In 1861, the American inventor Linus Yale, Jr., devised the modern pin-tumbler cylinder lock, which both defied picking and lent itself to inexpensive mass production. Improved versions of Yale's device remain the most-secure key-operated locks today.

LOOM

One of the earliest mechanical devices, the loom was being used to weave cloth before recorded history. Early weavers used simple frames of wood. Threads were connected to top and bottom pieces to create the warp. The weaver then used fingers or a needle to lace the threads from side to side (the weft) over and under the warp.

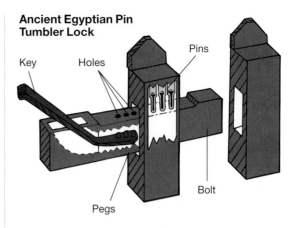

Ancient Egyptian Pin Tumbler Lock

Pins are positioned inside the lock so as to drop into holes in the bolt, thus holding the bolt in place. A series of pegs stick up from the key in positions corresponding to those of the pins. When the key is slid into the lock, the pegs raise all of the pins at once, thus allowing the bolt to slide free.

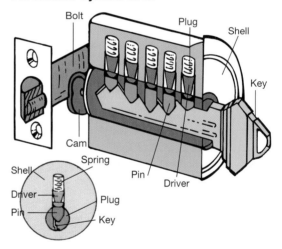

Pin Tumbler Cylinder Lock

The bolt is moved by turning the entire plug. In the locked position, the plug is prevented from turning because springs are pressing the drivers, which in turn are pressing the pins downward into the plug. The notches on the key force the pins to align with the surface of the plug. This allows the key to turn the plug and cam, thus moving the bolt.

The Egyptians showed looms in drawings on pottery made before 4000 B.C. The art depicts a loom made of two beams mounted horizontally across four leg posts. The weaver winds the weft thread around a spool and inserts it into a slim container called a shuttle, which is then slipped between the warp threads. A wooden slat (now called a heddle) is used to lift every other warp thread to create a gap through which the shuttle can be quickly passed. In this way, large quantities of cloth could be woven not only for clothing, but for curtains, tents, rugs, and other large items.

By about 2500 B.C., similar but more advanced looms appeared in China, where they were used to weave silk fabrics. These looms employed treadles (foot-operated levers) to lift the heddles that separated the warp threads for weaving.

Many early looms were vertical. The warp hung down from an upper beam. Such looms were used in Europe until late medieval times, and are still used by some Native American blanket weavers and Middle Eastern carpet makers.

By the 1500s, Chinese and European weavers had devised drawlooms for creating in-tricate cloth patterns. These were operated with the help of a worker, called a "drawboy," who sat on top of the loom pulling slip cords to raise certain weft threads during weaving. Mechanical drawboys were first used in the 1600s. These were perfected by the French inventor Joseph-Marie Jacquard soon after 1800. The first automated weaver, the Jacquard loom, used a revolving chain of punched cards to control the pattern being woven into the cloth. Such programming cards are still used in power looms today.

Even as Jacquard was improving loom technology, the English inventor Edmund Cartwright used steam to provide energy for the first power-driven loom in 1785. Modern industrial looms, though operated by powerful machinery at high speed, perform the same basic operations of warping, lifting, and wefting that were done by hand for thousands of years.

**Standard
Treadle Loom**

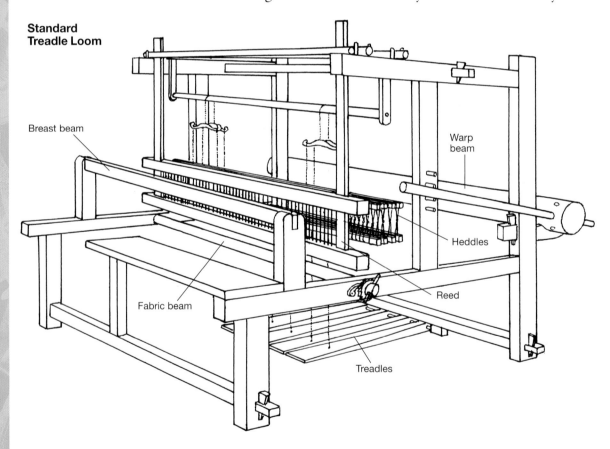

Breast beam

Warp beam

Heddles

Fabric beam

Reed

Treadles

Though treadle looms originated thousands of years ago, their basic design remains the same. Pressing down the treadles lifts the heddles, separating the threads strung between the warp and breast beams.

The Changing World 1460

A revolutionary explosive from the East, GUNPOWDER, has changed the rules of warfare that have been observed in Europe for centuries. Now even the strongest knight in shining armor can be felled by a peasant with a crude GUN. And even the stoutest castle wall can be breached with a CANNON.

Mightier than the gun is the new PRINTING PRESS invented by Johann Gutenberg just five years ago. Now common people can be seen reading pamphlets with revolutionary ideas about democracy and human rights. Gutenberg's press is also spreading new scientific theories at a record pace. For the first time, mathematicians, astronomers, and other scholars can learn of advances made in countries hundreds, even thousands, of miles away. Many are calling this new age of freedom and understanding a "renaissance," or "rebirth," contrasting it with the so-called Dark Ages that preceded it.

Europeans are also expressing a new sense of adventure. The Portuguese have ventured far into the perilous Atlantic, despite stories of sea monsters and devilish mermaids, and have even established farming communities on the edge of the known world—the Azores Islands, some 800 miles (1,288.3 kilometers) from the mainland of Europe. Some are predicting that the Azores will soon become a launching place for the greatest adventure of all time—a voyage around the world.

But few if any Europeans can imagine that an entire new world lies across the Atlantic. North America is home to more than a million people. With no common culture, the Americans still live in hundreds of separate tribes, most of which speak widely different languages.

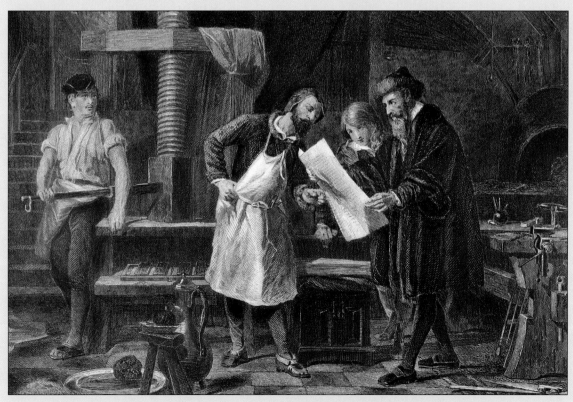

A 19th-century steel engraving depicts Johann Gutenberg taking the historic first printing from his movable-type press.

M

MACHINE GUN

Early firearms had to be loaded after every shot, which meant that a soldier could fire only once every few minutes. Repeating firearms made it possible to fire a few rounds without reloading. But the machine gun allowed a soldier to fire dozens—or even hundreds—of rounds a minute.

An ancestor of the modern machine gun was patented in 1718 by Englishman James Puckle. Mounted on a tripod, its barrel bore six to nine firing chambers, each with its own flintlock firing device. A crank turned the chambers so that after each shot, the next chamber moved into the barrel.

Then, in 1862, American Richard Gatling developed the Gatling gun, which had five to ten barrels that were rotated by a crank that also fed a continuous supply of bullets into its chambers. Five-barreled Gatling guns, able to fire seven hundred shots a minute, played a terrible role in the American Civil War and in later battles in the 1880s.

In 1884, Sir Hiram Maxim, an American-born inventor living in England, made the first truly automatic machine gun. Instead of being operated by a hand crank, it used the energy of its own recoil, or kick, to reload itself. The gun was mounted on a tripod, with an attached belt of ammunition.

Another automatic machine gun, a gas-operated weapon patented by American John Browning in 1892, was later developed for use in World War II. During that war, the Ger-

Gatling guns could fire 700 shots a minute. Firing each of its five to ten barrels in turn prevented any one barrel from overheating.

mans produced their own, remarkably light-weight machine guns, able to fire up to fifteen hundred rounds per minute (twenty-five per second). Machine guns fixed on fighter planes were effectively used by both sides.

MAGNETIC RESONANCE IMAGING

Magnetic resonance imaging, or MRI, ranks among the most important medical inventions of the twentieth century. Today, physicians use this high-tech device to see into the human body and create detailed images. X rays and related imaging devices are effective, but they expose patients to radioactivity, which can be harmful. By contrast, MRI uses only a magnetic field and radio waves.

MRI is based on discoveries by American physicists Edward Purcell and Felix Bloch in 1946. They learned that the nuclei of certain atoms such as hydrogen absorb very high-frequency radio waves when subjected to a strong magnetic field.

One of today's most widely used submachine guns is the Uzi, designed in the 1950s by Israeli army major Uziel Gal.

M

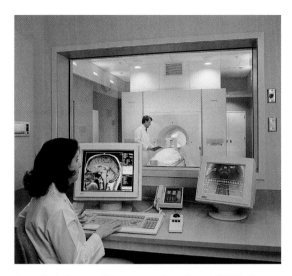

A technician positions a patient in an MRI chamber as a doctor analyzes the machine's computerized image of the patient's brain.

In 1981, British scientists introduced a practical medical imaging device that used the nuclear-magnetic-resonance phenomena. Their diagnostic machine, now called a magnetic resonance imager, or MRI, consisted of a tunnel-like chamber that surrounded a patient with a powerful magnetic field. Under the effect of the magnetic field, the atoms in the person's body become magnetized, lining up in an organized pattern. In this state, the atoms resonate or vibrate when the MRI's radio emitter sends high-frequency waves in short bursts. The responses of different atoms to the radio waves are fed into a computer, which produces an image of a very thin "slice" of an organ or other body part.

MRI can produce detailed images of blood vessels, body fluids, muscles, and ligaments. It even enables physicians to see through bone. MRI is especially useful for distinguishing between healthy and diseased tissue, and so is often used to find tumors. MRI has no known harmful effects to the body. But it can't be used on patients with implanted metal devices such as artificial joints, which can be dislodged by the strong magnetic field.

MAGNETIC TAPE AND RECORDER

In 1898, Danish telephone engineer Valdemar Poulsen invented the forerunner of the magnetic tape recorder. His "electromagnetic phonograph" registered the sound of human speech by changing the magnetic patterns along the length of a steel piano wire. In the 1930s, two German companies (AEG-Telefunken and BASF) developed tape made of plastic containing magnetic particles of iron oxide. This tape proved to have better recording characteristics than did wire.

To record sound, tape is moved past an ELECTROMAGNET (the recording "head") that realigns the particles in response to electrical signals generated by a microphone. Later, magnetized tape was used to record other types of signals—including computer programs and television images.

Americans John Mullin and Wayne Johnson demonstrated the first experimental videotape in 1952. Videotape was soon adopted by networks and stations for recording live shows for later rebroadcast.

In the 1960s, audiocassette tapes were introduced for home use and soon became popular. Later in the 1960s, the first home videocassette recorders were sold. In the 1970s, these VCRs became a popular home-entertainment device.

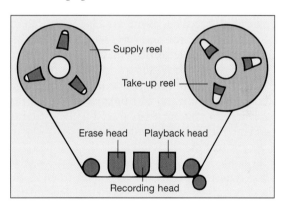

Sound is recorded on tape when the recording head arranges magnetic particles on the tape in a pattern that corresponds to the original sound waves.

MANUFACTURING

For hundreds of thousands of years, humans made everything they needed—all their tools and wares—by hand. This was the simplest form of manufacturing—slow, laborious, and limited by the accuracy of the human eye and the strength of the human hand. The first person to use a machine tool was an unknown

M

Middle Eastern potter, about 3250 B.C. He or she fashioned a turntable mounted on a post—the potter's WHEEL. A lump of clay could be rounded and hollowed out by spinning it on the wheel while shaping it with the hands. Like most machine tools, the potter's wheel made a task easier and faster, and it produced a better product than could have been made by hands alone.

Another important machine tool was the LATHE, which the Etruscans were using in present-day Italy before 700 B.C. Using this "turning machine," craftspeople could shape irregular wood blocks into precisely rounded forms. Seven hundred years later, the Chinese invented a water-powered trip-hammer. A system of rotating cylinders and shafts connected a waterwheel to the hammer, which helped produce beaten-metal items such as sickles and knives. The precision, power, and speed of machine tools lessened the need for human toil. As a result, manufacturers could produce more product with less labor, making useful and decorative objects available to more people.

Manufacturing took a giant leap forward with the invention of the STEAM ENGINE in the 1700s. Steam-powered tools ushered in the first Industrial Revolution (1760-1840). Among these tools were steam-powered hammers, punching machines, cylinder-boring machines, and forging presses. Most important of all, perhaps, was the steam-powered lathe, used to mass-produce screws and other machine parts in uniform sizes.

Indeed, it was the accuracy and speed of machine tools that made modern manufacturing possible. Before the Industrial Revolution, most manufactured products—from GUNS to PLOWS—were handmade by highly skilled workers. So no two were exactly alike, and repairs were difficult. Machine tools enabled manufacturers to create parts of identical size and shape. As a result, a worn or broken device could be easily and quickly repaired with a replacement part. This use of standardized parts, combined with the use of accurate machine tools, began the age of mass production.

Among the first mass-produced items were GUNS AND CANNONS, which soldiers needed to assemble and repair quickly in the field. In 1836, the American gun maker Samuel Colt began mass-producing record numbers of REVOLVERS using a factory full of milling machines, screw

machines, and mechanical presses that he had invented expressly for the job. Other manufacturers soon followed Colt's lead, mass-producing a broad array of products for the general public. By the end of the 1800s, mass production had brought such items as home SEWING MACHINES and BICYCLES within reach of the middle classes.

In many ways, the bicycle was a manufacturing benchmark. Though it was a complex machine, virtually all of its hundred-plus parts could be mass-produced in the 1800s. The one bottleneck in the process was assembly, which still had to be done by hand. It remained for pioneer carmaker Henry Ford to automate the factory assembly process on a large scale. Ford instituted the first true assembly line to produce his famous Model T AUTOMOBILE. A huge CONVEYOR belt moved the frame of the vehicle through the factory as each worker along the assembly line added his or her assigned part—be it a fan belt, door, or door handle. Using this method, Ford reduced the time needed to assemble a car from over twelve hours to just one and a half. As a direct

The wheel has long enabled potters to quickly "throw" small to medium-size objects such as bowls, plates, and pots.

M

Steam-powered locomotives (left) and mining equipment (background) greatly eased the labor of English coal miners in the early 1800s.

result, the price of a new Model T dropped from $850 in 1908 to just $360 in 1916.

Factory production grew still faster with the invention of machines that could control themselves. Automation became especially important in the large-scale manufacture of American weapons during World War II (1939-45). But the roots of automation trace back to a gadget called a governor, invented by James Watt in 1784. Watt's governor kept his newly invented steam engine running at a constant speed by closing the engine's throttle when the engine ran too fast, and opening it when the engine ran too slow. Such a "feedback loop" controls most modern engines.

Similarly, in 1801, the French weaver Joseph-Marie Jacquard invented a LOOM programmed to weave intricately patterned cloth. The loom's "program" consisted of a stiff paper card punched with a pattern of

Automation and assembly lines have remained essential to car manufacturing ever since Henry Ford used them to revolutionize the industry in 1913.

M

holes. As the card moved through a set of gears, each row of holes adjusted the loom to weave a different part of the pattern. This idea of controlling a machine with punch cards would later be used to put information into early electronic COMPUTERS. Computers, in turn, would become the brains of a new generation of automated machines in the last quarter of the twentieth century. Today, many computerized manufacturing processes require no human intervention, except troubleshooting. Bottles, cans, lightbulbs, and paper are examples of products manufactured by fully automated factories.

Over the course of the 1900s, automation did away with much of the drudgery and danger of factory work. Robots with mechanical arms and hands, for example, have replaced many assembly-line workers. Over the long run, however, automation actually created more jobs as high productivity contributed to a growing economy.

MATCHES

The first matches in reported history were used in China before A.D. 1000. Europeans may have experimented with them in the 1500s, but the first written account of experimentation with matches came from the great Anglo-Irish scientist Robert Boyle. In 1680, Boyle rubbed paper coated with phosphorus against a small stick covered with sulfur to produce a flame. Early matches emitted dangerous fumes, however, and frequently ignited spontaneously.

In 1855, Swedish inventor J.E. Lundstrom used a special form of phosphorus to manufacture the first safety matches. They were safer because they ignited only when struck against a second surface coated with the same chemical. In 1892, American Joshua Pusey patented the cardboard match. It was soon manufactured in the small packet of twenty that is still sold today.

MEDICAL TECHNOLOGY

Throughout history, the practice of medicine has advanced more through discovery than by actual invention. Early humans learned that chewing certain leaves settled the stomach, for example, and that a poultice made from another kind of leaf helped a wound heal. Some thirty-five hundred years ago, the Chinese discovered they could relieve many ills by inserting fine needles into special points on the body (acupuncture).

Even in modern times, many, if not most, drugs come from substances originally found in nature (ANTIBIOTICS from microbes, aspirin from willow bark, and so forth). The use of preventive VACCINES can be traced to the eighteenth-century discovery that exposure to a weakened or killed virus can protect a person from a live, disease-causing virus. Anesthesia comes from the nine-

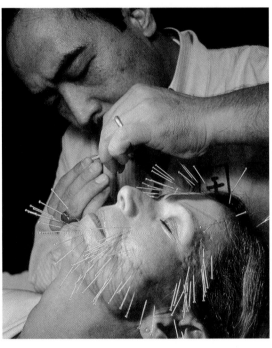

The modern acupuncturist employs his needles in much the same way as did his ancestors more than 3,000 years ago.

teenth-century realization that inhaling certain chemicals renders a person deeply unconscious. Modern-day researchers continue to find many new drugs by the trial-and-error process of mixing substances in test tubes and testing them in animals and human volunteers.

Only in the past two hundred years did medicine develop a sizable technology—a genuine war chest of inventions for diagnosing and treating disease and disability. These tools and machines have helped extend our average life expectancy. Similarly, medical devices ranging from hearing aids to artificial joints have greatly improved the quality of life for millions.

M

In 1796, the British physician Edward Jenner administered the first vaccine, an inoculation of cowpox germs that protected the patient against deadly smallpox.

A few medical devices predate the rush of invention that began in the 1800s. They include EYEGLASSES, first used to correct vision in the 1200s, and the first practical medical THERMOMETER, devised by the Italian physician Santorio Santorio in 1612.

By the early 1800s, scientists and physicians were beginning to understand the biological causes of different diseases. So they became more interested in being able to carefully examine their patients for specific signs and symptoms. The desire to listen to the heart and lungs, for example, led to the invention of the first STETHOSCOPE by the French physician René Laënnec in 1816. It was little more than a wooden tube with a trumpet-shaped sound collector at one end and an earpiece at the other.

In 1851, Hermann von Helmholtz, a German, invented the ophthalmoscope, a device that allowed the physician to examine the retina at the back of the eye. About this time, several similar instruments were devised for looking into the ear and throat. Alongside these medical tools, the nineteenth-century physician's kit also included the newly invented hypodermic syringe, used to inject medications directly into the muscles or veins.

The final years of the 1800s brought what may have been the nineteenth-century's greatest medical invention. In 1895, the German physicist Wilhelm Roentgen discovered X rays,

a kind of energy that passes through soft tissue but not through bone or other dense objects. He used his discovery to create the radiograph, or X-RAY-IMAGING device, which produced images of the human skeleton and could be used to detect bone fractures, dental cavities, tumors, and foreign objects such as bullets inside the body.

Soon after, in 1903, the Dutch physiologist Willem Einthoven devised the first simple ELECTROCARDIOGRAPH, enabling physicians to diagnose heart problems by reading changes in the patterns of the heart's tiny electrical currents.

The early 1900s also brought the invention of a stunning array of laboratory tests for detecting "hidden" health problems such as diabetes, kidney disease, and thyroid malfunction from samples of blood, saliva, or urine. These were followed, in the 1950s, by the first genetic tests, which enabled technicians to detect inherited disorders by examining the actual chromosomes carried in a person's cells.

Meanwhile, medical researchers of the 1920s had greatly expanded the use of X rays by introducing contrast materials (swallowed or injected) that made internal organs visible on radiographic images. In 1958, the Scottish physician Ian McDonald pioneered the use of ULTRASOUND, which used sound waves to

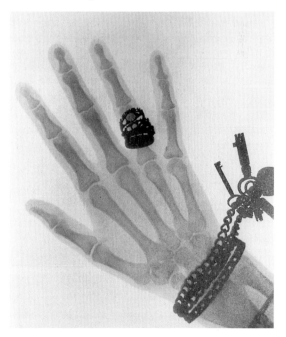

Wilhelm Roentgen, the inventor of X-ray imaging, produced this image of his wife's hand during his early experiments.

M

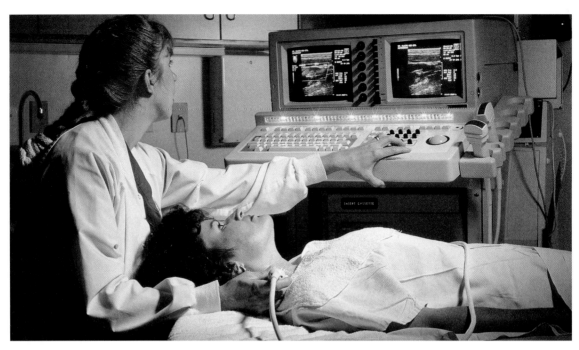

A medical technician uses ultrasound to evaluate blood flow in a patient's carotid artery. The computerized readings can reveal the presence of blockages due to atherosclerosis.

create images of internal organs and other structures.

The ability of doctors to diagnose internal problems took another giant step forward with the development of computer tomography (*see* X-RAY IMAGING) in the 1970s and MAGNETIC RESONANCE IMAGING in the 1980s. CAT (com-

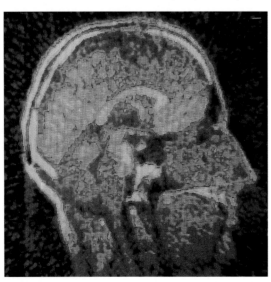

In the 1980s, magnetic resonance imaging (MRI) produced a new kind of window into the human body.

puterized axial tomography) scanners produce detailed cross-sections of the human body by sweeping a narrow beam of X rays across an area and interpreting the electrical impulses with a powerful computer. The MRI constructs pictures of internal organs by beaming radio waves through a patient's head, body, or limbs.

Such high-tech devices enabled physicians to look into the body indirectly. Another invention allowed them to look directly into the body—without cutting into it. That device was the ENDOSCOPE. Similar to a tiny microscope with a light, it was used in the early 1900s to search for internal causes of abdominal pain through a small slit in the patient's belly. By the 1970s, endoscopes were equipped with video cameras and miniature tools so that surgeons could perform surgery through a tiny incision. As a result, operations that once required extensive hospital stays and recuperation were being done on an outpatient basis.

Another invention that would revolutionize surgery was the LASER, an instrument that produces a narrow, highly concentrated beam of light. Invented by the American physicist Theodore Maiman in 1960, the laser was first used as a medical instrument two years later, in eye surgery. Today, medical lasers are used not only to restore sight, but also to stop

M

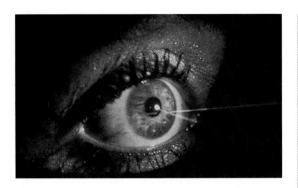

A precisely aimed laser beam enables a physician to diagnose the vision problem known as glaucoma.

internal bleeding, destroy tumors, remove disfiguring birthmarks, and clear clogged arteries.

The twentieth century also saw the development of ARTIFICIAL ORGANS. Notable among them is the artificial kidney, or dialysis machine. In the 1940s, the Dutch physician Willem Kolff invented the first such device to cleanse the blood of patients whose own kidneys had failed. American surgeons were the first to use artificial heart-lung machines in 1953. Then as today, the machines were used to keep a patient alive for an hour or more during open-heart surgery. The first artificial human heart designed for permanent use was the invention of American physician Robert Jarvik. In 1982, surgeons implanted the Jarvik heart in a patient who lived for 112 days. Today, improved versions of the Jarvik artificial heart serve as temporary replacements for patients waiting heart transplants. Researchers hope that the twenty-first century will bring artificial hearts sophisticated enough to serve as permanent replacements.

The spirit of invention finally came to drug development in the second half of the twentieth century. Instead of simply discovering drugs, scientists began actually designing chemicals to address specific medical needs, and then assembling them—molecule by molecule—in the test tube. This new approach, called "rational drug design," began with the work of American drug researchers Gertrude Elion and George Hitchings in the late 1940s. Together, Elion and Hitchings developed an array of new drugs effective against cancers, autoimmune disorders, and many different types of infection. By the end of the twentieth century, computers had greatly expanded scientists' ability to design new drugs

by rapidly predicting the effects of many possible chemicals.

An even more dramatic leap in drug development came in the 1980s with the development of the first GENETICALLY ENGINEERED DRUGS. In 1978, scientists spliced the gene for human insulin into the DNA of a common bacterium. The resulting "transgenic" bacteria churned out the valuable hormone along with its natural products. Beginning in 1982, drugmakers created a wide array of genetically engineered bacteria that produce a variety of human proteins, including those needed to treat growth deficiencies, hemophilia, multiple sclerosis, and many other diseases. Genetic engineers have even introduced foreign genes into higher organisms such as farm animals, which then produce valuable drugs in their milk.

MICROCHIP

See INTEGRATED CIRCUIT

MICROPHONE

When Alexander Graham Bell invented the telephone in 1876, it converted sound into electrical impulses very inefficiently. Many inventors and engineers were soon looking for a better device. The winner of the contest was Thomas Edison, and his invention became known as the microphone.

Edison made his 1877 microphone out of carbon granules packed into an insulated cup and covered with a thin metal membrane, or diaphragm. When sound waves struck the diaphragm, they caused a change in the electric current passing through the carbon. This type of carbon microphone is still widely used in telephone mouthpieces.

Other inventors independently designed microphones like Edison's at about the same time, causing long-simmering patent disputes. Also in 1877, American Charles Curtis and German Ernst Werner von Siemens independently developed dynamic, or moving-coil, microphones. A coil is attached to a diaphragm and suspended between the poles of a magnet. Sound waves striking the diaphragm move the coil back and forth between the poles, producing electric signals.

M

Sectional View of a Carbon Microphone

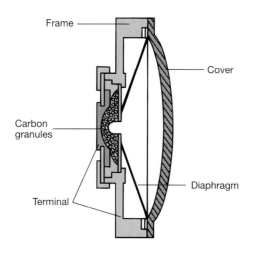

Carbon microphones, used in telephones, allow accurate voice communications and can withstand rough handling.

In 1923, the German inventors W.H. Schottky and Erwin Gerlach invented the ribbon microphone, a high-quality device still widely used in radio and television broadcasting and music recording. It operates by way of a metallic ribbon held between the poles of a magnet. When vibrated by sound, the ribbon cuts the magnetic lines of force between the poles, generating electric signals across the ribbon.

Also in 1923, American inventor A.G. Dolbear developed the crystal microphone that be-

Sectional View of a Crystal Microphone

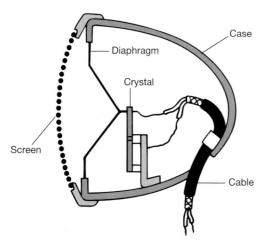

Crystal microphones are valued for their good sound quality and low cost, but they are sensitive to heat and humidity and must be handled gently.

came widely used in public-address systems, home-recording devices, and hearing aids. In this microphone, the diaphragm is linked to a piezoelectric crystal. The force of the diaphragm moving against such a crystal produces a small electrical discharge.

Today, the highest-quality recording and broadcasting work is performed with the capacitor microphone, developed by many different engineers over the twentieth century. In this microphone, a diaphragm bearing an electric charge is stretched tightly very near a metal electrode bearing the opposite charge. This creates a kind of electric field, called a charge capacitor, between the two surfaces. Sound waves vibrating the diaphragm create small electric signals in this field.

MICROPROCESSOR

See INTEGRATED CIRCUIT

MICROSCOPE, ELECTRON

In providing a closer look at things, optical microscopes greatly expanded our scientific understanding of the world. But visible light can reveal only objects larger than the light waves themselves. Since the average length of a visible light wave is 1/50,000 of an inch, or five thousand angstroms, an optical microscope can barely "see" bacteria and viruses, which are smaller. (*See* MICROSCOPE, OPTICAL.)

A scanning electron microscope creates a three-dimensional image of a solid object such as this dust mite by sweeping an electron beam over its surface.

In 1931, scientists determined to view smaller objects invented the first electron microscope. German physicists Ernst Ruska and Max Knoll built a microscope of the variety now called a transmission electron microscope. In principle, it operates much like an optical microscope. But instead of visible light waves, it uses a beam of electrons to illuminate a specimen. Electrons are subatomic particles that also behave as waves, with wavelengths only a fraction of an angstrom. So potentially, an electron microscope can magnify objects thousands of times more than an optical microscope.

In a transmission electron microscope, a beam of electrons bombards a specially sliced specimen just one micron (one millionth of a meter) in thickness. The thin specimen absorbs some of the electrons. Magnetic lenses focus the rest of the electrons onto a monitor screen or a special photographic plate. The parts of the specimen that absorb or scatter electrons appear dark; parts where the electrons pass through appear white. The result is a black-and-white image of stunning detail. Today, the most powerful of these microscopes can capture images of individual atoms.

In 1970, the British-American physicist Albert Crewe built the first practical scanning electron microscope (SEM). By scanning a beam of electrons over the surface of a solid object, this microscope creates three-dimensional images of surface details magnified up to fifty thousand times.

MICROSCOPE, OPTICAL

Before 1930, all microscopes were optical. That is, they used visible light to produce enlarged images of objects and details too small to be seen clearly with the naked eye. In the centuries since their invention, optical microscopes revolutionized science and medicine by allowing us to take a closer look at the world around us, as well as the cells and tissues that make up our own bodies.

The first and simplest optical microscope was the magnifying glass. In 1268, the English scientist Roger Bacon wrote about using this type of single-glass lens to study small objects. Around 1660, the Dutch naturalist Anton van Leeuwenhoek made several "simple," or one-lens, microscopes able to magnify objects more than two hundred times. With his inventions, he revealed for the first time a tremendous world of living things too small to see with the naked eye, including insect eggs and one-celled organisms such as protozoa. Even before Leeuwenhoek,

A scientist using a scanning electron microscope views his magnified specimen on a video screen, then selects the "snapshots" that capture the details he needs.

M

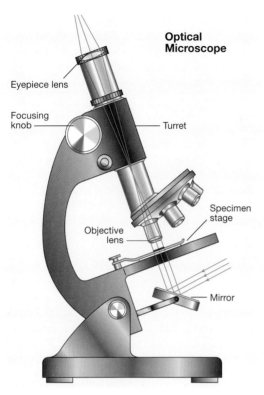

Optical Microscope

Eyepiece lens

Focusing knob

Turret

Objective lens

Specimen stage

Mirror

In an optical microscope, the objective lens produces an enlarged image inside the turret, which is then magnified by the eyepiece lens.

others were experimenting with the compound microscope which has two separate lenses, or sets of lenses. The first was made in 1590 by the Dutch spectacle makers Hans and Zacharias Janssen. In a wooden tube, the Janssens combined two double sets of curved-glass lenses. The ones near the eye are called the ocular lenses, and the ones near the object are the objective lenses. Unfortunately, the techniques for grinding lenses in that day were crude. So the Janssens' magnified images were very fuzzy.

In 1610, German astronomer Johannes Kepler devised better lenses, which were soon used in telescopes and microscopes. But even these improved microscopes failed to provide a clear view of living tissues because they distorted colors, making objects difficult to see. Biologists had to stain most cells to make them clearly visible under the microscope, and stain usually killed the cells.

In 1830, the Englishman Joseph Lister developed a lens for microscopes that greatly reduced color distortion. During the rest of the 1800s, the microscope played an important part in advancing medical science by allowing scientists to see the organisms that cause many diseases.

A hundred years after Lister, Dutch physicist Frits Zernike invented the phase-contrast microscope. His instrument enhanced differences in the way light waves pass through different parts of a living cell, making some parts brighter and others darker than normal. The result was high-contrast microscopic images, that showed much finer detail than scientists had ever seen before.

Scientists continued to improve optical microscopes with better lenses and finer focusing controls. In most laboratories today, monocular microscopes (with one ocular lens) have been replaced by binocular microscopes, through which the viewer looks with both eyes at once. Specialized microscopes have been developed for "viewing" specimens with ultraviolet light or infrared light, X rays, or radar waves. (*See also* MICROSCOPE, ELECTRON.)

MICROSCOPE, SCANNING TUNNELING

The world's most powerful microscope, the scanning tunneling microscope (STM), has a magnification power of one hundred million, and can reveal the contours of a single atom.

This remarkable device, invented by Gerd Binnig and Heinrich Rohrer at the IBM Zurich Laboratory in Switzerland, bears no resemblance to any of the microscopes that preceded it. It has no lenses, nor does it "magnify" in the ordinary sense of the word. Instead, a scanning tunneling microscope operates by exploiting a phenomenon of quantum mechanics known as vacuum tunneling. "Tunneling" electrons cross thin barriers and travel narrow distances no wider than a few atoms.

Most scanning tunneling microscopes operate in a vacuum, though some have been used in a liquid. The instrument's working parts include a tungsten probe whose tip tapers down to the size of a single atom. The probe is attached to three tiny pieces of a ceramic material called piezoelectric crystal. Such crystals compress and stretch in response to minute changes in electric current.

During operation, an electric current of a few millivolts passes through the crystals and into the tungsten probe. When the probe is held to a surface, electrons begin tunneling, or flowing, across the gap between its tip and the specimen. As the probe moves across the specimen, the changing flow of electrons feeds back to the crystals. Their electric response, in turn, is fed into a computer to produce a three-dimensional map of the specimen's surface.

In addition to using the STM to study atoms, scientists have also used it to physically move atoms one at a time. In 1990, IBM scientists in California produced the world's smallest graffito. Using the probe of a scanning tunneling microscope, they spelled out the initials of their company using individual xenon atoms on a nickel plate.

MICROWAVE OVEN

In the mid-1940s, the American scientist Percy Spencer was walking through a radar test room in his laboratory at the Raytheon Company in Waltham, Massachusetts. Suddenly he noticed that a candy bar in his pocket was getting warm and melting. Spencer had discovered the working principle behind microwave ovens.

In the following years, Spencer and his colleagues at Raytheon developed the first such oven—the Radarange. It was built around a magnetron, a type of electron tube originally used to power RADAR sets. The radiation, or microwaves, produced by the magnetron excite the molecules in the food's water and fats, causing them to vibrate more rapidly. This produces heat and cooks the food.

In 1953, Raytheon offered Radaranges for sale, but they were far too big and costly for household use. Weighing about 750 pounds (340.1 kilograms) and costing up to some $3,000, they were bought primarily for use in restaurants and on ships and trains. In the late 1960s, countertop microwaves became practical, thanks to the invention of a smaller magnetron tube by Japanese engineer Keishi Ogura. Today, millions of homes have microwave ovens, which are used to cook and warm a wide variety of foods.

MILKING MACHINE

Before the invention of milking machines, dairy farmers had to milk their cows twice each day by hand. The milking machine became an important labor-saving device, speeding up the process and making it easier to protect the milk from contamination and spoilage.

The first milking machines were introduced to the United States from Great Britain in 1905, followed by more efficient models around 1915. Powered first by steam engines and later by

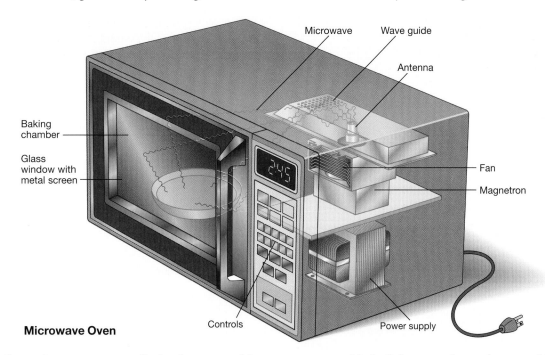

Microwave Oven

In a microwave oven, radiation is generated by a magnetron, a kind of electron tube, and scattered by a small fan to the oven's metal walls for uniform heating. The radiation causes liquid molecules in food to vibrate and warm.

M

Today, even family dairy farms rely on machines to speed milking, ensure sanitation, and record daily production.

gasoline motors and electricity, such machines transformed dairying from a small family operation into the factory system known today.

Milking machines operate by emptying the cow's udders with suction applied through flexible tubes placed on the teats. In modern machines, the milk first passes through a fluid meter that measures quantity, and then is piped directly into a storage and cooling tank.

MIRROR

The morning act of gazing into the mirror is a habit quite recent in human history. Only in the 1800s did the looking glass become a common household object.

The ancient Egyptians and Babylonians created mirrors around 2500 B.C., using highly polished bronze, gold, and silver. There is evidence that the Romans learned to make mirrors from glass, and that the process continued in the Middle Ages. But glass mirrors were rare and valuable, used only by the rich and powerful.

In the 1500s, the glassmakers of Venice (now part of Italy) perfected a process of coating the back of a glass plate with tin or mercury. For generations, they provided the high-quality mirrors for all of Europe. Then, in the 1840s, German chemist Justus von Liebig developed a way to coat a glass surface with a thin layer of silver. This process led to mass-produced mirrors, and soon nearly every household had several.

Today, manufacturers mass-produce mirrors by mechanically spraying molten aluminum or silver onto one side of a glass plate in a vacuum.

MORSE CODE

Soon after the American inventor Samuel F.B. Morse devised the TELEGRAPH (the first practical electrical system for long-distance communication), he invented the first signaling code for converting letters and numbers into symbols and back again. Introduced in 1840, the code was elegantly simple—a series of dots and dashes that a telegraph operator could create with short and long bursts of electric current. Eleven years later, an international convention met to make improvements in the code.

At first, receiving stations used primitive "printers" to write out letters and numbers as they arrived. But telegraph operators soon saw that they could "read" and transcribe messages more reliably than the machine could. For fifty years, quick and accurate telegraph operators were in brisk demand. Then improved coding and decoding machines replaced many operators.

Morse code rapidly gained worldwide acceptance, since it readily fit any language with an

INTERNATIONAL MORSE CODE

A	B	C	D	E	F
G	H	I	J	K	L
M	N	O	P	Q	R
S	T	U	V	W	X
		Y	Z		
1	2	3	4	5	
6	7	8	9	0	

In Morse code, letters and numbers are represented by dots and dashes. An electric current of short duration causes a dot to be printed, and a longer-duration current causes a dash to be printed. A dot followed by a dash represents the letter *A*.

alphabet. When radio was introduced in 1897, Morse code became the universal signaling system between ships at sea. The improved international Morse code adopted in 1851 remained in use through the 1900s, but was gradually replaced by more advanced electronic-communications devices.

MOTION PICTURES

Thomas Edison is often credited with being the first to develop motion pictures. But many inventors contributed to this technology. Among the first and most important was the English-born American photographer Eadweard Muybridge, who in 1877 designed both a way of taking photographs in quick succession and a "magic lantern" that could project the images in rapid order on a screen.

In 1889, Edison employee William Dickson made a major breakthrough when he tried recording pictures on CELLULOID film. Tough but supple, celluloid could be manufactured in the long rolls needed for motion photography. Dickson and Edison also invented a motion-picture camera (the Kinetograph) and a peep-hole viewing machine (the Kinetoscope).

After studying Edison's machines in the 1890s, the French brothers Louis and Auguste Lumière invented a vastly superior device—the Cinématographe—which became the model for modern-day movie cameras and projectors. The Lumières' small, hand-cranked camera could expose about sixteen frames per second.

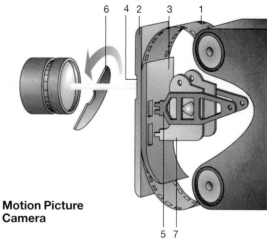

Motion Picture Camera

Unexposed movie film (1) passes between a camera gate (2) and the pressure plate (3) behind the aperture (4). A registration pin (5) holds the film steady as the shutter (6) opens, allowing light to expose the frame. After the shutter closes, a claw (7) pulls the next frame into position.

The movie era is said to have officially begun on December 28, 1895, when the Lumières projected a program of brief silent movies to a paying audience in a Paris café.

The era of talking films began in 1927, with the enormously popular "talkie" *The Jazz Singer*. It was created using a method that synchronized the picture with a separate phonograph record. This awkward system was soon replaced by a process called Phonofilm, which recorded a movie's sound track alongside its pictures on the same strip of celluloid. Phonofilm was developed by inventor Lee De Forest in the early 1920s, but was not adopted by movie studios until 1929.

In 1877, Eadweard Muybridge produced this revolutionary photo sequence using 24 trip wires triggered by the movements of a galloping horse.

Successful filmmaking combines technology, art, and business to produce a powerful form of communication.

M

The Changing World 1785

America's war for independence may finally be over. But the world remains at the height of an even greater revolution—the Industrial Revolution. At the center of this global transformation is England, where hundreds of thousands are abandoning family farms and traditional cottage crafts to work the powerful machinery of modern textile mills and factories.

The transition has not always been peaceful. Fearing the loss of their livelihood, hand spinners have destroyed dozens of the new mechanized SPINNING JENNIES. Mobs of weavers have burned down the first factories daring to use automated LOOMS. But the march of progress cannot be stopped. Textile industrialist and inventor Richard Arkwright has now established an entire system of factories with machinery to assist in every phase of cloth making from carding yarn to spinning and weaving.

Though some of Arkwright's factories are still powered by the WATERWHEEL, he has joined the many factory owners who have recently switched to steam power. In the three years since JAMES WATT introduced his improved, double-acting STEAM ENGINE, the device has become the new workhorse of industry. For the first time, industry no longer depends on the forces of wind and water or the muscles of man and animal to do its work.

The power of Watt's steam engines has likewise revolutionized English mining, pumping water and lifting coal from depths never before imagined possible. Yoked to air pumps (*see* PNEUMATIC TOOLS), these same engines are fanning powerful blast furnaces hot enough to burn coke (a fuel made from coal) instead of charcoal. As a result, coke is now the fuel of choice for the rapidly growing iron and STEEL industries.

Meanwhile, in the newly independent United States of America, Delaware miller Oliver Evans is using both waterpower and steam power to operate the world's first fully automated factory. In his flour mill, grain is dumped onto a moving CONVEYOR belt that carries it through every step of processing without human assistance.

The Industrial Revolution begun in England in the mid-1700s had spread through Europe and North America by the end of the century. Textile mills such as this one provided an abundance of low-wage jobs for women and children.

NUCLEAR-POWER REACTOR

In the 1940s, scientists learned how to unleash the energy contained in the nucleus, or core, of an atom. The world first witnessed this energy in the form of the atomic bomb (*see* NUCLEAR WEAPONS). Since that time, scientists have succeeded in harnessing nuclear energy as a source of electric power. They do so with the nuclear reactor.

The tremendous power produced in nuclear reactors comes from the fission, or splitting, of atomic nuclei. In the process, a small amount of mass (physical substance) is converted into a huge amount of energy. The fission of uranium 235—the fuel most commonly used in nuclear reactors—produces about 160,000 times as much energy as an equal weight of coal.

The story of nuclear reactors began in the 1930s when Europeans probed atoms of heavy metals with nuclear particles. When uranium 235 was bombarded with neutrons, a strange thing happened: the bombardment produced energy and atoms of barium, a much lighter element. Otto Hahn reported these results, and

Lise Meitner suggested the explanation—uranium atoms had been split! Soon afterward, the Swiss-born American physicist Felix Bloch suggested that the atom splitting could be made continuous. He proposed building a reactor in which the splitting of one atom of uranium 235 would trigger the breakup of other uranium atoms. The first sustained reaction was created by an American team in 1942, directed by Italian physicist Enrico Fermi.

Because the United States was at war with Germany and Japan, the main interest in this new source of energy was its promise as a colossal new weapon—the atomic bomb. But after the war, scientists set about taming the nuclear chain reaction to produce useful energy. The nuclear-power reactors they devised share the following features:

The reactor's core contains three essential elements: fuel, moderator, and coolant. The radioactive fuel generally consists of small pellets of uranium packed inside long metal rods. As many as fifty thousand of these fuel rods stand upright in a reactor's core.

The moderator consists of a substance such as water or graphite that surrounds the fuel rods to slow the speed of the particles released

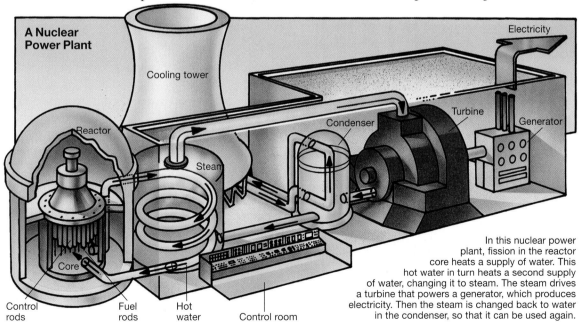

A Nuclear Power Plant

Electricity

Cooling tower

Reactor

Steam

Condenser

Turbine

Generator

Core

Control rods

Fuel rods

Hot water

Control room

In this nuclear power plant, fission in the reactor core heats a supply of water. This hot water in turn heats a second supply of water, changing it to steam. The steam drives a turbine that powers a generator, which produces electricity. Then the steam is changed back to water in the condenser, so that it can be used again.

N O

during fission. By doing so, the moderator increases the chance that these particles will remain within the fuel, where they can split more atoms.

The coolant, in turn, carries away the heat produced by the fission reaction. In many reactors, the coolant is used to boil water for steam power, which can drive turbines to produce electric power.

Other important parts of the reactor include control rods made of a material such as cadmium. This metal absorbs some of the nuclear particles produced during fission. Thus, these control rods can be lowered into the core to slow a nuclear reaction, or stop it entirely in an emergency.

The entire reactor core is housed inside a reactor vessel with heavy steel walls. The reactor vessel itself lies within a containment building made of thick concrete. Such structures are designed to prevent the escape of radioactivity.

In December 1951, an experimental nuclear reactor in Idaho became the first to generate electric power. Three years later, the U.S. Navy launched the first nuclear-powered submarine. A nuclear-power plant in England began operation in 1956, and in 1957, Duquesne Light Company began generating electricity from America's first commercial atomic-power plant, in Shippingport, Pennsylvania. In 2000, more than one hundred nuclear-power plants provided about twenty percent of the electricity used in the United States.

Because it doesn't pollute the air or use up the world's limited supplies of fossil fuels, nuclear energy has great promise. But problems remain. Foremost in the public's mind is the danger posed by rare but catastrophic nuclear-reactor accidents such as the one that occurred in 1986 at the Chernobyl nuclear-power plant in the Ukraine. Nuclear reactors also produce radioactive wastes, whose safe disposal remains difficult. In addition, the cost of building and running a safe nuclear-power plant remains high. The future of nuclear power will depend on how these problems are solved in the twenty-first century.

NUCLEAR WEAPONS

Nuclear weapons are the most powerful tools of war ever created by humankind. A nuclear explosion produces destruction on a scale that dwarfs that of any conventional bomb. Moreover, nuclear weapons produce harmful effects that linger far longer and cover a far larger area than the immediate effects of the explosion itself.

When World War II began in Europe in 1939, German physicists had succeeded in splitting the atom and were exploring the use of atomic energy in weapons. When the United States entered the war in late 1941, the government quickly began a top-secret effort to develop atomic energy. It was called the Manhattan Project. Soon project scientists had created the first atomic chain reaction, and established a secret laboratory in Los Alamos, New Mexico.

The first test of an atomic bomb was conducted on July 16, 1945, in the New Mexico desert. By this time, Germany had surrendered and the war in Europe was over. But fighting against the Japanese in the Pacific continued. On August 6 and 9, American planes dropped atomic bombs in the Japanese cities of Hiroshima and Nagasaki, killing many thousands of people. Days later, Japan surrendered.

After World War II, the Soviet Union soon developed and exploded its own atom bombs. In 1952, the United States developed the hydrogen bomb, some seven hundred times more powerful than the first atom bombs. The Soviet Union followed suit nine months later. Today, as many as twelve nations possess nuclear weapons, and several others are thought to be developing them.

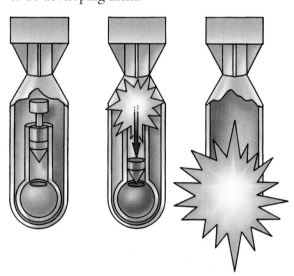

Inside an atomic bomb, a conventional explosive such as TNT serves as a trigger, forcing together fissionable material such as uranium-235 to spark an atomic chain reaction.

Inside a hydrogen bomb, TNT triggers a fission device, which in turn triggers the fusion of deuterium and tritium, two forms of hydrogen, to produce an even greater explosion.

The awesome power of nuclear weapons comes from the energy released from the nucleus, or core, of an atom. This energy may be released in two ways: through the splitting of the nucleus, called nuclear fission, or through the joining of two nuclei, called nuclear fusion.

The first nuclear weapons—atomic bombs—were the fission type. In such weapons, many nuclei undergo fission so rapidly that, in effect, they split at the same time, releasing a tremendous amount of energy. Only a few materials will support this type of nuclear chain reaction. They include the radioactive elements uranium 235 and plutonium 239. An explosive chain reaction also requires a certain amount of fissionable material. An atomic bomb contains separate pieces of fissionable material, each too small to support a chain reaction by itself. The bomb also contains a conventional explosive. When this explosive is triggered, it pushes the pieces of the fissionable material together with great force, starting the chain reaction.

Fusion bombs are often called hydrogen bombs because they depend on the fusion of many hydrogen nuclei. Fusion releases even more energy than fission for the same weight of nuclear material. Fusion is also more difficult to achieve. For fusion to take place, the hydrogen nuclei must be confined and heated to several million degrees. Because of this heat requirement, fusion weapons are also known as thermonuclear weapons.

At the heart of a thermonuclear weapon are forms of hydrogen such as deuterium and tritium, which undergo fusion more readily than does ordinary hydrogen. The weapon also contains a fission, or atomic, bomb. The atomic bomb's explosion produces the extremely high temperature and pressure needed to cause the deuterium and tritium nuclei to fuse—producing the most massive explosion ever achieved by humans.

In the 1950s, the world became concerned about the dangerous radioactive fallout produced by nuclear-test explosions. In 1963, an international treaty banned the testing of nuclear weapons in the atmosphere, in space, or underwater. Since then, most tests have been conducted underground. In addition, some 120 countries, including the United States and the former Soviet Union, have committed themselves to preventing the spread of nuclear weapons. But such agreements are unlikely to eliminate nuclear weapons as long as the leaders of some nations place their own ambitions above the best interest of humanity.

NUTS AND BOLTS

Sometime in the early 1500s, the European makers of armor and clocks began using a new kind of metal fastening system: the nut and bolt. The nut consisted of a small, square block with a threaded center hole that fit over a matching bolt. The bolt was a small cylinder with a broad head and with a spiral ridge—or threads—along its length. These small devices held a tremendous advantage over nails: they could be easily disassembled and reassembled without damage.

The first nuts and bolts had to be tightened and loosened by hand. Around 1550, someone devised an adjustable wrench, or spanner—a strong metal lever for gripping a nut.

In 1835, the English engineer Sir Joseph Whitworth proposed that nuts and bolts be made in standard sizes, and in 1900, Guest, Keen, and Company became the first to mass-produce them. Soon nuts and bolts were being sold and used by the millions—becoming an integral part of the machinery of modern industry.

NYLON

Nylon was the first of the "miracle" yarns made entirely from chemicals, rather than from natural ingredients. It was the brainchild of American chemist Wallace Carothers, who in the 1930s chemically linked long chains of carbon-based molecules to create a fiber with unprecedented strength and flexibility. Nylon soon proved to be cheaper and longer-lasting than silk for women's stockings. It had many other advantages, including better fit and washability.

Nylon's strength and durability gave it a vital role in World War II, when the material was woven into parachutes, flak jackets, tents, and aircraft tires. In the years since, manufacturers have fashioned nylon into thousands of products and have added nylon to natural fabrics to make them more durable.

Quality-control experts check nylon at the DuPont plant in Seaford, Del., where the fiber has been manufactured since 1939.

OFFICE TECHNOLOGY

The first business transactions were no doubt simple—a basket of grain was traded for a clay pot, for example—and so required no records.

But by 4000 B.C., the merchants of ancient Mesopotamia (modern-day Iraq) were buying and trading entire shiploads of goods. Record keeping became important, and someone devised the first office machine—the ABACUS, a simple calculating device still used throughout China today.

The first improvement on the abacus came in 1642, when the young Frenchman Blaise Pascal—bored with the task of adding long columns of figures in his father's office—invented a mechanical adding machine. It operated by a series of hand-cranked counting wheels that displayed a total through small windows in the machine's cover.

Pascal's ADDING MACHINE and similar items remained the only mechanical office devices for nearly two hundred years. But office work in those days depended on many smaller, simpler inventions. Among the most important were the ERASER, invented around 1752; the graphite PENCIL around 1564; and the quill PEN, first used by the Spanish monks around A.D. 600.

The Industrial Revolution of the 1800s greatly expanded trade, and intensified the need for office paperwork. A great labor saver came with the invention of CARBON PAPER by Englishman Ralph Wedgewood in 1806. Previously, the only way to duplicate a document had been to copy it word for word. Even more revolutionary was the invention of the TYPEWRITER in 1864. In the years following its introduction, female typists all but replaced the legions of male clerks who once recorded all business transactions.

In 1887, the American inventor A.B. Dick patented the first office copy machine—the mimeograph, or stencil duplicator, which could make up to five thousand copies from a single wax stencil. In the same decade, Alexander Graham Bell's newly invented TELEPHONE enabled businesspeople to communicate across town without ever leaving their offices. An invention of Thomas Edison's—the PHONOGRAPH—became the first office dictation machine in 1887.

The year 1900 brought the invention of two now ubiquitous office devices—the PAPER CLIP, patented by Norwegian Johann Waaler, and the FACSIMILE (FAX) MACHINE, invented by the German physicist Arthur Korn. It would be another seventy years before businesses realized the usefulness of Korn's ma-

N
O

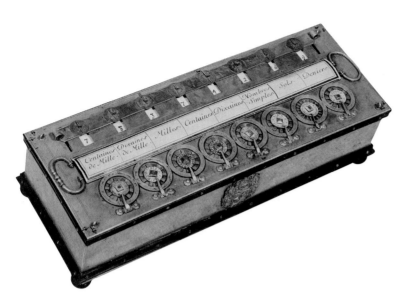

The first practical adding machine performed only addition, with numbers entered by means of dials and gears.

have become standard equipment in practically all businesses, churning out billions upon billions of copies a year.

The second half of the twentieth century brought the invention of a seemingly endless array of special-purpose machines that automated many aspects of business. To give just one example, a company that generates a large volume of mail may employ folding machines to pleat letters, as well as inserting machines to stuff them into envelopes; optical scanners to sort the envelopes by ZIP code, and automatic postal scales to weigh them and print the required postage.

Yet all these labor-saving machines pale in comparison to a modern-day office COMPUTER programmed to perform a wide variety of tasks. International Business Machines introduced the first widely

chine. But the paper clip was an immediate hit. Other small but useful office inventions of the twentieth century included transparent tape, invented by Richard Drew in 1930; the ballpoint pen, invented by Laszlo Biro in 1943; correction fluid, invented by Bette Nesmith Graham in 1959; and sticky "Post-it™" notes, invented by Arthur Fry in 1980.

Among the more substantial office inventions of the early twentieth century was the electric typewriter. The German Blickensderfer Typewriter Company introduced the first office model in 1908, but electric typewriters did not become popular in offices until the 1940s and 1950s.

In 1914, the German-American inventor Edward Kleinschmidt devised the teleprinter, or Teletype, which businesses used to transmit and receive printed messages over telephone lines. Teletype remained a vital link between national and international businesses until fax machines and computer modems replaced them in the late 1970s.

The PHOTOCOPIER, developed in 1940 by the American inventor Chester Carlson, would enter the office in 1951—the first machine to reproduce copies of ordinary (not specifically prepared) documents. Since then, photocopiers

In 1873, the original Remington typewriter featured a ratchet roller to create even line spaces, and a keyboard with letters in almost exactly the same positions we know today.

N O

American inventor Chester Carlson (center) demonstrates his revolutionary xerography, or "dry printing," process in 1948.

used office computer, the IBM 701, in 1953. In the 1960s, the development of INTEGRATED CIRCUITS, or computer chips, greatly reduced the size and cost of computers, making them a common fixture even in small businesses. By the 1970s, many companies relied on computers to handle important data such as personnel records, payrolls, inventories, customer records, invoices, and receipts—responsibilities that once kept millions of workers busy all day. Computers also sped the task of word processing, now one of their most popular applications. In the 1990s, computers even changed the way businesses communicated, with e-mail and Web pages (*see* INTERNET) replacing many traditional forms of correspondence and advertising.

A computer network enables dozens of clerks at an airline reservation center to simultaneously book flights and issue tickets to customers across the country.

By the end of the twentieth century, virtually every office task could be eased, if not fully automated, by a machine.

OPTICAL CHARACTER RECOGNITION

Until the early 1990s, the only way to turn a paper document into a computer file was to manually enter each letter and symbol by striking the keys of a computer keyboard. Though much faster than handwriting, keyboarding seemed slow and error-prone when compared to other computer tasks. So in the early 1980s, computer programmers and engineers around the world set about the task of designing the hardware and software needed to allow a computer to read and process text automatically.

Scanning a page of text and reproducing it electronically is the basis for the modern FACSIMILE (FAX) MACHINE. But a facsimile is only an image, or "picture," of the page. The text can't be revised electronically because a computer does not recognize the individual letters. To solve this problem, computer programmers devised software that could compare each optically scanned letter to a digital "alphabet" and select the most closely matching letter, then convert the image of the letter to the appropriate electronic signal. By the early 1990s, improvements had made document imaging fast and accurate enough for wide use.

OSCILLOSCOPE

In 1897, the German physicist Karl Ferdinand Braun succeeded in focusing a narrow stream of electrons (then called cathode rays) on a screen of fluorescent material. The electrons caused the screen to glow briefly at whatever point they struck it. This improved cathode-ray tube (CRT) was an early ancestor of modern television picture tubes.

Braun then demonstrated that he could use the stream of electrons to show the characteristic patterns, or oscillations, of electromagnetic waves. His cathode-ray oscilloscope has been adapted to show many other kinds of waves, including sound waves and electrical patterns of the human heart and brain. (*See* ELECTROCARDIOGRAPH.)

OVEN

Until a few thousand years ago, all food was cooked by grilling on an open fire or on a heated rock. When early farmers who grew grain learned to cook doughy mixtures on hot surfaces, they also began to experiment with the oven—a confined space that is heated to a high temperature. By 2000 B.C., the ancient Egyptians were using large, rounded clay ovens. The baker built a fire inside the chamber. Then, when the clay walls were very hot, the coals were raked out, and the dough was baked in the lingering heat. Similar ovens of clay or brick remained common until about 1800.

The Red Willow people of the Taos Pueblo (New Mexico) still bake bread and fire pottery in the adobe ovens their ancestors built more than 1,000 years ago.

In 1795, the American-born British scientist Benjamin Thompson built a front-opening iron box heated by a fire in a separate chamber called the firebox. The fire also heated the stovetop, which could be used to warm foods in metal kettles or pans. The introduction of gas and electric heat ushered in the conventional ovens we use today. (*See also* MICROWAVE OVEN.)

P

PAPER

For centuries, paper has been the basic material of written communication. It's also used in packaging, disposable toweling, and hundreds of other materials. By definition, paper is a matted sheet formed by pressing a watery mix of plant fibers. The Chinese official Ts'ai Lun spread a wet mixture of wood pulp and cloth fibers onto a piece of fabric and pressed it into a sheet about two thousand years ago, the earliest documented creation of paper as we know it. Paper was not made in Europe until about one thousand years later.

Early paper was made one sheet at a time. Then, in 1798, the Frenchman Nicolas-Louis Robert invented a conveyor-belt machine that manufactured paper in a continuous sheet. This and other industrial advances rapidly brought paper into common use in the nineteenth century.

PAPER CLIP

Open almost any desk drawer, and you're likely to find several of those twisted metal fasteners we call paper clips. Cheap and handy, they are designed for temporarily attaching papers together without marring a single sheet. The Norwegian inventor Johann Waaler twisted the first paper clip into shape, patenting his clever device in 1900. The time was right for Waaler's gadget. Thousands of offices needed it, and machinery was available that could quickly and cheaply cut, twist, and package the clips by the millions. Today's clips are often plastic-coated (in a rainbow of colors). Some are even gold- or copper-plated.

Making Paper

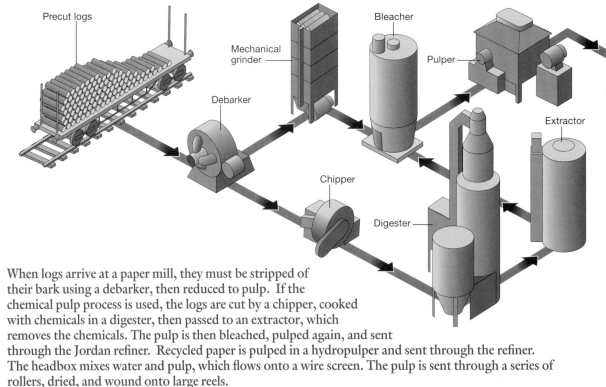

When logs arrive at a paper mill, they must be stripped of their bark using a debarker, then reduced to pulp. If the chemical pulp process is used, the logs are cut by a chipper, cooked with chemicals in a digester, then passed to an extractor, which removes the chemicals. The pulp is then bleached, pulped again, and sent through the Jordan refiner. Recycled paper is pulped in a hydropulper and sent through the refiner. The headbox mixes water and pulp, which flows onto a wire screen. The pulp is sent through a series of rollers, dried, and wound onto large reels.

PARACHUTE

Chinese acrobats used crude, umbrella-like parachutes as early as the 1100s. Leonardo da Vinci sketched his own design of one around 1495. The modern parachute, however, traces back to a bulky canvas device created by the French balloonist Jean Pierre Blanchard in 1785. Later balloonists discovered that silk made a better parachute, but their designs were still crude, swinging the parachutist violently and sometimes collapsing.

The need for parachutes increased greatly in the early 1900s with the invention of the airplane. Designs improved rapidly. Then, in the 1940s, the new synthetic fabric NYLON was employed in parachutes used in World War II. Parachutes saved the lives of many thousands of fliers whose planes were shot down. They were also used by special forces called paratroopers for surprise attacks. Today, parachutes are also used to drop supplies into remote areas, and to slow drag-racing cars and some space vehicles during their descent through the atmosphere.

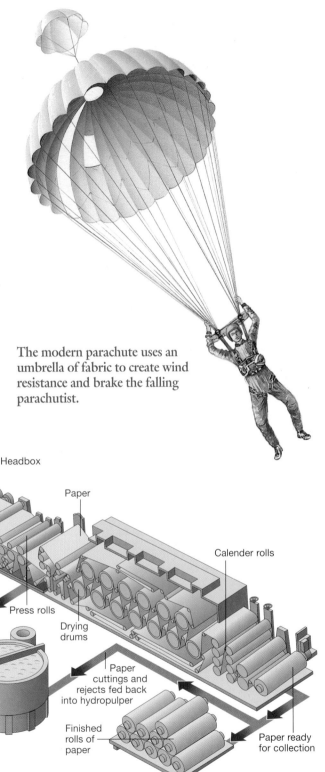

The modern parachute uses an umbrella of fabric to create wind resistance and brake the falling parachutist.

Headbox

Jordan refiner

Paper

Calender rolls

Filter

Press rolls

Drying drums

Recycled paper

Hydropulper

Paper cuttings and rejects fed back into hydropulper

Finished rolls of paper

Paper ready for collection

P

PARTICLE ACCELERATOR

A particle accelerator is a high-energy device that produces a beam of fast-moving, electrically charged atomic particles. Since the 1930s, particle accelerators have been an important research tool, helping us understand the fundamental building blocks of matter and the forces that hold them together. Physicists use particle accelerators to shoot particle beams at atoms and study how the atoms break apart. For this reason, particle accelerators are often called "atom smashers."

Credit for the first particle accelerator is given to the English physicist Sir John Cockcroft and the Irish physicist Ernest Walton, who developed a single-step accelerator and used it to bombard various atoms with high-speed particles in the early 1930s. In 1931, the American physicist Ernest Lawrence invented a more powerful device—the cyclotron, or circular accelerator. And in 1947, the American physicist Luis Alvarez invented the linear accelerator. Both circular and linear accelerators use electric fields to produce and accelerate beams of high-energy particles. These particles flow in a single direction through a chamber that's been emptied of air.

The great challenge in accelerator technology is to ensure that the machine's electric fields accelerate the charged particles in only one direction. In linear accelerators, this is accomplished by sending the particles through a straight line of tube-shaped vacuum chambers, called drift tubes. Between each tube is an electric field called an accelerating gap. The longer the line of tubes and gaps, the more energy the particles gain.

Circular accelerators use large magnets to bend the path of the charged particles so that they travel in a circle. In this way, the particles can pass through the same accelerating gap over and over again, gaining energy with each pass.

PEN

A pen is a tool for writing or drawing with fluid INK. The Egyptians made the first known pens around 1500 B.C., using bamboo reeds whose tips had been split, frayed, or carved. Pens continued to be made solely from reeds for some two thousand years.

The fall of the Roman Empire gave rise to the next important type of pen. In the early 600s, European monks could no longer get

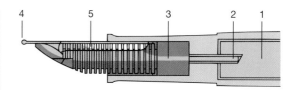

A modern fountain pen features an ink cartridge (1) pierced by a tube (2) that channels ink through the nib (3) to the tip (4). A vent hole (5) allows air to enter as the ink empties.

the Mediterranean reeds they needed for writing. So they devised a way to split and carve a goose-feather quill so it would hold and deliver ink from its tip. Quills had the disadvantage of holding only enough ink to write a few words at a time. In addition, their writing tips wore out quickly, and so required frequent replacement.

For centuries, people tried to design better pens. Finally in 1830, steelmakers in England found a way to produce affordable, long-wearing steel points for quill pens. These steel "nibs" gave quill pens both a longer life and a finer writing tip.

Then, in the 1880s, the American Lewis Waterman invented a writing instrument that would rapidly replace the quill pen. It was the fountain pen, able to store a generous amount of ink in a hollow reservoir without leaking or clogging. Waterman's pen had to be filled carefully with an eyedropper. "Automatic" fountain pens, which filled themselves with the pull of a lever, followed in 1913.

For half a century, the fountain pen remained the writing instrument of choice. A crude version of the ballpoint pen was invented in 1888 by the American John Loud. But the first practical ballpoint was developed fifty years later by Laszlo Biro of Hungary. In the 1950s, improvements in the ballpoints made them the most popular writing instrument.

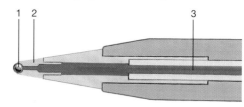

The working parts of a ballpoint pen consist of a metal ball (1) that rotates inside a brass point (2) connected to an ink tube (3) anchored inside the pen barrel.

They were far cheaper and easier to use than fountain pens. In 1964, Japanese manufacturers introduced felt-tip pens, or "markers." These were used at first for marking and poster making. Very-fine-tipped models were offered later and became popular for everyday writing.

PENCIL

Four hundred years after its invention, the graphite pencil remains the world's most popular writing instrument. This simple device dates back to 1564, when an English farmer discovered a soft black substance in his pasture. He found he could mark his sheep with the stuff and it wouldn't wash off. Soon this substance—named "graphite," from the Greek word meaning "to write"—was being cut into lengths and sold as writing sticks. The graphite was wrapped in string to keep fingers clean. At first some scientists believed that graphite was an ore of lead, and the dark part of a pencil is still called its lead. But graphite is really a form of the element carbon.

The new "pencils" proved easier and neater to use than quill pens. Best of all, their marks could be erased, when desired, with a piece of rubber. Modern pencils contain a mixture of powdered graphite and clay encased in cedar, a wood that sharpens easily without splintering.

PENDULUM

A pendulum is a simple device that consists of a weight suspended so that it can swing freely with the force of gravity. In 1581, Galileo discovered an important property of pendulums while watching chandeliers swinging from the

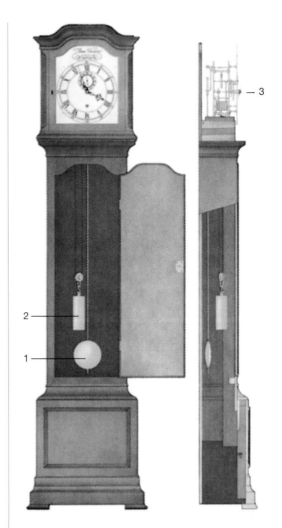

The pendulum (1) of a 19th-century grandfather clock is driven by a descending weight (2) hung from a series of geared wheels and escapements (3).

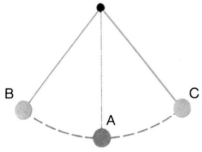

A simple pendulum uses the force of gravity to keep a swinging weight (A) moving between two points (B and C).

ceiling of a cathedral on long ropes. He noted that the time required for a pendulum to complete its swing is virtually the same whether it is swinging vigorously or barely moving. In other words, the duration of a pendulum's swing is determined only by the pendulum's length, not by the width of its swing.

The Dutch scientist Christiaan Huygens developed a pendulum clock in 1656, ushering in a new age in accurate timekeeping. The value of the pendulum was its ability to accurately control a clock's ESCAPEMENT through the constancy of its swing. Earlier clocks ran fast when their spring was tightly wound, and slow when it was nearly unwound. With a pendulum, the clock would run at a uniform speed and keep better time.

PESTICIDES

Scientists estimate that there are some sixty-seven thousand different kinds of pests that attack farm crops around the world. Since ancient times, farmers have used various natural mixtures to discourage them. For example, one early weapon against insects was pyrethrum, a powder made by Chinese farmers from dried chrysanthemum flowers. But in the twentieth century, "chemical warfare" between farmers and pests (both plant and animal) reached a new stage of intensity.

In the 1940s, British agricultural researchers developed 2,4-D, a herbicide (plant killer) that fought weeds by causing them to grow abnormally. About the same time, the Swiss chemist Paul Müller discovered that a chemical called DDT had an extraordinary ability to kill insects by interfering with their nervous system. In the late 1940s and the 1950s, DDT helped revolutionize agriculture by attacking major insect pests. It also reduced world levels of the human disease malaria by helping kill the mosquitoes that spread it.

It was soon discovered that both plant and insect pests can develop resistance to pesticides. So hundreds of new pesticides were created. Production soared more than thirty times over, to an estimated 2.5 million tons worldwide by 1990.

It also became clear in the 1960s that many pesticides such as DDT and 2,4-D harm wildlife and desirable plants—and might also harm humans. DDT was causing the gradual disappearance of many species of birds and beneficial insects such as bees. It was outlawed in the United States in the early 1970s. Still, the widespread use of pesticides remained a major environmental problem, encouraging an urgent search for safer ways to protect crops and reduce human disease.

PHONOGRAPH

The term phonograph was coined by THOMAS EDISON in 1877 for his first sound-recording device. While working on improvements for the newly invented TELEPHONE, Edison noticed that he could feel the vibrations of the small

Though it fueled a "green revolution" by dramatically increasing crop yields, the widespread spraying of agricultural pesticides has also endangered the health of many desirable plants, animals, and humans.

P

disc inside the earpiece when someone was speaking. He could feel the vibrations more clearly if he attached one end of a needle to the disc and put the other end against his finger.

Soon after, Edison made a related discovery. While working on a gadget to improve the telegraph, he noticed that when he ran telegraph tape with raised impressions representing the dots and dashes of telegraph code over a steel spring, odd "singing" sounds somewhat resembling speech were produced.

Putting his two discoveries together, Edison set up an experiment: He used his own voice to vibrate a metal disc to which a needle was attached. At the same time, he rapidly moved a paper coated with wax under the needle. As Edison hoped, the needle made impressions on the wax. Next, Edison tried making impressions on tin foil stretched around a cylinder. On one occasion, Edison turned the cylinder with a crank, and began shouting out the lyrics to "Mary Had a Little Lamb," causing the "recording" needle to produce impressions in the foil. Then he set up a second needle to "replay" the sound. When he cranked the cylinder, he heard his own voice reciting the rhyme.

Edison's invention set off great excitement around the world. In 1895, the German-born American inventor Emile Berliner improved on Edison's invention with his "gramophone,"

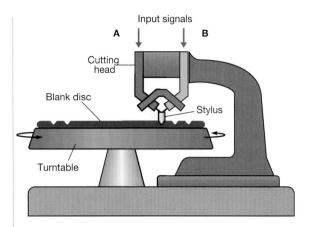

In making a stereo phonograph record, separate channels of amplified sound (input signals) vibrate a cutting stylus, which chisels a groove with different vibration waves on its right and left walls.

using wax-covered metal discs instead of cylinders for recording sound. In 1901, Berliner found an effective way to manufacture hundreds of these "records" from a single master.

Early records had rather large grooves, and turned at a standard speed of seventy-eight rotations a minute. They held less than five minutes of music, and were difficult to hear because of the scratchy noise of the records' surface. They also wore out after being played many times—the heavy replay needle ground down the impressions on the record surface. In 1948, American engineer Peter Goldmark developed the long-playing, microgroove record. It was designed to spin only thirty-three and one-third times per minute, and the fine, thin replay stylus required only a small weight. The discs produced clear sound and played for up to twenty-five minutes on one side. When the new phonographs were connected to wide-range speakers and powerful amplifiers, they produced "high-fidelity" sound and were known as "hi-fi" sets.

In 1957, engineers created stereophonic sound. They cut two separate tracks into the groove of a record, and designed the phonograph to play the two tracks through separate speakers. This made recordings sound even more lifelike.

Phonographs remained tremendously popular for a full century, but they were replaced after 1970 by new recording and playback methods. CASSETTE tape players produced sound that was recorded magnetically on recording

Thomas Edison posed with his favorite invention, the tinfoil phonograph, at the National Academy of Sciences in 1877. He later demonstrated its "magic" at the White House.

P

tape. LASER-DISC (or CD) players used a laser beam to "read" sound that was recorded as a pattern of hills and valleys in microscopic grooves on a CD.

PHOTOCOPIER

In 1934, while pursuing a career as a patent lawyer, the American inventor Chester Carlson hated spending hours hand-copying the many complex documents his work required. He vowed to create a fast, inexpensive machine for making copies.

For years, Carlson conducted experiments, first in his own kitchen and later in a make-shift laboratory in the back of his mother-in-law's beauty shop. In 1938, he got his first patent for what he called electrophotography—a means of duplicating documents with dry chemicals and electrostatically charged plates. But Carlson lacked the money to build a machine that could actually produce copies. Finally, in 1944, he reached an agreement with the Battelle Memorial Institute, which funded the machinery he needed. The company also gave Carlson's invention a catchier name—"xerography" from the Greek words meaning "dry writing."

Photocopiers have been greatly improved in the years since Carlson's original, but they still work on the same principles. At the heart of the device is a drum coated with the chemical selenium. At the beginning of the copying process, the drum is given a positive electric charge. Flashlamps illuminate the document to be copied (placed facedown on a glass plate). Printed areas on the document block areas of the drum from this light. But areas of the drum beneath unprinted areas are illuminated and so lose their electric charge. Next, a negatively charged dark powder called toner passes over the drum surface. Only those drum areas retaining their positive charge (those beneath printed areas of the paper) hold the toner. At the same time, an ordinary piece of paper is fed into the machine, which rolls against the drum surface. The toner from the drum transfers to the paper, which is then heated to fuse the toner particles to the paper. Finally, the drum automatically cleans itself of leftover toner and stands ready for the next copy.

The first office copiers using Carlson's process were produced by the Xerox Corporation and went into service in 1958. Though they weighed some 600 pounds (272.1 kilograms), they were a great hit. Since then, refinements have made office copiers smaller, faster, and easier to operate. In 1973, the Japanese company Canon introduced a color photocopier. Many machines also employ electronically controlled conveniences such as automatic sorting and stapling of documents.

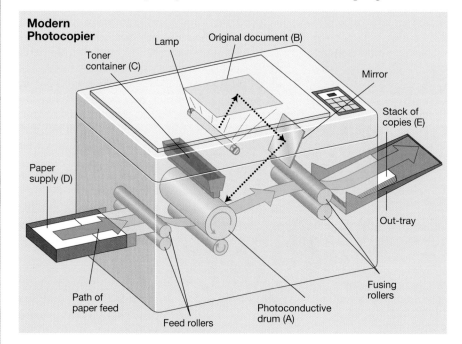

Modern Photocopier

Toner container (C)
Lamp
Original document (B)
Mirror
Stack of copies (E)
Paper supply (D)
Out-tray
Path of paper feed
Feed rollers
Photoconductive drum (A)
Fusing rollers

In photocopiers that print electrostatically, a photoconductive drum (A), coated with selenium, is positively charged. It is then exposed to the document (B) to be copied, and covered with negatively charged toner (C), which forms a positive image on the copying paper (D). Heat fuses the toner to the paper, producing a permanent image (E).

PHOTOELECTRIC CELL

In 1839, French physicist Edmond Becquerel discovered that certain metals produce a small electric current when exposed to light. In 1887, Heinrich Hertz, a German scientist, found that shining a light on an electrically generated spark changed the spark's length. Then, in 1899, Philippe Lenard, a German, and Sir Joseph Thomson, an Englishman, proved that light causes metals to give out a stream of electrons, which form an electron current. The discovery of such "photoelectric effects" led to the development of three types of important devices: light meters, electric eyes, and solar batteries.

Light meters, technically known as photoconductive cells, are among the oldest photoelectric devices, developed in the late 1800s. When light shines on a photoconductive cell, it strengthens an electric current already flowing from an attached battery or other power source. If the device is a simple meter, it can be used by a photographer to judge how to set a camera (the camera lens is opened wider to compensate for diminished light). But the change in current can also be used to turn streetlights on when it gets dark, and to turn them off when light returns in the morning.

Electric eyes, technically known as photoemissive cells, operate such devices as automatic doors, motion detectors, and smoke alarms. They employ a beam of light that, when interrupted (by an intruder, for instance, or by a particle of smoke), opens an electric circuit that powers the desired mechanical response (opening a door or sounding an alarm).

The third type of photoelectric device is the solar cell, or photovoltaic cell, which converts light directly to electricity. The American

Solar panels power the light and bell of a buoy that automatically warns passing ships of an underwater obstruction.

scientist Charles Fritts developed the first solar battery in the 1880s, using selenium coated with a fine layer of gold. The first practical solar cells were not devised for almost one hundred years. Today, small solar cells help provide power for space probes and satellites. Finding an economical way to convert solar power to electricity for general use could solve major environmental problems caused by burning fossil fuels.

PLASTIC

See CELLULOID

PLOW

The plow—a device to break up and turn over soil before planting—has been called the most important invention in the history of agriculture. The first Stone Age farmers no doubt used deer antlers and forked branches to scratch the soil before planting. About 3000 B.C., the first human-built plows appeared in

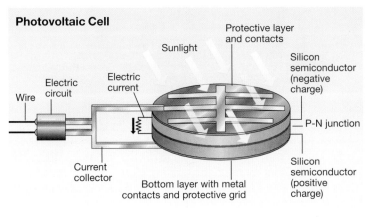

Photovoltaic Cell

Sunlight
Protective layer and contacts
Electric current
Electric circuit
Wire
Silicon semiconductor (negative charge)
P-N junction
Current collector
Bottom layer with metal contacts and protective grid
Silicon semiconductor (positive charge)

When sunlight strikes the P-N junction inside a photovoltaic cell, it causes electrons in the atoms of the cell's two semiconductor layers to move between them, creating an excess of electrons in one layer (treated to attract electrons) and a shortage in the other (treated to give up electrons). When a wire, electric circuit, or other device connects the layers, the motion of the electrons, called an electric current, continues in an attempt to restore the atoms in each layer to a state of balance. This current can be collected and used as a power source to operate many different and useful objects.

P

By the Middle Ages, European plows featured a metal colter, or cutting blade, in front of the plowshare to help break up heavy soils.

the Middle East. Their basic design consisted of a pointed wedge of wood with a handle that one farmer could use for guiding, and a beam to which other farmers could yoke themselves for pulling.

By Roman times, farmers were using stronger plows equipped with iron blades, or plowshares. Over the following centuries, plows changed little in basic design. But they became larger and heavier, were sometimes mounted on WHEELS, and were eventually pulled by oxen and then by horses (*see* HARNESS).

Early plows were good for cutting through light soil. But they didn't turn the soil over, nor did they work well in the heavier soils of northern Europe. Between A.D. 1000 and 1100, the Slavs in Eastern Europe invented the moldboard, a curved metal surface placed behind the plowshare to automatically turn the soil over as the plow passes. The moldboard plow also dug deeper into the earth than could older plows, better loosening the soil for strong crop growth.

English and American inventors greatly improved the plow in the eighteenth and nineteenth centuries. In 1720, the Englishman Joseph Foljambe invented the first moldboard plow sheathed in iron. In 1797, the American Charles Newbold built a cast-iron plow. About the same time, Thomas Jefferson was designing better moldboards. In 1819, New Yorker Jethro Wood used one of Jefferson's designs in a cast-iron plow featuring standard-size, interchangeable parts.

Wood's sturdy plow proved ideal for the rocky soils of eastern America. But it didn't scour itself of the heavy, sticky soil of the Midwest. In 1838, the Illinois blacksmith John Deere developed a plow made of saw-blade steel that cut the prairie soil cleanly. His plow enabled Midwestern farmers to cultivate more land with fewer horses than ever before, and helped transform their region into the vast grain belt it remains today.

In 1842, the Cravath brothers of Bloomington, Illinois, introduced the disc plow, featuring sharp, curved steel discs that easily rolled through hard, dry soil as they sliced it. The first

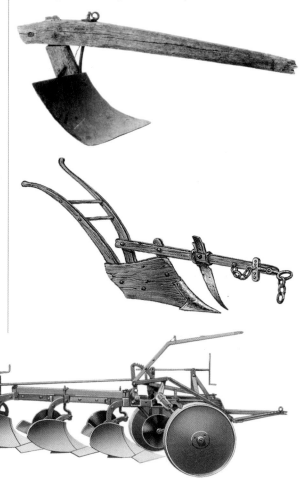

Deere's steel plow (top) was able to slough off the stickiest prairie soil. Still used in traditional farming, the walking plow (middle) is pulled by draft animals and guided by the farmer. The tractor-pulled gang-plow (bottom) cuts several furrows at once.

successful steam-powered plow followed in the 1860s, and gasoline-burning tractors appeared in the 1890s. But most American farmers continued to rely heavily on animal power until the 1930s and 1940s. Today's tractors can pull assemblies of more than twenty plows, able to till more than 150 acres (60.75 hectares) in a day.

PLYWOOD

Plywood is made from thin layers, or plies, of wood glued together in a precise way. This layering gives plywood a greater strength and durability than that of ordinary wood. In addition, a thin layer of expensive wood can be used on the surface to produce a beautiful yet strong panel at low cost.

For maximum strength, plywood is always made from an odd number of layers arranged so that the grain of one layer lies at a right angle to those next to it. This cross-layering gives plywood its remarkable strength and resistance to splitting and swelling.

To produce plywood, manufacturers debark a log and soften it with steam, then rotate it against a blade to produce a continuous sheet of thin wood.

The ancient Chinese and Egyptians made simple forms of plywood. In 1830, the cabinetmaker Michael Thonet became the first European to do so, building chairs out of layered wood. But plywood didn't become widespread till the introduction of mass-production methods in the early 1900s. In 1905, the U.S. Plywood Corporation opened the first manufacturing plant in Portland, Oregon. Then as now, manufacturers shaved off large, thin sheets of wood, which were then glued together with various ADHESIVES such as resin. The core layers of a plywood sheet typically consist of softwood such as Douglas fir, with an attractive hardwood such as oak or cherry as the outside face.

PNEUMATIC TOOLS

Pneumatic tools are power machinery driven by compressed air. The air powering the pneumatic tool is fed to it through hoses from a compressor that draws air and uses pistons or rotors to compress, or pressurize, it. A valve between the air line and the tool allows the operator to control the tool's pneumatic power. Among the most important tools are pneumatic drills and hammers.

Pneumatic tools have a number of advantages over conventional power tools. Because the compressor can be located some distance from the tool itself, a pneumatic tool can be considerably smaller and lighter than an electric tool with the same power. Also, pneumatic tools do not produce electric shocks or sparks. They are especially useful in projects where wet conditions or explosive materials are nearby.

The ancestor of today's pneumatic devices is the hand bellows, a simple kind of air compressor invented around 1500 B.C. in Egypt.

The air pump above was invented in Germany by Otto von Guericke, who used it to prove the existence of vacuums.

About A.D. 1650, the German engineer Otto von Guericke used the idea of mechanically compressing air to create an air pump. Von Guericke used his air pump for scientific experiments.

It would be another century before anyone thought to harness an air pump for powering machinery. About 1800, the Englishman George Medhurst used one to drive a motor inside a

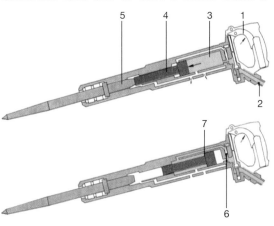

Pressing the control lever (1) of a pneumatic hammer triggers the entrance of compressed air into the inlet (2) and inner chamber (3), forcing the piston (4) down against the tool bit (5). The diaphragm valve (6) reverses the airflow, drawing air into an outer chamber (7) and forcing the piston back up to complete the cycle.

mine. By the late 1800s, pneumatic drills and hammers were in wide use. Their great power made possible the building of America's first large-scale rock tunnel—the Hoosac Tunnel, a railway passage in the Berkshire Hills of western Massachusetts.

PNEUMATIC TUBE

See TIRE

POLYESTER

Among the many synthetic fibers and plastics used today, nearly half are polyesters—made by chemically linking various acids and alcohols into long-chain molecules. In 1937, chemists with Britain's Imperial Chemical Industries created the first polyester—polyethylene, a lightweight plastic still commonly used for plastic bags, milk cartons, other packaging, and insulation. In the following decades, chemists around the world created dozens of similar polyester substances. Today, they're commonly used in hundreds of products such as knit fabrics, bottles, hoses, photographic film, and carpeting. Because polyester is readily broken down and reused, it has become the world's most heavily recycled fiber.

POLYMERASE CHAIN REACTION

In 1993, the American biochemist Kary Mullis won the Nobel Prize in chemistry for his invention of polymerase chain reaction (PCR). This process rapidly multiplies a small sample of DNA—genetic material from a person or other living thing. Today, machines designed to carry out this biochemical technique can generate billions of copies of DNA fragments in a few hours. Medical and police laboratories and scientists use the reproduced fragments in many important medical and forensic tests. Before the invention of PCR, tests of genetic materials were difficult and slow because there was only a tiny amount of the material to be tested.

In essence, PCR is a three-step biochemical reaction. First, the desired sample—a fragment of genetic material—is heated to unravel the two strands of the DNA molecule. Second,

Polymerase Chain Reaction

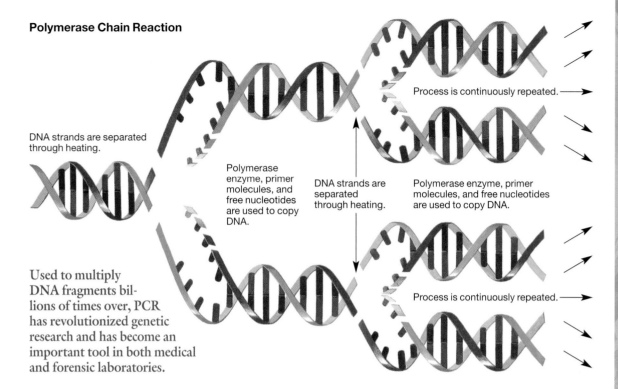

DNA strands are separated through heating.

Polymerase enzyme, primer molecules, and free nucleotides are used to copy DNA.

DNA strands are separated through heating.

Polymerase enzyme, primer molecules, and free nucleotides are used to copy DNA.

Process is continuously repeated. ⟶

Process is continuously repeated. ⟶

Used to multiply DNA fragments billions of times over, PCR has revolutionized genetic research and has become an important tool in both medical and forensic laboratories.

segments of artificially prepared DNA, called primers, are attached to each strand to prepare it for copying. Finally, the natural enzyme DNA polymerase is added, prompting each DNA string to make a copy of itself. By repeating these three steps about twenty times, a sample of DNA can be copied a million times over in about an hour.

Today, doctors can use PCR to identify genetic disorders from DNA in a patient's blood sample. Police use it to identify suspects from blood or hair found at the scene of a crime. Biologists have used it to study the genetic makeup of ancient humans and extinct animals from bits of forty-thousand-year-old tissues.

POLYSTYRENE

Polystyrene was born when industrial chemists of the late 1930s devised ways to link thousands of small hydrocarbon molecules known as styrene. The result was a strong, inexpensive substance that proved to be an excellent insulator. Among the most familiar polystyrenes is Styrofoam, used to make cushiony, insulating containers such as disposable cups, ice chests, and egg cartons. The popularity of disposable polystyrene products has created environmental

problems because of their extremely long lifespan—hundreds or even thousands of years. Chemists continue to look for ways to make them degrade more quickly.

POLYVINYL CHLORIDE

Tough, insulating, nonflammable, and resistant to moisture, decay, and insects, polyvinyl chloride, or PVC, was recognized as an ideal building material in the second half of the twentieth century. Made from the toxic gas vinyl chloride (first prepared in 1835), PVC has been made into "vinyl" flooring tiles, house siding, rain gutters, and many other building materials. Today, its greatest use lies in durable PVC pipes and pipe fittings. Credit cards are also made of PVC.

PORCELAIN

The glassy ceramic we call porcelain is one of the world's first human-made materials. The Chinese created it before 620 B.C. by mixing kaolin, a fine clay, with powdered petuntse, a mineral found in granite. At extremely high temperatures (about 2400 degrees Fahrenheit

P

A porcelain pillow of the Sung dynasty (11th-12th century) epitomizes the strength and beauty of Chinese porcelain.

or 1315.6 degrees Celsius), the two materials fuse to produce a ceramic of great strength and beauty. The secret to creating true porcelain remained in China for well over a thousand years. But English potters created a very similar, high-quality porcelain, called bone china, using charred and ground bone around 1800.

POWER GENERATION

In the ancient world, as in undeveloped areas today, the muscles of people or animals were the primary source of power. Only in the past two thousand years have nonliving power sources been extensively employed by mankind to do work.

The first power generator appears to have been the WATERWHEEL, mentioned in Greek writings as far back as the first century B.C. Early waterwheels, described by the Roman architect Vitruvius, required a fast-moving stream flowing beneath the wheel to catch and move its paddles. The wheel was attached to a millstone that was able to grind about 330 pounds (149.7 kilograms) of grain per hour—more than forty times the amount a slave could grind by hand. Over the centuries, water mills improved in efficiency and spread throughout the world, wher-

In a traditional water mill (right), a paddle wheel (1) connects to a pair of grindstones (2) by a system of gears.

American windmills remained important sources of power for milling and manufacturing well into the 19th century.

ever there was flowing water to move their paddles or buckets.

Where moving water was scarce, people looked to the wind for power. The first WIND-MILLS in recorded history appeared on the parched, windy plains of the Middle East some

In 1830, a race between a horse-drawn car and the tiny steam locomotive *Tom Thumb* convinced American railroad officials of the practicality of steam power.

thirteen hundred years ago. Their basic design included an upright shaft holding a spinning wheel of horizontal sails. Before A.D. 1000, a different kind of windmill appeared in Europe—the now-familiar "post mill" with a horizontal shaft jutting out of a building or post holding a vertical wheel of sails. Like the waterwheel, early windmills were used to grind grain. But in the late 1500s, the Dutch adapted their windmills to pump water from tidal lands. For centuries, windmills remained an important source of mechanical power across the flatlands of Europe and the arid plains of the Middle East.

The science of generating power made a major leap with the invention of STEAM ENGINES in the 1700s. The steam driving these engines was created by heating water over burning coal or wood. The expanding steam moved pistons that could be harnessed to do useful work.

In 1712, the Englishman Thomas Newcomen built a practical steam engine to pump water out of flooded mines. Though grossly inefficient by today's standard, Newcomen's engine could empty out as much water in two days as twenty workers and fifty horses could pump in a full week. Another Englishman, James Watt, began improving on Newcomen's design in 1763. By 1785, Watt had created a steam engine able to power an entire cotton mill with a single revolving shaft. Watt coined the term "horsepower" as a measure of the number of horses his engines replaced.

By providing a reliable, low-cost source of energy, steam engines drove the Industrial Revolution of the late eighteenth and early nineteenth centuries. They powered boats, locomotives, and TRACTORS, as well as factories throughout Europe and the United States.

Today, steam produced by the burning of fossil fuels turns gigantic TURBINES to produce most of the world's electricity.

But the power of electricity was not harnessed for practical purposes until the 1880s. The Italian physicist Alessandro Volta built the first electric BATTERY in 1800 by stacking zinc and silver disks in a tank of salt water. In 1831, the English chemist and physicist Michael Faraday invented the first ELECTRIC GENERATOR, producing an electrical current by spinning a magnet inside a coil of wire. Faraday's "dynamo" remained a scientific curiosity. He left it to others to improve his design and put it to practical use. Among them was the American Thomas Edison, who in 1882 opened the first electric-power stations in New York City and London to provide power to customers who used his new invention—the INCANDESCENT LAMP, or "lightbulb."

In 1882, Edison's first New York City power station supplied enough electricity to light 1,284 incandescent lights for 59 customers in a square-mile area.

P

Since the 1880s, electricity has had an ever increasing role in reducing human toil and increasing comfort and convenience. It's now used to power everyday objects from toasters to TELEVISIONS, furnaces to AIR CONDITIONERS, power tools to industrial machinery. Indeed, the nations that generate the most electricity per person are able to produce more with less human effort than other countries, and in doing so enjoy the highest standards of living.

A different kind of power generator revolutionized modern transportation in the early twentieth century. As far back as the 1600s, scientists had dreamed of creating an INTERNAL-COMBUSTION ENGINE. Such an engine would burn fuel internally—that is, inside its own chambers. So it would be more efficient than an external-combustion system such as the steam engine, which burns fuel in a furnace separate from its moving parts.

The French engineer Jean-Joseph Étienne Lenoir built the first practical internal-combustion engine in 1859. The Lenoir engine operated smoothly on coal gas from Paris's street-lighting system. But it was not very powerful. The next advance came with the invention of the four-stroke engine, which compresses fuel and air to create a faster, more efficient burn. The German engineer Nikolaus Otto built the first four-stroke engine in 1876. Many of his engines were built to drive industrial machines. But they were too slow and heavy to power moving vehicles. In the 1880s, two other German engineers, Gottlieb Daimler and Karl Benz, created smaller, lighter engines that ran on gasoline. Daimler and Benz used their new engines in early motorcycles and AUTOMOBILES.

Today, internal-combustion engines power tens of millions of cars as well as most ships, AIRPLANES, tractors, and power tools from chain saws and lawn mowers to air PUMPS and CRANES. Internal-combustion engines also generate power for institutions such as hospitals in times of electrical outages, as well as for homes and small industries in remote areas out of the reach of power lines.

A major drawback of engines and power plants that burn fossil fuels (gas, oil, or coal) is that they release huge quantities of pollutants into the air. Concern for human health and the environment has spurred great interest in "alternative" sources of energy such as windmills, solar-energy collectors, and geothermal plants,

Nuclear-power plants generate electricity from the tremendous amounts of energy released by the splitting, or fission, of atoms.

which provide power without air pollution. NUCLEAR-POWER REACTORS are one possible alternative source of energy. But they generate highly dangerous radioactive waste, which is difficult to dispose of safely.

PRINTING PRESS

The invention of the printing press in the fifteenth century represents one of the great landmarks in human history. It ushered in an age in which books and other reading materials became widely available. More people learned to read and became educated. For the first time, scientists and inventors could easily share information across long distances. Europe entered a period of growth and exploration.

The invention of the printing press is credited to Johann Gutenberg, a German printer. In reality, his great contribution lay in assembling all the elements that make up printing, elements that had been known, at least in the Far East, for centuries.

Though more elaborate in cabinetry and typeface than Gutenberg's revolutionary 15th-century press (artist's reconstruction above), European presses of the 17th century (below) still operated on the same basic principles.

Around A.D. 100, the Chinese began carving symbols standing for words on stone, inking the raised surfaces, and making impressions. About the same time, the Chinese official Ts'ai Lun developed PAPER.

By A.D. 500, the Japanese were carving text on wooden blocks. As early as A.D. 1041, the Chinese printer Pi-Sheng was casting individual symbols out of pottery and using them as movable, reusable type. By the 1300s, the Koreans were casting symbols in bronze. In Gutenberg's time, several kinds of INK were available. The kind most suited to printing was a combination of linseed oil and carbon black.

All these elements came together in the printing press Gutenberg developed in the 1440s. Precisely what his first press looked like, we don't know. Most likely, it consisted of two upright timbers, connected by a low cross beam that supported a flat bed of wood or stone, on which the type was placed and inked. A second, raised cross beam held a heavy wooden screw with a flat board, or platen, on its lower surface. The press operator turned the screw with a lever to press the flat board against a piece of paper lying atop the inked type. Gutenberg not only built the printing press itself, he created

P

the technology needed to cast large quantities of metal type from molds prepared for each character. The type could be used to print one page, then broken apart and used on the next page. This made possible the printing of a long complex book, such as the Bibles for which Gutenberg became famous.

The Industrial Revolution ushered in advancements such as the mechanical ink roller (1810) and the steam-powered press (1822). Another major advance came in 1846, when the American Richard Hoe devised the rotary press, which feeds paper between several cylinders with inked printing surfaces. Hoe's rotary press became the forerunner of modern, high-speed newspaper presses. The 1800s also brought photoengraving techniques for printing photographs. In the 1900s, presses went electronic, with computer controls and laser-light printers that continued to speed reproduction while improving quality and reducing costs. (*See also* LITHOGRAPHIC PRINTING.)

PULLEY

The pulley ranks among the simplest yet most important of machines. A typical pulley con-

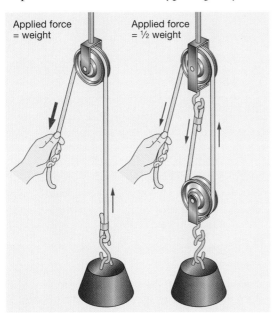

In simple fixed pulley (left), lifting the weight requires a pulling force equal to the weight. Additional pulleys reduce the amount of force needed to lift the same weight (right).

sists of a WHEEL with a grooved rim that carries a rope, chain, or belt. If one end of the rope is secured to a heavy object, a work crew can lift the object by pulling downward on the other end. When used in combination, pulleys can allow workers to lift an object many times heavier than they could lift without these devices.

Pulleys have been aiding human muscles as far back as 600 B.C., when Homer wrote of Greek sailors using pulleys with wooden wheels to hoist ship sails. Around 225 B.C., the Greek mathematician Archimedes devised a system of interconnected pulleys for dragging a ship onto dry land. And by 30 B.C., the Romans had combined the pulley with the recently invented CRANE.

Together with the wheel, SCREW, axle, LEVER, and wedge, the pulley is considered one of the six simple machines.

PUMP

Pumps—devices used to move or compress liquids or gases—are among the oldest and most widely used machines. The Greeks and Persians devised one early pump, called Archimedes' screw, before 200 B.C. This rotating machine removed water from the holds of large ships. Around A.D. 100, another Greek, Hero of Alexandria, devised a piston-and-cylinder suction pump to raise water from wells. It worked much like a modern-day syringe, drawing water up below a piston, which fitted tightly inside a cylinder. In the Middle Ages, piston-and-cylinder pumps were improved with

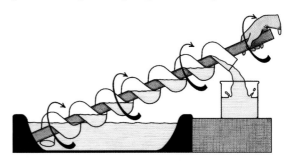

One of Archimedes' many inventions is the pump called Archimedes' screw. As it turns, water is scooped into the lower end and moves up through the coils. You can make this simple device with a few feet of flexible tubing, a sturdy rod such as a broomstick, and some cloth tape to hold the top and bottom ends of the tubing in place.

the addition of valves that let water or air escape between strokes of the piston.

By the 1600s, Europeans were using simple pumps to raise water to field level for irrigation. They used oxen to turn a WATERWHEEL. In Holland, wind power from WINDMILLS helped pump water out of low area as the Dutch reclaimed land from the sea.

The first steam pumps were developed around 1700, but did not become widespread for more than one

How A Suction Pump Works

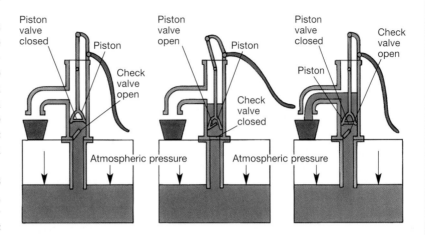

Profile: Archimedes

"Give me a place to stand, and I can move the world." The man credited with these words was Archimedes, a Greek mathematician and inventor who lived some twenty-two hundred years ago. A pioneer in the science of mechanics, Archimedes understood that a person with a LEVER could move many times his or her own weight. Challenged by

the king to prove his point, Archimedes did so. He reportedly designed a device that allowed the monarch to move a large ship by himself.

Archimedes was born around 287 B.C., in Syracuse, a Greek settlement on the island of Sicily. Little is known about his personal life except that his father was an astronomer and may have been related to the king of Syracuse. We also know that Archimedes studied for a time in Alexandria, Egypt, a center of Greek culture.

Archimedes' fame rests on his many inventions and the legends that grew up around them. They include, among others, the pulley, the crane, an ingenious pump known as Archimedes' screw, and a sphere that imitated the motions of celestial bodies.

When Archimedes was an old man, the Romans attacked Syracuse. He turned his creative mind to the city's defense and invented several weapons to hold off the enemy. Among them, legend holds, was a huge system of mirrors that burned Roman ships by focusing the sun's rays on them. Syracuse, however, was defeated in 212 B.C., and Archimedes was killed. The story goes that he was drawing mathematical figures in the sand when a Roman soldier struck him down. But Archimedes was so highly respected that the Roman commander buried him with full honors.

P hundred years, when advances in engineering and technology made it possible to build sturdy machines with metal parts. In the 1800s, pumps were used to drain mines, raise water from ever deeper wells, and create early water-supply systems for cities.

Today, pumps are among the most common mechanical devices and are often powered by electric motors. Many pump gases rather than liquids, as is the case with the compressor pumps in AIR-CONDITIONING systems and REFRIGERATORS.

The Changing World 1840

Some doctors are warning their patients not to travel on the new railroads that are being built around the country. The speed of travel—up to 50 miles (80.5 kilometers) an hour—may be harmful to the human body, they warn. Nonetheless, many Americans are enjoying train travel. Pulled by powerful STEAM ENGINES, the new passenger lines provide year-round service, regardless of winter freezes or spring mud. Already, the railways are transforming the Atlantic Coast states, with new towns, mills, and farms springing up wherever their track is laid. Steam power is shrinking the distance between America and Europe as well, with steamships making the transatlantic crossing in just fifteen days. Among the finest are the luxury steamers built by the New York millionaire Cornelius Vanderbilt.

On the home front, iceboxes have transformed the American kitchen, enabling families to keep fresh milk, meat, and vegetables readily at hand. The only drawback is the muddy tracks left by delivery men hauling ice blocks into the house twice a week. Families can also preserve foods in vacuum-sealed glass jars, and grocers are beginning to carry food in vacuum-sealed tin cans (see CANNING). Still needed is a handy method for opening the thick metal cans, which require a chisel and hammer to unseal.

As the decade progresses, the daguerreotype becomes a sensation (see CAMERA AND FILM). No longer is it necessary to hire a skilled artist to paint a family portrait. Studios in many cities offer the new picture-making technique perfected by the Frenchman Louis Daguerre. Unfortunately, most children find it difficult to sit motionless before the camera for the several minutes required to capture their image on a metal plate.

But the best news of all in the 1840s is the continuing conquest of the terrible contagious disease—smallpox. Perhaps the greatest killer in the history of mankind, smallpox appears to be no match for the cowpox VACCINE now available in many doctors' offices. Once inoculated, both adults and children appear to enjoy lifelong protection from the deeply scarring and often-fatal disease.

The railroad station stood at the center of mid-19th-century America, a land of small towns, family farms, and vast distances.

Q-R

QUARTZ-CRYSTAL TIMEPIECE

The invention of quartz-crystal timepieces has been called the single greatest contribution to precision timekeeping. The tiny motions that govern the most accurate of these clocks are so regular are that they lose no more than one second every ten years. Quartz movements in inexpensive clocks and watches may vary by as little as a few minutes in a year.

New Jersey clockmaker Warren Marrison built the first full quartz-crystal clock in 1929. But his invention was made possible by an earlier discovery by the French physicists Pierre and Jacques Curie. In 1880, the Curie brothers discovered that certain crystals such as quartz, a common mineral, produce a small electric current when they are compressed. Conversely, applying a small electric current to such a crystal causes it to change shape ever so slightly. This phenomenon was dubbed the "piezoelectric effect."

Marrison harnessed the piezoelectric effect for timekeeping by applying an alternating electric current to a small ring of quartz that he suspended by threads and enclosed in an insulated chamber. Because alternating current is constantly reversing direction, it caused the quartz crystal to vibrate with an extremely steady frequency. This frequency was far too high for practical time measurement. So Marrison used a gear-and-motor system to reduce the vibration one million times to correspond with each "tick" of his clock's second hand.

In 1971, Texans George Theiss and Willy Crabtree greatly reduced the size of the quartz-crystal clock by replacing its motor and gears with an INTEGRATED CIRCUIT. In doing so, they produced the first quartz-crystal watch—the digital "Pulsar." Today, there are millions of quartz watches and clocks, making it possible for people to have inexpensive but accurate timepieces at home, in automobiles, and on their wrists.

RADAR

Radar is a device that locates objects and determines their speed and direction with shortwave radio waves, or microwaves. The U.S. Navy coined the word "radar" during World War II, as an acronym for *radio detecting and ranging*. Radar detects a target by sending a radio signal through the air or water, and then registering the radio echoes that bounce back from objects in its path. Radar "ranges," or determines the distance to the target, by calculating the time between transmitting the signal and receiving its echo.

In this way, radar operators on the ground can locate aircraft, ships, even spacecraft thousands of miles from Earth. They can detect such targets regardless of darkness, smoke, clouds, fog, or rain. Ships equipped with radar can detect icebergs as well as other ships in their path. Airplanes equipped with radar can navigate through clouds. Weather forecasters use radar to track storms.

By continually monitoring the distance to an object, radar can be used to determine how fast and in which direction that target is moving.

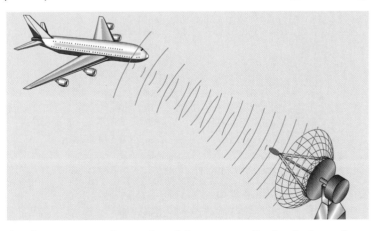

A radar antenna emits a series of shortwave radio signals that reflect back from objects in their path. The timing of the signals' return reveals each object's distance.

Radar enables air-traffic controllers to guide the many pilots approaching, landing, and taking off from a busy airport.

This information can be used in many ways, from directing missiles to guiding astronauts in space. Police commonly use handheld radar "guns" to determine the speed of cars, just as baseball and tennis officials use them to measure the speed of balls.

In 1900, the Croatian-born American radio pioneer Nikola Tesla discovered that large objects produce reflected radio signals strong enough to be detected by an electromagnetic device. He predicted that such echoes could be used to locate ships at sea. But little was done to develop the idea until the 1930s.

In 1935, the Scottish physicist Sir Robert Watson-Watt developed the first practical radar system. In the years leading up to World War II, several countries secretly developed similar systems. Radar played a crucial role in that war. It helped the British win the Battle of Britain against the powerful German air force, and enabled the Allies to win the Battle of the Atlantic against Germany's submarine fleet.

After the war, radar was developed for peacetime uses, such as air-traffic control, satellite tracking, and weather forecasting, especially severe-storm warnings. Today's radar sets range in size from missile-guidance systems no larger than a coffeepot to radar telescopes the size of multistory buildings for studying distant planets.

RADIO

Radio is a means of communication using electromagnetic waves that travel through space at the speed of light. The electromagnetic waves used for radio communication are similar to light and heat waves, but are lower in frequency.

Since radio was invented at the dawn of the twentieth century, it has become one of our most popular and reliable forms of communication. Personal radios, car stereos, and clock radios are just some of the many kinds of radio receivers we use in everyday life.

In 1864, the Scottish physicist James Clerk Maxwell first predicted the existence of radio waves. Noting how light consists of radiating waves, he suggested that similar waves, with different frequencies, must exist. In 1888, Maxwell's ideas led the German physicist Heinrich Hertz to experiment with producing such waves by passing an electric current through special metal rods.

Hertz never communicated by radio. The first to do so was the British scientist Sir Oliver Lodge, who in 1894 sent a Morse-code signal a

How Radio Signals Reach Us

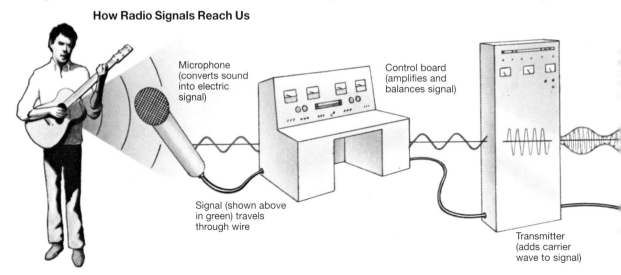

Microphone (converts sound into electric signal)

Control board (amplifies and balances signal)

Signal (shown above in green) travels through wire

Transmitter (adds carrier wave to signal)

Q
R

At age 22, Marconi posed with the wireless receiver he would later use to send the first radio message across the Atlantic.

half mile, where it was detected with a receiver, or "tuner," of his own invention. The Italian inventor Guglielmo Marconi put all the pieces together in 1901, when he succeeded, on his first try, in sending and receiving radio signals across the Atlantic Ocean between England and Canada. In effect, Marconi's radio was a wireless telegraph, sending a simple signal of dots and dashes.

The next great advance in radio technology came with the invention of the first practical ELECTRON TUBE by the English electrical engineer Sir John Fleming in 1904. The electron tube made it possible to transmit speech, music, and other sounds beyond the electrical buzz of Morse code. The American inventor Lee De Forest improved on Fleming's tube in 1906, making it possible to use a radio loudspeaker strong enough to project sound into a room. Previously, radios had to be held up to the ear.

Still, radios were used primarily as "wireless" telegraphs for ships at sea. Then, in 1920, the American engineer Frank Conrad started a series of music broadcasts that were enthusiastically received by radio hobbyists. Conrad went on to develop the world's first radio station with regularly scheduled broadcasts—KDKA in Pittsburgh—in 1920.

Radio technology continued to advance with the invention of FM, or frequency modulation, by the American radio pioneer Edwin Armstrong in 1933. FM transmissions greatly reduced static and so produced higher-quality sound. Another advance came with the invention of the TRANSISTOR in 1948. By replacing bulky radio tubes, transistors made the first pocket-size radios possible.

RAYON

In 1664, the English scientist Robert Hooke speculated that it might be possible to create a human-made fiber as useful as natural silk. Over the following two hundred years, many chemists tried and failed. Finally, in 1889, the French chemist Hilaire de Chardonnet perfected a process in which chemically treated wood pulp was dissolved in a mixture of ether and alcohol, then forced through fine jets to form a continuous, strong thread. Fabrics made from Chardonnet's "artificial silk" caused a sensation. Fifty years later, it became known as rayon, the first artificial fiber and still among the most popular.

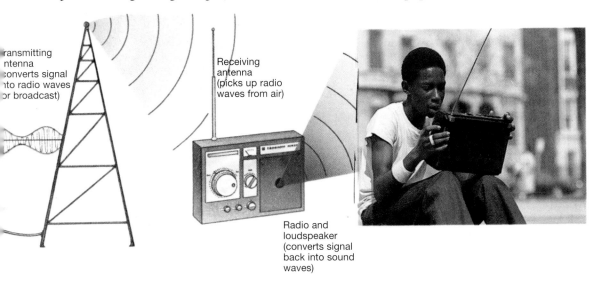

Transmitting antenna (converts signal into radio waves for broadcast)

Receiving antenna (picks up radio waves from air)

Radio and loudspeaker (converts signal back into sound waves)

Razor

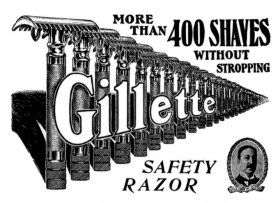

An early ad for safety razors promised freedom from "stropping," the laborious sharpening and smoothing required to maintain a straight-edge blade.

The term razor refers to any sharp-edged instrument used for shearing body hairs off at the skin. People have used razors since antiquity to shave faces, heads, and other body parts for both cultural and medical (in preparation for surgery) reasons. The first Stone Age razors probably consisted of clamshells, natural glass, or shark teeth. In fact, such items are still used for shaving by primitive cultures.

The first metal razors appeared in the Bronze Age, some four thousand years ago. The development of finely tempered steel in the seventeenth century produced the straight-edged razor, with its broad, curved blade. Such razors remain unsurpassed in durability and sharpness. But they can inflict serious cuts, and they have to be repeatedly sharpened with a stone, then smoothed with a leather strap.

Much more convenient is the "safety razor," invented in 1895 by the American manufacturer King Camp Gillette. Gillette's safety razor used thin, disposable blades that were clamped between two plates of a chamber, exposing only a narrow cutting edge. Other types of safety razors followed, including those with cartridge-style blade injectors, and others in which the entire unit is thrown away after use.

In 1928, another American manufacturer, Jacob Schick, invented the first practical electric razor, or "shaver." Like later models, the Schick shaver had a metal shield with one or more flexible heads perforated with slots. As the shield passes over the skin, hairs that stick through the slots are sheared off by razors moving inside the heads. Though quick and convenient, electric shavers don't cut as closely as simple razors.

Reaper

For centuries, the world's farmers were limited in how much they could grow by the speed with which they could harvest, or reap, their crops. Grains left too long in the field risked being ruined by bad weather and rot. Even a large number of laborers could not always bring in a harvest quickly enough by hand. Besides, few farmers could afford to hire many workers.

Reapers

Mechanical reapers were made more than 2,000 years ago by the Romans, who used an ox to push a two-wheeled cart fitted across the front with jagged iron teeth that skimmed off the heads of grain into the cart (A). Cyrus McCormick's widely used mid-19th-century reaper was a horse-drawn, two-wheeled vehicle equipped with a revolving wooden reel that flattened the stalks against a vibrating knife blade (B). Subsequently, harvesters were developed with special mechanisms that both reaped and bound the cut grains into sheaves or bundles (C).

So it was a great need that spurred the invention of a mechanical reaper, a machine able to cut grain quickly and efficiently. The first recorded patent for a mechanical reaper was issued to the Englishman Joseph Boyce in 1799. Soon after, many reapers appeared, using a variety of revolving cutters or vibrating knives. But none worked well enough to become popular.

Then, in 1832, the American farmer Cyrus McCormick demonstrated a horse-drawn reaper that cut grain with a series of mechanical knives and claws, and caught it in a metal receptacle. Though several similar reapers were invented around the same time, none worked as well or grew as popular as McCormick's.

Historians credit McCormick's reaper with helping transform the North American prairie into a vast wheat-growing belt. In the early years of the twentieth century, it was replaced by COMBINE HARVESTERS, able not only to cut the grain but to thresh and clean it as well.

used a similar system to create the first practical ice-making machine. His ice maker used the chemical ether as a refrigerant. Evaporation of liquid ether produced the cooling effect. Then the ether gas was compressed by a hand-operated compressor and cooled until it condensed. The ether could then be released to evaporate again, producing more cooling.

In 1844, the American John Gorrie built a much larger refrigeration machine that used compressed air rather than a liquid for cooling. His invention led to the modern AIR CONDITIONER. In the 1850s, Ferdinand Carré of France invented yet another type of refrigerator, using ammonia as its refrigerant. By the 1930s, chemists had created new chemicals such as Freon, which worked as efficiently as ammonia, but without ammonia's strong smell.

Since then, refrigerators have changed little in basic design. Their three basic components are a compressor, a condenser, and an expansion device such as a valve. The compressor can be a piston that presses the refrigerant gas

REFRIGERATOR

Refrigerators are mechanical devices that remove heat from an enclosed space to lower its temperature. As a modern household appliance, refrigerators are used to store food at temperatures cool enough to slow spoilage.

Since ancient times, people used naturally cool places to store foods. Artificial refrigeration can be traced to two discoveries in the 1700s: the fact that liquids absorb heat when they evaporate, and that a gas can be turned into a liquid by compressing, or pressurizing, it.

The first known example of artificial refrigeration is credited to the Scottish scientist William Cullen. In 1748, Cullen evaporated the chemical ethyl ether to lower temperatures in a laboratory chamber. Cullen never made practical use of his device. But in 1834, Jacob Perkins, an American engineer living in London,

Inside a Household Refrigerator

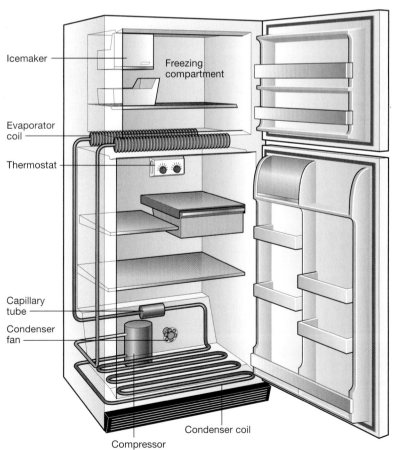

Icemaker

Freezing compartment

Evaporator coil

Thermostat

Capillary tube

Condenser fan

Condenser coil

Compressor

Q
R

in a sealed chamber. The condenser is a long, winding tube that passes through circulating air or cold water. Compressed gas moving through the condenser gets rid of heat energy, turning into a liquid. When it passes through the expansion valve, the liquid evaporates suddenly and turns back into a gas, taking up heat from its surroundings and causing a cooling effect.

Most home refrigerators today have separate compartments for frozen and fresh foods. Evaporation coils built into the walls of the freezer compartment keep it colder than the rest of the refrigerator—generally about zero degrees Fahrenheit versus 35 degrees Fahrenheit (-17.8 degrees Celsius versus 1.8 degrees Celsius). The temperature is kept steady by means of a thermostat (*see* THERMOMETER).

REVOLVER

Early firearms had to be reloaded after every shot. Gunmakers experimented with schemes that would allow a gun to "repeat"—shoot several times before reloading was necessary. Not until 1835, however, did the American inventor Samuel Colt manufacture the first successful revolver—a firearm with a rotating cylinder equipped with six firing chambers.

In the 1860s, Colt's "six-shooter" became the most widely used pistol of the Civil War. In the 1870s, his Peacemaker model became the "gun that tamed the West." Colt's basic design is still used in modern revolvers. For military use, the revolver has been replaced by MACHINE GUNS, which can fire continuously.

ROCKET

In its simplest form, a rocket is a tube of fuel closed at one end and open at the other. When the fuel at the open end is ignited, hot gases

An ancient Chinese warrior prepares to ignite an early military rocket. The attached stick gave the missile stability in flight.

rush out of that end and propel the rocket in the opposite direction. The faster the gases rush out, the faster the rocket moves forward.

A rocket, unlike a JET ENGINE, carries both fuel and an oxidizer within itself. (A jet carries fuel, but needs oxygen from the air around it.) So rockets can operate in space, which is airless, while jets cannot. In fact, rockets operate best in outer space, where there is no drag from the atmosphere, and where exhaust gases can reach their maximum speed.

In the twentieth century, the rocket enabled humankind to achieve the age-old dream of reaching the Moon. It likewise

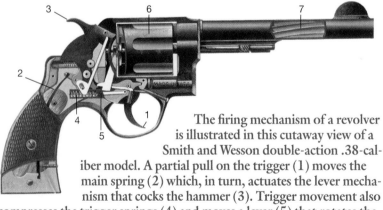

The firing mechanism of a revolver is illustrated in this cutaway view of a Smith and Wesson double-action .38-caliber model. A partial pull on the trigger (1) moves the main spring (2) which, in turn, actuates the lever mechanism that cocks the hammer (3). Trigger movement also compresses the trigger springs (4) and moves a lever (5) that rotates the cylinder (6), bringing a cartridge into firing position. Pulling the trigger all the way back releases the hammer, which drops forward to strike a charge in the cartridge, firing the bullet down the rifled barrel (7). Double-action revolvers cock and drop the hammer with a single pull of the trigger. With single-action revolvers the hammer must be cocked manually.

made possible SPACE PROBES to explore the planets of our solar system.

The Chinese invented the first crude rockets in the 1200s. They did so by stuffing gunpowder into bamboo tubes. For centuries, small rockets such as these were used as weapons, signaling devices, and fireworks.

Important advances came in the 1800s, when bamboo and paper rocket shells were replaced by metal casings. In 1805, the British artillery expert William Congreve added a flight-stabilizing guide stick (a "fin") to his rockets and built the first practical launching pad. During the War of 1812, Congreve's rockets were more spectacular than accurate, but reports of their success encouraged further research around the world.

The early twentieth century brought the foundations of modern rocketry. In 1903, the Russian inventor Konstantin Tsiolkovsky developed ideas for using gyroscopes to guide rockets,

Profile: Robert Goddard

Robert Goddard, the father of modern rocketry, was born in 1882 in Worcester, Massachusetts. Early on, he discovered his love of experimentation and invention, designing new kinds of kites and performing chemical experiments in an attic workshop. As a teenager, Goddard began reading science-fiction stories about space travel. Though the rockets of that time were used only as fireworks and short-range weapons, he became convinced that astronauts might one day ride rockets into space.

After high school, Goddard studied and taught at several universities. He experimented with gunpowder rockets, and in 1919 published a famous report in which he proposed a way of reaching the Moon with a multistage rocket. The most powerful stage would be placed on the launching pad, with the next most powerful stage placed on top of it, and so on. Goddard's report brought both fame and ridicule as reporters labeled him the "moon rocket man." Soon after, Goddard began experimenting in secrecy with a new kind of rocket that burned liquid fuel and liquid oxygen. He had realized that such novel fuels would produce much more power than solid fuels such as gunpowder. During this period, Goddard also married Esther Kisk, who became his most valuable assistant, keeping a motion-picture record of his rocket work for some twenty years. She was filming on March 16, 1926, when Goddard launched the world's first liquid-fuel rocket. The ten-foot rocket (3.05 meters) rose only forty-one feet (12.5 meters), but proved that the principle of liquid-fuel rocketry was sound.

In the following years, the famed aviator Charles Lindbergh took a great interest in Goddard's work, and persuaded a wealthy benefactor to fund an experimental rocket station near Roswell, New Mexico. There, Goddard developed larger and better rocket engines and steering devices. And in 1935, one of his rockets flew at the speed of sound. During World War II, Goddard worked for the U.S. government developing rocket aircraft. His wartime work produced more than two hundred patents for inventions in the fields of rockets, GUIDED MISSILES, and space exploration.

But during his lifetime, Goddard never convinced military experts of the vast potential of liquid-fuel rocketry. It was only after his death, in 1945, that the U.S. government launched its massive rocketry and space program. It was then that scientists realized the importance of Goddard's work. In 1961, the first American reached space. In 1969, the first person stepped onto the Moon. Both were carried into space by the multistage, liquid-fuel rockets of Goddard's dreams. Today, his space-age vision is kept alive at the Goddard Space Flight Center in Greenbelt, Maryland.

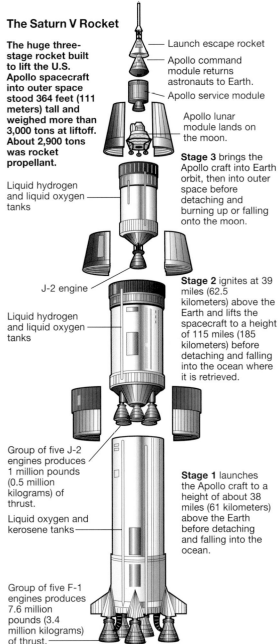

The Saturn V Rocket

The huge three-stage rocket built to lift the U.S. Apollo spacecraft into outer space stood 364 feet (111 meters) tall and weighed more than 3,000 tons at liftoff. About 2,900 tons was rocket propellant.

— Launch escape rocket

Apollo command module returns astronauts to Earth.

Apollo service module

Apollo lunar module lands on the moon.

Stage 3 brings the Apollo craft into Earth orbit, then into outer space before detaching and burning up or falling onto the moon.

Liquid hydrogen and liquid oxygen tanks

J-2 engine

Liquid hydrogen and liquid oxygen tanks

Stage 2 ignites at 39 miles (62.5 kilometers) above the Earth and lifts the spacecraft to a height of 115 miles (185 kilometers) before detaching and falling into the ocean where it is retrieved.

Group of five J-2 engines produces 1 million pounds (0.5 million kilograms) of thrust.

Liquid oxygen and kerosene tanks

Stage 1 launches the Apollo craft to a height of about 38 miles (61 kilometers) above the Earth before detaching and falling into the ocean.

Group of five F-1 engines produces 7.6 million pounds (3.4 million kilograms) of thrust.

and multistage "booster" rockets to reach outer space. Then, in 1917, the German scientist Hermann Oberth proposed replacing gunpowder with liquid fuel for rockets.

In 1926, the American engineer Robert Goddard made practical use of these ideas, building and launching the first liquid-fuel rockets. As his liquid fuel, Goddard used a mixture of gasoline and liquid oxygen. Though few realized it at the time, his suc-cess marked a turning point in the history of rocketry.

During World War II, Wernher von Braun led a team of German scientists in developing the first long-range, guided rockets. After the war, he came to the United States to help develop other rocket vehicles, including the Saturn V rocket that launched U.S. astronauts to the Moon in 1969. Since then, rockets have become ever more powerful and efficient, providing the motive energy for many space probes. Military rockets include many with sophisticated guidance systems, and some that are small enough for a soldier to carry.

RUBBER, SYNTHETIC

Until World War II, the production of tires and industrial cables, belts, and hoses depended on the availability of natural rubber, extracted from a variety of tropical trees. So, when the war in the Pacific cut off the Allies' supply of natural rubber, the United States quickly organized a huge wartime program—second in scale only to the nuclear-bomb project—to create a synthetic substitute. American chemists hit upon the right formula with styrene and butadiene—two chemicals readily available from petroleum. By 1945, U.S. plants were producing one million tons of styrene-butadiene rubber a year.

Other synthetic rubbers designed for special purposes include neoprene, a rubber developed in the United States in 1931 from acetylene gas and hydrogen chloride. Neoprene's ability to withstand harsh chemicals make it ideal for uses such as gas hoses and electrical insulation that comes in contact with oil or strong sunlight. Polyurethane, developed in Germany in 1937, is familiar as the soft foam rubber used in cushions and mattresses. It is also spun into the amazingly stretchy fabric spandex.

RUBBER, VULCANIZED

Even after the invention of SYNTHETIC RUBBER in the 1940s, natural rubber remained a much better material for making aircraft tires, engine mountings, and many other products. But the so-called "natural" rubber used in manufacturing is not entirely a gift of nature. In its natural state, rubber is soft and sticky when hot, stiff

Goodyear had been experimenting with rubber for years before a lucky stove accident produced "vulcanization."

dropping some rubber mixed with sulfur on a hot stove. The resulting chemical reaction produced a tougher, more elastic material suitable for manufactured products—especially tires.

RUDDER

The first rudder, used in Egypt around 3000 B.C., may have been little more than an oar hung off the side of a boat. By the Middle Ages, the rudder was moved to the stern, or back, of the boat, where it was easier to use. This simple steering device consists of a flat blade that extends below the water's surface. If the blade is turned when the boat is moving, the boat turns in the opposite direction.

As ships became bigger and more powerful, various mechanical arrangements were invented to provide the greater leverage needed to turn the rudder. Rudders of modern ships are moved by cables, gears, and hydraulic lines controlled by powerful gas, steam, or diesel engines. Many aircraft are likewise steered by rudders, via rudder bars or pedals in the cockpit.

and brittle when cold. The American inventor Charles Goodyear made rubber into a far more useful material when he devised the process of "vulcanization" in 1839. Goodyear's invention came about in part by chance rather than by design, as a consequence of his accidentally

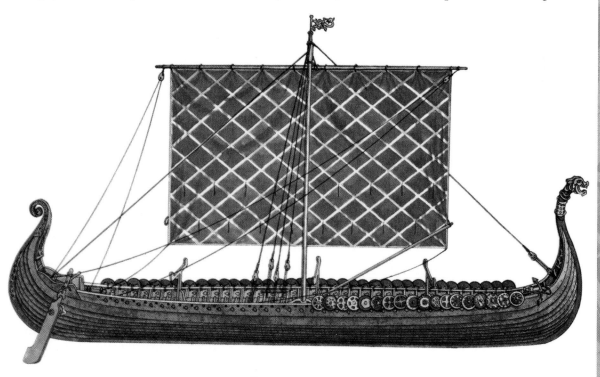

The master seamen of their age, the Vikings equipped their 9th-century dragon ships with oarlike rudders similar in design to those used by the ancient Egyptians.

The Changing World 1920

Is the horse and buggy obsolete? It seems so, with some fifteen million AUTOMOBILES registered in the United States alone. No longer a plaything of the rich, cars are now coming off of the assembly line with price tags under $400—well within reach of millions of ordinary people.

Americans have many automobile models from which to choose. Should they buy a Cadillac, Chevrolet, Maxwell, Milburn Electric, Packard, Peerless, or Pierce-Arrow? Or should they remain loyal to the basic Model T—Ford's most popular car. Catering to the thousands of new automobile owners, entrepreneur J.G. Kirby has opened the first drive-in restaurant in Dallas. "People with cars are so lazy," says Kirby, "that they don't want to get out of them to eat."

As cars continue to crowd city streets, so do record numbers of people. This year's census makes it official: more than half of Americans now live in urban areas, and less than 30 percent remain on farms. A dizzying array of entertainment beckons the city dweller. Families can stay home and listen to Enrico Caruso or Dame Nellie Melba on the PHONO-GRAPH, or enjoy the

antics of Charlie Chaplin or Mary Pickford in the air-conditioned comfort of a sparkling new movie theater.

In Hollywood, radio pioneer Lee De Forest has announced he's invented a process for recording sound for MOTION PICTURES. But major studios remain uninterested, and theaters continue to embellish silent films with live piano music.

As yet, few people other than pilots have had the thrill of flying in an AIRPLANE. But anyone can send an airmail letter from coast to coast. The U.S. Post Office has inaugurated bicoastal airmail service from New York City to San Francisco, with more routes promised soon.

But why settle for a letter across the country, when rockets may soon be delivering mail to the Man in the Moon? Newspaper headlines are trumpeting the futuristic ideas of "moon rocket man" ROBERT GODDARD. Goddard's recent scientific papers explain how to build a missile that can reach space. But the reclusive physics professor seems embarrassed by all the fuss. Reports are that he is now experimenting with a new kind of "liquid-fuel" rocket on his Aunt Effie's farm in Auburn, Massachusetts.

Early coast-to-coast airmail traveled by plane only during the day, with mail sacks transferred to trains for nighttime ground travel. By 1924, a string of flashing beacons and emergency landing fields permitted the first true, round-the-clock airmail flights.

S

SAFETY PIN

In 1849, New Yorker Walter Hunt invented the modern safety pin, allegedly on a dare. Challenged to make something useful out of a simple piece of wire, Hunt came up with a small but ingenious clothing pin with a shield to prevent the user from getting pricked. Most clever of all, a circular twist in the middle of Hunt's pin acted as a spring to keep the point from slipping out of its cover.

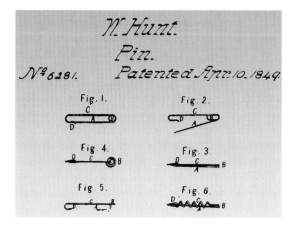

Walter Hunt's 1949 patent application illustrated several variations of his ingeniously simple device.

SATELLITE (ARTIFICIAL)

The Earth's Moon is a natural satellite, as are the moons circling other planets. In 1687, the English mathematician Sir Isaac Newton used his theory of gravity to show that it was possible to place artificial satellites in orbit as well. It would be more than 250 years, however, before the development of the modern ROCKET made it possible to do so.

In 1955, both the United States and the Soviet Union announced plans to launch an artificial satellite, an object that would go into orbit around the Earth. The Soviets were the first to succeed, placing *Sputnik 1* in orbit on October 4, 1957. The first *Sputnik* contained a thermometer and a radio transmitter for sending signals to Earth. The second *Sputnik*, launched

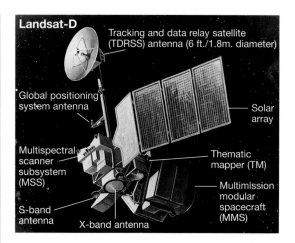

Since the 1970s, the United States has launched a series of observation satellites dubbed Landsat, all of which produce detailed images of the Earth's surface.

a month later, carried a dog to show that life could survive in space in a pressurized capsule. The United States sent its first satellite into orbit in 1958. *Explorer 1* was equipped with cameras and scientific equipment for studying Earth's upper atmosphere.

Since the 1950s, thousands of satellites have been placed in orbit, providing services that have become a part of daily life. We rely on them for weather forecasting and storm tracking as well as global communication via radio, television, and telephone signals. Still other satellites are used for military surveillance, navigation, and scientific research. Beginning in the 1980s, satellites have even been used as microgravity factories where certain drugs and other high-tech materials can be manufactured free of defects caused by gravity.

Whatever their purpose, artificial satellites have certain features in common. Many generate their power from the Sun with PHOTOELECTRIC CELLS, storing that power with rechargeable BATTERIES for use in darkness. Most satellites can automatically maintain their proper altitude with radar navigational systems linked to thrusters, small rockets that can fire briefly to change the craft's position. Other types of control equipment move antennas and sensors,

S

according to directions from operators on the ground. Radio receivers and transmitters enable satellites to communicate with those operators.

SCALES AND BALANCES

By the Middle Ages, the ancient balance had progressed from a crude stick-and-string device to a system of weighing pans suspended from a metal fulcrum.

Hieroglyphs show Egyptians using mechanical devices for weighing as far back as 5000 B.C. The simplest such devices consisted of a beam precisely balanced on a fulcrum, or pivot point, at its center. By placing an object of unknown weight on one end, then placing objects of known weight on the other until the beam balanced, one could determine the unknown weight. Then as today, such measuring played a vital role in commerce (determining the quantity of a trade), medicine (precisely measuring drugs), and industry (weighing ingredients for recipe products such as bread or bricks). Later balances were improved by hanging pans from either end of the beam. In the 1700s, a knife-thin fulcrum, or pivot, improved accuracy further.

A Dutch cheese wholesaler uses a simple but gigantic scale to weigh his product at market.

Later still came spring scales, in which the weighing pan was either hung from or rested on a spring whose tension took the place of a counterweight. The twentieth century brought electronic scales, more accurate than any spring scale or mechanical balance. In electronic scales, the tiny movement of the pan accepting a weight is translated into an electrical current that registers as a measurement on a digital screen or printout.

SCIENTIFIC INSTRUMENTS

Since the English philosopher Roger Bacon began using a magnifying glass for scientific research in the 1200s, a long parade of improved scientific instruments have continued to expand our knowledge of the world around us.

The first great rush of scientific invention began in the seventeenth century. In 1609, GALILEO GALILEI built the first astronomical TELESCOPE, and used it to discover mountains on the Moon, the satellites of Jupiter, the phases of Venus, sunspots, and many new stars. In 1673, the Dutch biologist Anton van Leeuwenhoek built a microscope powerful enough to reveal creatures invisible to the naked eye. (*See* MICROSCOPE, OPTICAL.) In the 1630s, the English astronomer William Gascoigne invented the micrometer, a device used to make extremely accurate linear measurements. Gascoigne used his micrometer in a telescope to measure the angular distance between stars. During the Industrial Revolution (1760–1840), it would be used to achieve new standards of precision in manufacturing.

Micrometer

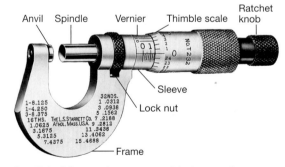

A solid object to be measured is inserted between the anvil and spindle of a micrometer, and a knob is then rotated to hold the object tight. Fractional measurements appear on the sleeve of the micrometer.

The 1600s also saw the dawn of scientific weather forecasting, thanks to three inventions. They were the first reliable BAROMETER (air-pressure gauge), invented in 1643 by the Italian mathematician Evangelista Torricelli; the first reliable THERMOMETER, invented in 1654 by Cardinal Leopoldo de Medici; and the first hygrometer (humidity gauge), invented in 1687 by the French physicist Guillaume Amontons. In 1714, the German physicist Daniel Fahrenheit greatly improved the accuracy of temperature measurements with the invention of a practical mercury thermometer, and developed the temperature scale that still bears his name.

American physicist Ernest Lawrence explored the mysteries of the atom using the cyclotron he invented in 1929.

The early twentieth century brought a flurry of innovations that enabled scientists to separate the chemical ingredients of life. Among them was CHROMATOGRAPHY, invented in 1903 by the Italian-born Russian botanist Mikhail Tswett. The chromatograph was used to separate and identify chemical compounds such as amino acids from complex mixtures such as body fluids. A few years later, the British physicist Sir Joseph John Thomson invented the SPECTROMETER to analyze the many chemicals being identified with the chromatograph. Thomson's device revealed the structure of these complex molecules by sorting their fragments in electric and magnetic fields.

In 1908, the German physicist Hans Geiger invented the first radiation detector, or GEIGER COUNTER, enabling scientists to study the newly discovered phenomenon of radioactivity—the high-energy product of decaying atoms. In the following years, physicists realized that such subatomic forces could reveal the fundamental laws that govern the universe. To further their explorations, they began building fantastically powerful machines called PARTICLE ACCELERATORS, designed to bombard atoms with subatomic particles to understand the relationship between matter and energy.

Biologists, meanwhile, continued to deepen their study of life with the aid of more and more powerful microscopes. Their science took a great leap forward in 1931, when German physicist Ernst Ruska invented the electron microscope (see MICROSCOPE, ELECTRON). Able to look at structures even smaller than a wave of light (one fifty-thousandth of an inch), the electron microscope more than tripled the magnification power of the best optical scopes. It revealed for the first time the physical structure of viruses as well as many unknown cell structures.

The same year, the amateur astronomer Grote Reber of Illinois expanded humankind's

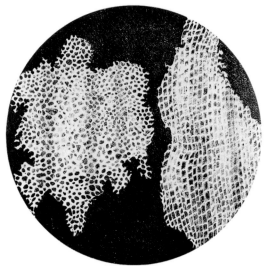

In 1665, Robert Hooke drew the tiny structures he saw when viewing a slice of cork through a primitive microscope. He called them "cells."

S

A U.S. weather satellite tracks several tropical storms moving across the Atlantic Ocean in 1995.

view in another direction. Reber's invention of the radio telescope—consisting of a bowl-shaped antenna—enabled him to map thousands of unseen stars by their radio signals, and opened an entirely new way to study the universe.

By the 1940s, explorations into the world of atomic forces and particles had given rise to the new field of nuclear physics, first revealed to nonscientists with the explosion of the atomic bombs in 1945, the first NUCLEAR WEAPONS. Soon afterward, scientists turned their attention to the design of NUCLEAR-POWER REACTORS, which could use the terrific energy of nuclear reactions for more positive purposes.

After World War II, scientists began exploiting COMPUTERS as the ultimate scientific

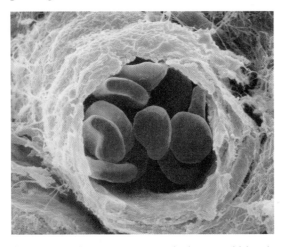

A scanning electron micrograph shows red blood cells traveling through an artery.

tool. In 1949, the British biochemist Dorothy Hodgkin became the first to use a computer to determine the structure of an organic chemical—the ANTIBIOTIC penicillin. Soon other scientists were likewise using computers to create complex models of real-life phenomena.

In the mid-1950s, the U.S. Weather Bureau, U.S. Air Force, and U.S. Navy formed a research group to produce the first simple but continuous computer forecasts of the weather. Computers were likewise at the controls of the first weather SATELLITE, *TIROS 1*, launched by the United States in 1960. Today, meteorologists rely on high-speed supercomputers to gather, organize, and graphically display weather data. Other computers analyze huge amounts of weather information to generate increasingly accurate forecasts. Computers are likewise employed to predict both local and global results of human changes in the environment (pollution, habitat destruction, and so forth).

Today, computers also control a vast array of scientific instruments with a precision far surpassing that of a human eye or hand. A fine example is the scanning tunneling microscope (*see* MICROSCOPE, SCANNING TUNNELING). Invented in a Swiss IBM (International Business Machines) laboratory in 1981, the device features a probe that tapers down to a point the size of a single atom. Using computer controls, a scientist working with this device can produce a three-dimensional map of individual atoms on the sample's surface.

SCISSORS

The origins of that ingenious cutting device—scissors—are lost in antiquity. Somewhere in Asia more than three thousand years ago, early scissor makers began working with bronze and then iron. They ground twin blades, then connected them between the cutting ends and the handle ends. These scissors or shears could cut through thin layers of material cleanly.

Oddly, the type of scissors that first appeared in Europe, about 1500 B.C., was unlike the familiar pivot blades described above. Instead, they operated around a C-shaped spring that arched between the two handle ends. Pivoting scissors reached Europe in the 1500s, becoming widespread with the introduction of cast steel in the mid-1700s.

SCREW AND SCREWDRIVER

The Greek scholar ARCHIMEDES is often credited with inventing the screw before 200 B.C. But his screw was a kind of water PUMP. Spiral-threaded screws to be employed as fasteners were probably invented around the same time, but they were not widely used because each screw had to be made by hand. Screws resurfaced in Europe in the 1400s, when they were used to assemble armor. Made of metal, they had hexagonal or octagonal heads and were tightened down by hand or with a crude wrench.

A century later, gunsmiths discovered that nails held better if given a little twist. They applied the twist with a small hand tool—the first screwdriver—inserted into a slot in the nail head.

The modern era of screws, nuts, and bolts arrived in the 1800s when machine tools could mass-produce screws of any size and diameter.

They were used to fasten both metal and wood (wood screws were given sharp points).

SCUBA GEAR

See AQUA-LUNG

SEISMOMETER (SEISMOGRAPH)

An earthquake shakes a desert valley in central California. Within seconds, the vibrations register on hundreds of sensitive instruments around the world. The instruments are seismometers, or "shake measurers," which gauge the large and minute earth motions, or seismic waves, produced by quakes, explosions, and other ground-shaking events. Taken together, the data from three or more seismic stations can pinpoint the location of such an event, as well as determine its strength. Studying such information has helped scientists understand

Some Common Types of Screws and Bolts

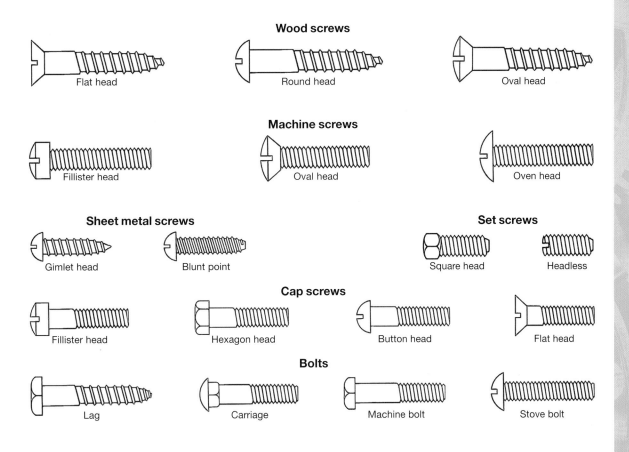

Wood screws

Flat head · Round head · Oval head

Machine screws

Fillister head · Oval head · Oven head

Sheet metal screws

Gimlet head · Blunt point

Set screws

Square head · Headless

Cap screws

Fillister head · Hexagon head · Button head · Flat head

Bolts

Lag · Carriage · Machine bolt · Stove bolt

S

Elegantly simple, the first known seismometer recorded tremors in 1st-century China. This working model stands on display at London's Natural History Museum.

the structure of the Earth far below the surface, as well as estimate the risk of future quakes.

Though the term seismic (Greek for "shaking") wasn't coined till the mid-1800s, the Chinese scholar Chang Heng invented a kind of seismometer around A.D. 132. It consisted of a cylinder with eight dragon heads on the upper rim, each with a tiny ball balanced on its tongue. Directly below were eight open-mouthed frogs. A quake in the surrounding region, though too weak to be felt by a person, would cause one or more of the balls to drop from a dragon's mouth into a frog's.

The modern seismometer is usually called a seismograph, or "shake writer," because it records seismic waves on a continuous graph. The first seismograph was built by the British geologist John Milne in 1880.

It consisted of a horizontal (sideways) PENDULUM suspended from a string so that its motion lagged behind that of the rest of the instrument when rocked. During an earthquake, this difference in movement was recorded with reflected light as a graph on photosensitive paper.

Various scientists and engineers greatly improved the seismograph in the 1950s. Today's machines generally contain three seismometers for registering motion in three directions. A weight on a spring is used to register vertical (up-and-down) motion, by noting changes in the distance between the suspended weight and the seismometer's frame. Two weights on swinging pendulums register sideways motions, one moving generally east-west, the other north-south.

Today's skilled technicians also use seismometers to recognize various kinds of seismic waves, using differences in their arrival times to calculate the distance and strength of a natural or human-made quake. In these ways, thousands of seismic events are recorded each year.

Since the 1950s, governments have used seismographs to monitor underground nuclear explosions. Most recently, geologists have begun using portable seismographs to locate mineral and oil deposits. They do so by setting off small explosions in an area and recording how fast or slow the seismic waves travel through the ground.

November 30, 1992, North Atlantic Ocean, Magnitude = 5.7, Depth = 10 km, Distance = 3,461 km

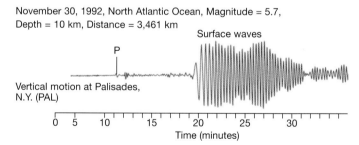

Seismometers (left) work by measuring a gap between a suspended weight and a frame that moves with the ground when an earthquake occurs. A seismogram (above) is a record of how the ground moves at a particular place—in this case, at Palisades, New York, during an earthquake on November 30, 1992. The largest waves shown here are surface waves, which last for several minutes.

Seismometer

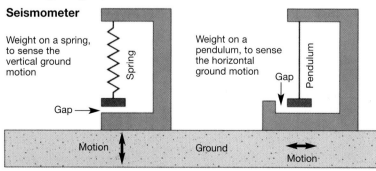

SEMICONDUCTOR

Most substances are either electrical conductors (an electrical current can run through them) or insulators (electrical current can't run through them). But a few special materials are both conductors and insulators, depending on conditions. They are called semiconductors.

Natural semiconductors such as the elements silicon and germanium have a limited ability to carry an electric current, depending on the arrangement of their atoms. But in the 1940s, U.S. scientists at Bell Laboratories discovered that they could greatly increase and control the conductivity of semiconductors by adding tiny amounts of impurities, or "dopants." In doing so, they created the first semiconducting device—the TRANSISTOR—and ushered in the "age of electronics." The transistor, in turn, led to the revolutionary semiconducting device known as the INTEGRATED CIRCUIT. Today, the circuitry of most electronic devices, from COMPUTERS to pacemakers, is etched into semiconductor "chips."

The production of such semiconductor devices requires the manipulation of matter on an atomic level. Typically, this begins with the manufacture of semiconductor crystals far purer than the crystal found in nature. Silicon—the main ingredient in sand—is melted at high temperature, and any impurities are removed. Then cooled crystalized silicon is sliced into microscopically thin wafers. The result is crystal with almost perfect order among its atoms. The wafer must be so clean and smooth that its surface varies in height by no more than a few atoms.

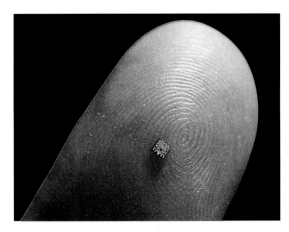

A silicon chip a few millimeters across holds millions of microscopic components.

The second step involves coating the silicon wafer with a fine layer of silicon dioxide. Then circuit patterns are etched into the oxide with lasers.

Finally, dopants are added to the exposed silicon, atom by atom, to create regions with different semiconducting properties.

SEWING MACHINE

A labor-saving device for stitching cloth and other materials, the sewing machine was not so much invented as slowly developed over two centuries. In 1790, the English cabinetmaker Thomas Saint patented the first known sewing machine, a crude boot-stitching device that used a hand crank and a hooked, crochet-type needle to carry thread through pre-punched holes. The first machine used for large-scale sewing jobs was invented by the French tailor Barthélemy Thimonnier in 1830. By 1841, eighty of his machines were being used to sew army uniforms. But his factory was destroyed by a mob of tailors because the invention threatened their jobs.

About the same time, the American Walter Hunt devised a sewing machine that featured an eye at the point of its needle. Convinced his invention would throw poor seamstresses

Howe's 1846 sewing machine (above) could sew 250 stitches per minute—five times faster than the speediest seamstress. But the device didn't become popular until Singer turned it into an easy-to-use home appliance in 1851.

A 19th-century mother introduces her child to the wonders of a foot-treadle Singer sewing machine, one of the first household appliances sold on credit.

out of work, Hunt abandoned it. But in 1846, another American, Elias Howe, patented a machine much like Hunt's, with an eye-pointed needle and a shuttle that moved back and forth to feed cloth beneath the moving needle.

Then, in 1850, yet a third American, Isaac Singer, put all the pieces together. His sewing machine had an overhanging arm with an eye-pointed needle and a presser foot to hold the material in place. A table supported the cloth, with a wheel feeding it under the moving needle. Most important, Singer's machine featured a foot treadle instead of a hand crank, leaving both hands free for maneuvering the cloth. Within a decade, the name Singer became a household word as sewing machines became as popular in homes as in factories.

During the 1930s, electric motors began to replace foot treadles. In the late 1940s came machines with needles that could move from side to side as well as up and down, allowing even inexperienced sewers to make zigzag stitches for buttonholes and the like. In 1968, the Pfaff Company of Germany introduced the first electronic sewing machines.

SEXTANT

Early seafarers guessed their position by following the Sun, Moon, and stars. But they were never quite sure of their whereabouts because their measurements from the deck of a bobbing ship were not very accurate. An important breakthrough for navigation was the sextant, invented independently by the American Thomas Godfrey and the Englishman John Hadley in 1730.

Shaped like a pie wedge whose edge forms one-sixth of a circle, the sextant has a movable arm with a mounted mirror, and a fixed arm holding a small telescope. To "shoot the Sun" (or Moon or star), the navigator views the horizon through the telescope, then moves the mirror arm until the Sun's reflection and the horizon appear to merge. At this point, the sextant's scale shows the Sun's altitude—how many degrees it is above the horizon. This information, together with the accurate time, can tell the sailor the ship's position from tables in a navigational almanac. This technique can still be used, but it is being replaced by modern satellite-based positioning.

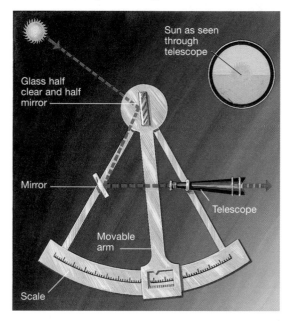

Mariners used sextants to find latitude by measuring the angle between the horizon and the Sun or a star.

SOAP

We know soap as a substance that removes dirt when dissolved in water. But its inventors—the Phoenicians of 600 B.C.—used it in medicine and clothmaking. Soap's cleansing properties remained unknown until the second century A.D., when the Greek physician Galen discovered that soaping helped cure skin diseases.

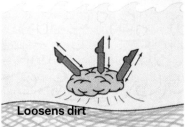

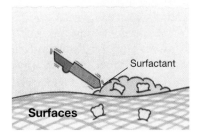

Surfaces　　Surfactant

Loosens dirt

Suspends dirt

Surfactants are the substances in both detergents and soap that do the actual cleaning. One end of each surfactant molecule is attracted to oily dirt. The other end is attracted to water and thus suspends the dirt particles so that they can be rinsed away easily.

To make a barrel of soap, the colonial woman mixed water and wood ashes to make lye (an alkali), then added fat drippings from her kitchen.

Early soapmakers created their product by mixing plant ashes and animal fats. Today, we understand that soap is produced by the reaction between an alkali substance (such as ashes) and fat or oil. The ancient Greeks spread their knowledge of soapmaking throughout Europe. But it remained a rarity and a handicraft until the 1800s, when new manufacturing methods and formulas led to large-scale production.

SOLAR BATTERY

See PHOTOELECTRIC CELL

SONAR

In the early 1900s, physicists suggested that it might be possible to create a device that would use underwater sound waves to detect icebergs and enable ships to navigate around them. The sinking of the *Titanic* in 1912 and the threat of submarines as World War I began in 1914 spurred interest, and many tried to build such a

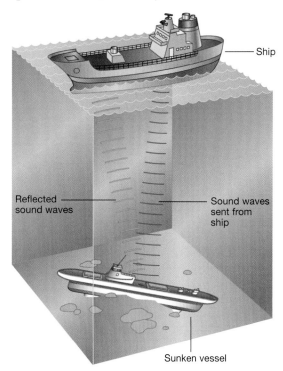

Ship

Reflected sound waves

Sound waves sent from ship

Sunken vessel

The ship's sonar system transmits sound pulses and receives the echoes from an underwater object. In a typical sonar system, the reflected signals activate a visual display that reveals both the object's direction and its distance.

S

device. Around 1915, the French physicist Paul Langevin succeeded. The key to Langevin's invention was his use of crystals such as quartz that change shape when subjected to an electric charge. In this way, such "piezoelectric" crystals can be used to convert electrical energy into acoustic energy, or sound waves.

Langevin mounted his crystals in an oil-filled chamber and used them to produce powerful pulses of sound. Traveling through the water, the sound bounces off objects in its path, and the echoes are picked up by a separate set of crystals within the device. The time that elapses between sending the signal and receiving its echo indicates the distance of a large object and its direction of travel (away from or toward the detector).

By 1918, Langevin's "echolocation" device was being used by the British to hunt German submarines. The U.S. Navy perfected the system just before World War II, giving it the name sonar, for *s*ound *n*avigation *r*anging. Today, sonar's peacetime uses include hunting schools of fish and mapping ocean bottoms. Geologists use specially adapted sonar sets to search for underground oil and gas deposits and to study the nature of deep layers of rock. A form of sonar adapted for medical use is commonly known as ULTRASOUND, and an image created by ultrasound is called a sonogram.

SPACE PROBES

In 1959, two years after they placed the first SATELLITE into orbit, the Soviets launched the first space probe—the first human-made object to escape the gravitational force of Earth. This unmanned vehicle sent back information about radiation levels near the Moon. In the 1960s, the United States followed with the first of many successful deep-space probes to our solar system's planets and beyond.

Space probes have much technology in common with satellites and manned spacecraft. But their unique missions—the unmanned exploration of outer space—require the use of special systems for launch, navigation, and long-distance space travel.

When launched, space probes require an extra boost to escape the Earth's gravity. Typically, this "escape velocity" is provided by an upper stage on the launch ROCKET. The probe must, in fact, exceed escape velocity. Otherwise, it would

simply drift into an orbit around the Earth. Even though the craft has escaped the pull of Earth, it will be influenced by the gravity of other bodies, including Earth's Moon. Launch engineers must precisely time the probe's journey past these moving bodies so that it will reach its destination.

Probes also require sophisticated in-flight guidance systems. These involve computers, both in the craft and at ground stations, that calculate the probe's present position and motion. Radio signals from ground operators can direct the firing of thrusters (small rocket engines) to change the craft's direction and speed to keep it on its planned course. Space probes also have internal guidance systems such as GYROSCOPES and star-sighting devices that keep its pointing direction, or attitude, steady.

Measuring the changing position of a space probe is a complex task. Satellites can be tracked by powerful radar stations and telescopes on Earth. But when the probe travels beyond the reach of such devices, trackers on the ground rely on radio signals sent back from the craft. Sophisticated computer models compare the direction and nature of these signals to give a best estimate of the probe's position.

Electricity is needed to power the craft's navigation and steering systems and its scientific instruments. Probes traveling toward the Sun

Launched in 1997, the mission of the Cassini space probe is to make a detailed survey of the planet Saturn, its rings, and its moons.

from Earth typically use solar energy captured with PHOTOELECTRIC CELLS. Probes that explore the outer planets and beyond may be equipped with small NUCLEAR-POWER REACTORS.

SPACE SHUTTLE

In 1981, space travel entered a new era with the launch of the first space shuttle. A reusable space vehicle, the shuttle is half rocket, half airplane. The building of the space shuttle tied together technology developed over the entire twentieth century. The shuttle combines elements of the pioneer AIRPLANE flown by the Wright brothers in 1903, the ROCKET technology developed by ROBERT GODDARD in the 1920s, and a vast array of small but powerful electronic circuitry developed since 1950 (*see* COMPUTER and INTEGRATED CIRCUIT).

The U.S. space shuttle was designed in the 1970s to be launched into orbit as a rocket, to operate as a spaceship during a five- to twenty-eight-day mission, and to fly back through the atmosphere as a hypersonic glider, landing on a conventional runway. The first shuttle, *Columbia*, roared into space and back in April 1981.

The shuttle consists of three main components: the orbiter itself, with three main engines; an external fuel tank; and two solid-fuel rocket boosters. At launch, the shuttle stands more than 184 feet tall (56.1 meters), weigh-

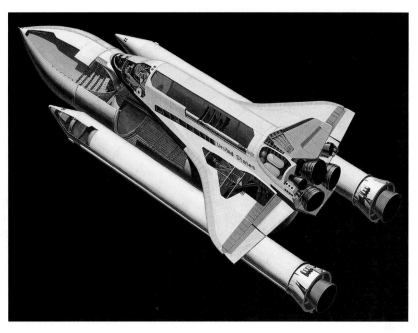

The space shuttle, America's manned reusable space transportation system, has enhanced the operational capability of our space program.

ing some 4.5 million pounds (2.04 million kilograms). The large cargo bay of the shuttle (60 feet by 15 feet or 18.3 meters by 4.6 meters)

The thundering launch of the orbiter *Discovery* in August 1984 marked the debut of NASA's third space shuttle (after *Columbia* and *Challenger*).

makes it an all-purpose spacecraft, able to carry up to 65,000 pounds (29,478.5 kilograms) of satellites, space-station components, space-repair equipment, and scientific instruments. The shuttle's huge cargo doors swing open immediately after it reaches orbit, and remain open until just before reentry. Solar panels and heat radiators on the open doors power some shuttle systems while cooling the crew cabin at the front of the craft.

The shuttle's flight crew uses five independent computers to monitor and control the craft's systems. The flight demands near-constant coordination between the crew and the computerized controls. The crew's living and working quarters occupy two equipment-jammed decks. Life-support systems recycle waste products to provide fresh air and water. The craft's systems are powered, in part, by fuel cells that produce energy by combining hydrogen and oxygen, then converting it to electricity.

The shuttle is large enough to carry passengers in addition to its flight crew. It also launches at a lower speed than previous space vehicles. For these reasons, it's well suited for carrying scientists and other nonastronauts.

The U.S. shuttles are the only models in active use, but the European Space Agency (ESA) has plans for its own shuttle and space planes.

SPECTROMETER, MASS

The mass spectrometer is an invention whose great impact on modern life remains largely invisible to the public. It is an instrument for sorting atoms or molecules on the basis of their differences in mass. In effect, it enables scientists, engineers, and physicians to obtain a molecule-by-molecule chemical analysis of almost any substance—be it an air sample, drop of blood, or Moon rock.

Mass spectrometers have enabled biologists and medical researchers to understand the chemical processes of life, from plant photosynthesis to human metabolism. Geologists use the device to analyze the content of unknown samples, including meteorites and the first lunar rocks. In industry, mass spectrometry is used to assure the chemical purity and safety of products. In most cases, the device can detect smaller amounts of a substance than can any other instrument, sometimes less than one trillionth of a gram. This ability is especially cru-

cial in the production of superpure materials such as SEMICONDUCTORS, where a tiny amount of contamination can spell failure.

A mass spectrometer consists of four basic parts—a handling device, accelerator, analyzer, and detector—all of which lie inside a vacuum chamber. The handling system inserts the sample material into the accelerator. The accelerator imparts a charge to the molecules within the sample and propels them forward as a beam of charged particles, or ions. The beam passes through the analyzer, which produces an electric field that separates the particles according to their mass. Finally, the detector registers the separated ion beams and records their individual mass and abundance.

In 1913, the British physicist Sir Joseph John Thomson built a crude form of such a device. He simply passed a beam of ions through an electromagnetic field and allowed the separated ion beams to strike a photographic plate. The British physicist and chemist Francis Aston continued Thomson's work and in 1919 built a spectrometer that allowed him to separate and identify rare gases in a sample of air. Since then, mass spectrometers have been used to discover many previously unknown chemical elements and compounds.

In the electronic age, mass spectrometry has become extremely sophisticated, with computers and data-handling systems to provide near-instant analysis of an unknown sample. Results are often combined with gas and liquid CHROMATOGRAPHY for the rapid separation and analysis of especially complex mixtures. Such techniques continue to further our investigation of the great chemical mysteries of life.

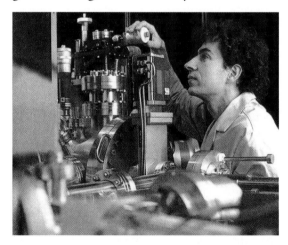

A geologist uses a mass spectrometer to determine the makeup and age of a rock sample.

SPHYGMOMANOMETER

A fairly simple device with a big name, the sphygmomanometer (sfig-mo-ma-NOM-e-ter) measures blood pressure—one of the most important indicators of bodily function. The heart pushes blood through the circulatory system of blood vessels. The sphygmomanometer can measure whether that pressure is in the normal range. Blood pressure that is too high or too low may cause health problems. Today, sphygmomanometers, or blood-pressure measurers, are used in virtually every medical exam.

Measuring blood pressure has become a standard part of medical exams.

The device consists of a cloth cuff that contains an inflatable chamber. The chamber is connected to two tubes. One leads to a squeeze bulb or air pump, and the other leads to a dial or digital display. Typically, a doctor or nurse wraps the cuff around the patient's arm above the elbow and inflates the cuff to cut off circulation to the arm. Placing a stethoscope over the main artery of the arm, he or she then listens for pulse sounds while slowly deflating the pressure cuff with a valve. The pressure at which blood is heard returning to the artery (as seen on the display) is called systolic pressure. The pressure at which no sound can be heard (and the blood is moving most slowly between heartbeats) is the diastolic pressure.

Modern sphygmomanometers trace back to a device used by the British scientist Stephen Hales around 1705. Hales studied the blood pressure of various animals such as horses by attaching a long glass tube to an artery and recording the height to which the blood rose in the tube. The first practical sphygmomanometer for humans—able to measure blood pressure without puncturing an artery—was invented and used by the Italian physician Scipione Riva-Rocci in 1896.

SPINNING JENNY

The invention of the FLYING SHUTTLE in 1733 greatly speeded and mechanized the weaving of fabric. But work often ground to a halt because spinners couldn't hand-spin thread fast enough to supply the weaving machines. A breakthrough came in 1764, when the English weaver James Hargreaves invented the spinning jenny—a machine that spun multiple threads at one time.

Hargreaves is said to have conceived his idea when his daughter Jenny's spinning wheel accidentally tipped over and its spindle continued to revolve in an upright rather than a horizontal position. Hargreaves realized that by building a machine with many vertical spindles connected together, one spinner could turn them all at once, producing a dozen or more threads instead of just one.

Local handspinners, afraid that the new machine would put them out of work, destroyed Hargreaves's first models. But by 1780, spinning machines were being operated by power machinery able to do the work of hundreds of hand spinners.

Spinning Jenny

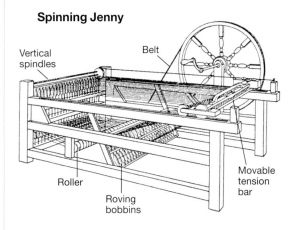

Using an improved version of Hargreaves' spinning jenny, an operator could spin about 16 threads at once.

S

SPINNING WHEEL

Before the SPINNING JENNY, there was the spinning wheel, itself a revolution in the making of thread and yarn. Spinning is the process by which cotton, wool, or other short fibers are twisted together to produce yarn or thread for weaving or sewing. Since prehistoric times, people have spun without tools, simply twisting fibers between their fingers, or between the palm and thigh. Around 3000 B.C., the Egyptians began fastening the drawn-out fibers onto a dangling wooden rod, or spindle, that could be whirled to twist the fibers into thread. The spinning wheel mechanized this process, appearing first in Asia in the first century B.C., and in Europe around 1300.

The key to the spinning wheel's operation is a driving belt or gear that connects the large

wheel and a small spindle. By turning the wheel (either by hand or with a foot pedal), the spinner rotates the spindle to quickly draw out the thread. The spinning wheel's smooth action produced a much stronger, more uniform thread than could be spun by hand.

SPOON

The spoon was the first tool made solely for eating. Archaeologists speculate that it was invented when prehistoric hunters began stewing their meat, creating the need for a utensil to bring hot liquids to the mouth. The oldest known spoons, shaped and smoothed out of clay, date back about seven thousand years. The Egyptians followed with spoons carved from wood, ivory, or stone, while the ancient Greeks crafted spoons from silver and bronze.

STAPLER

What office or classroom today doesn't have a stapler for tacking together sheets of paper? This office "necessity" is the 1868 invention of Charles Gouldin, whose original design has remained basically unchanged. All staplers feature a channel that feeds a strip of U-shaped wires (the staples) to a slot beneath a blunt blade. When the top of the stapler is pressed, the blade breaks off an individual wire, forcing it through papers placed over a small metal anvil. A set of grooves in the anvil bends the wire tips flat beneath the papers, fastening them together.

Today, many busy offices use electric staplers that automatically shoot staples through paper at high speed. Construction workers use electric staplers, or "tackers," that drive heavy wire staples into wood or other material without bending them.

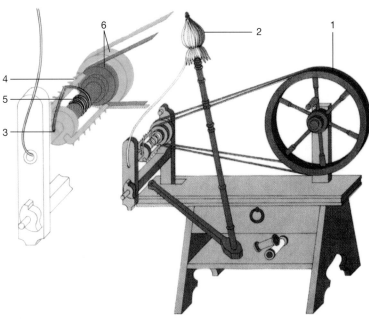

This late-15th-century wheel represented a revolution in hand spinning, since it both spun and wound the yarn simultaneously. Powered either by hand, as in the wheel shown here, or by foot-treadle, it had two wheel-mounted belts that turned pulleys connected to a spool and a U-shaped flyer. As the right hand turned the driving wheel (1), the left hand drew fiber from the mass of loose yarn topping the distaff (2). The fiber passed through a small eye on the spindle shaft (3) and was caught over one of the hooks on the flyer (4), which, while turning, wound it around the spool (5). With its lager pulley (6), the flyer revolved more slowly than the spool. The yarn shifted from one hook to another as the spool filled with thread.

STEAM ENGINE

When water turns into steam, it expands to about seventeen hundred times its liquid volume. Steam engines harness the tremendous energy of this expansion to do their work. The steam TURBINE, in which steam turns huge, fan-like wheels, is a type of steam engine. But most engineers use the term "steam engine" to refer to a kind of reciprocating engine, which means that steam power is used to drive a piston back and forth inside a cylinder.

The story of the practical steam engine begins in the 1600s, when flooding was a serious problem in English mines. Mine owners installed huge pumps powered by horses to raise the water to the surface. But what they wanted was a machine that didn't require food, stables, or daily care. Many English inventors tried to build such a "mechanical

Newcomen Steam Engine

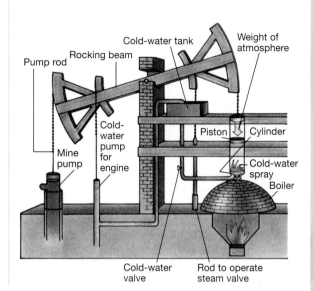

Labels: Cold-water tank · Weight of atmosphere · Pump rod · Rocking beam · Piston · Cylinder · Cold-water pump for engine · Cold-water spray · Boiler · Mine pump · Cold-water valve · Rod to operate steam valve

Profile: James Watt

According to science legend, the great Scottish inventor James Watt spent many childhood hours watching a teakettle on the fire. Sometimes he would hold a spoon at the spout and watch the steam condense into water. Impressed by how steam could lift the kettle lid, he is said to have remarked: "If only I could trap enough of that steam in the right way, I could do mighty things." Whether or not the story is true, Watt did go on to make steam do mighty things. He did so with the STEAM ENGINE for which he is famous.

Born in Renfrew County, Scotland, in 1736, Watt had little schooling but eagerly read books and spent many hours building mechanical toys in his father's carpentry shop. At seventeen, he moved to Glasgow to work for an instrument maker, studied mathematics for a time in London, then moved back to Glasgow to become a mathematical instrument maker at the university there.

While working at the university in the 1760s, Watt was asked to repair a model of Newcomen's engine, a steam-powered water pump used in English mines. Newcomen's engine was the first practical steam engine. But Watt saw that it wasted a

tremendous amount of energy. Over the next decade, Watt built a steam engine very different from Newcomen's in design. Watt's invention used less fuel and produced more power. Moreover, it could be harnessed to power machinery in factories and mills, riverboats and locomotives.

By 1785, Watt had created a steam engine mighty enough to power an entire cotton mill. For the first time, textile and flour mills didn't have to be built alongside rivers to get their power through WATER-WHEELS. Watt's engine provided a far better source of power, enabling factories to move into cities and use larger machines. Watt's steam engine is widely credited with ushering in the modern Industrial Age. Watt retired a wealthy man in 1800, yet kept researching and inventing till his death in 1819. The units of power we call the "watt" and "kilowatt" are named in his honor.

S

How A Simple Steam Engine Works   1

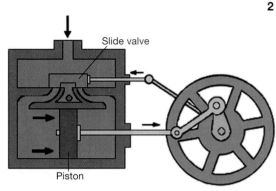

Steam inlet from boiler
Steam port
Slide valve
Steam chest
Flywheel
Exhaust
Piston rod
Piston   Cylinder

Steam entering the left-hand side of the chamber will move the piston to the right.

2

Slide valve
Piston

As expanding steam continues to push the piston to the right, the slide valve closes and no more steam enters the chamber.

horse." And in 1712, Thomas Newcomen finally succeeded, building one that really worked.

Newcomen's steam engine looked unlike any modern-day engine. It featured one piston suspended by a chain from one end of a huge wooden rocker beam. When the piston moved down into the cylinder, the other end of the beam pulled a rod out of a suction pump to extract water. Boiling water produced the steam that pushed the piston up. Condensing the steam with a spray of cold water pulled the piston down again. Newcomen's engine could pump as much water in two days as fifty horses and twenty workers could pump in a week.

The first all-purpose steam engine was invented by the Scottish engineer James Watt. After repairing a Newcomen engine in 1763, Watt

realized he could build a much more efficient engine by keeping the cooling, or "condensing," chamber separate from the rest of the engine. Watt patented his engine in 1769. In 1782, he doubled its power with a sliding valve that allowed the piston to do work on both its downstroke and upstroke. Watt also invented the "governor"—a mechanical control that automatically kept the engine running at a constant speed.

Watt's greatly improved steam engine was first used in mines. But it also proved to be an efficient power source for factories. It could, for example, raise water for turning waterwheels that, in turn, drove machinery.

Beginning around 1800, steam engines were adapted to power boats and railroad locomotives. By 1820, steamboats carried passen-

Manufacturing Steel

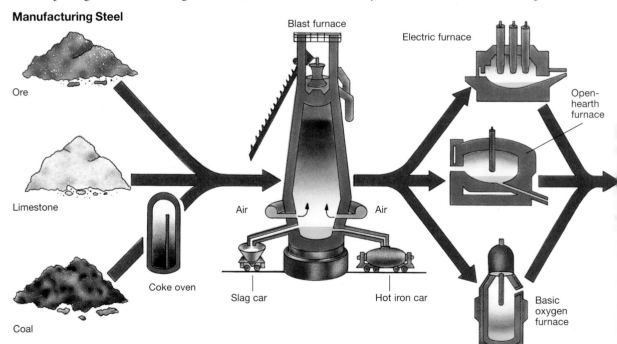

Blast furnace
Electric furnace
Ore
Open-hearth furnace
Limestone
Air   Air
Coke oven
Slag car   Hot iron car
Basic oxygen furnace
Coal

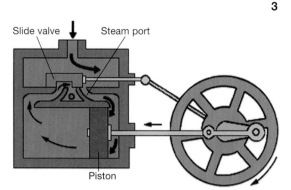

Slide valve Steam port

Piston

When the piston is all the way to the right again, the steam rushes into the right-hand side of the chamber and pushes the piston back to the left.

gers and freight on major rivers. And by 1840, the United States alone had nearly three thousand miles of railroad track. In 1860, there were thirty thousand miles.

In 1900, steam engines remained the industrial world's chief power source. But by 1950, they had been largely replaced by ELECTRIC MOTORS and INTERNAL-COMBUSTION ENGINES.

STEEL

Steel, more than any other metal, transformed civilization in the 1800s and 1900s. Its strength, affordability, and versatility made possible the building of huge machines, ships, trains, airplanes, automobiles, factories, and high-rise

3 buildings. Centuries from now, an archaeologist studying the period between 1850 and 2000 might call it the Age of Steel.

Egyptian ironworkers appear to have been the first to create small amounts of steel more than two thousand years ago. They did so by melting iron bars inside intensely hot charcoal furnaces, then rapidly cooling the molten iron with cold water. Though they did not understand it at the time, these early steelmakers had produced an alloy, or mixed metal, consisting of about 99 percent iron and 1 percent carbon. The result, which we call steel, was a material of greater strength and flexibility than had ever been found on Earth.

For many centuries, steel could be made only a few pounds at a time. So it was reserved for the making of special items such as swords and knives. Then, in 1856, the British engineer Sir Henry Bessemer patented a process for producing steel with blasts of cold air. In this process, large amounts of molten iron were placed in a huge, pear-shaped container called a Bessemer converter, whose bottom was pierced by hundreds of small holes through which the cold air was blown. For the first time, steel was being produced in large quantities at low cost. Production grew rapidly. By 1880, U.S. steel factories were churning out some 1.2 million tons a year.

In the years since, manufacturers have built several different types of steelmaking furnaces.

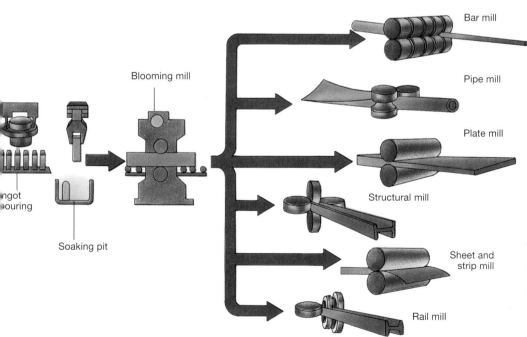

Bar mill

Pipe mill

Blooming mill

Plate mill

Structural mill

ngot ouring

Soaking pit

Sheet and strip mill

Rail mill

The basic steps in the manufacture of steel begin with the raw materials used to convert iron ore to iron, which is further refined to make steel. The final steps involve the shaping and finishing of steel products.

Metallurgists, in turn, have created thousands of different types of steel by adding small amounts of different metals such as chromium, nickel, and tungsten. With the right combination of these "alloying elements," steel can be made so hard that only a diamond can scratch it, or so soft that it can be bent by hand; so strong it can support the tallest skyscraper, or so delicate it can be spun into fibers.

STETHOSCOPE

Since the days of Hippocrates in the 400s B.C., physicians have listened to the noises of internal organs, especially the heart and lungs. But not until the 1800s did someone invent an instrument to amplify these faint sounds. In 1816, the French physician René Laënnec devised the first stethoscope—a wooden tube about 12 inches (30 centimeters) long, with a broad end to be placed against the patient's chest and a narrow end placed near the physician's ear. In 1840, the American physician George Cammann improved Laënnec's design, creating the stethoscope seen in medical offices today. It consists of two earpieces connected by flexible rubber tubes that join before connecting to a cup or diaphragm that is held against the chest. In this way, the physician can clearly hear the many internal sounds used to diagnose problems of the heart, lungs, stomach, and blood vessels.

STIRRUP

For some two thousand years, the horse-riding tribes of central Asia controlled their horses with only a BRIDLE. But only the most skillful riders could keep their balance in this way.

Then, in the 200s B.C. in China, came the first stirrup—a leather strap bound around the horse's body just behind its front legs and ending in a loop on either side of the horse. The first leather stirrups may have been used for quick mounting. The Chinese dramatically improved stirrups with metal footholds around A.D. 100. This important innovation was not adopted by Europeans for about seven hundred years.

By giving riders a more secure hold of their horses, metal stirrups made mounted combat possible. In fact, some historians credit the stirrup with revolutionizing warfare and enabling

feudal lords to control vast areas of land and peasants during the Middle Ages in Europe.

STOVE

Stoves produce, contain, or direct heat for a special purpose. When designed solely for cooking, they are often called ranges, and this is the form we know best today.

Early humans no doubt realized that an open fire was an inefficient way to cook a meal or heat a home. The first crude stoves may have been rings of rocks and mud set about a fire to retain its heat. The Chinese used iron before A.D. 200 to build better stoves, pouring molten iron into sand molds. Cast-iron stoves appeared in Europe in the 1400s.

Stovemaking was an important industry in America beginning in the 1650s. Many early American stoves were designed to be inserted into a fireplace, not for cooking, but to direct heat into a room. By the 1700s, fireplace stoves were being built with a top hole for inserting a pot of water. The Franklin stove, invented by Benjamin Franklin in 1742, incorporated these designs while burning wood with great efficiency. It warmed houses and frontier cabins for over a century.

The year 1802 brought the invention of stoves that burned coal for heat. By the 1890s, gas ranges had become popular for cooking in towns and cities. Electric ranges first appeared in restaurant kitchens around 1890, and were adapted for home use in the 1920s.

SUBMARINE

Engineers and inventors have been trying to build practical undersea vessels for almost two thousand years. The earliest recorded attempt was around 300 B.C., when Alexander the Great was lowered into the sea in a barrel with glass portholes. The first craft actually piloted underwater was constructed in 1620 by the Dutch engineer Cornelis Drebbel. Drebbel demonstrated his submarine beneath the Thames River. He submerged the craft by partially flooding the hull, propelled it underwater with oars sealed in their locks with leather gaskets, and brought it to the surface by pumping the hull out again. A pipe that extended into the air allowed Drebbel to breathe.

Early in the history of submarines, people recognized their potential as weapons of warfare.

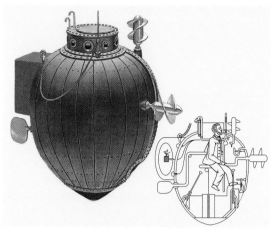

Bushnell made his hand-cranked *Turtle* out of oak planks bound with iron straps and coated with tar. The operator submerged and raised the vessel with foot pumps that filled or emptied a water compartment.

During the Revolutionary War, the Connecticut inventor David Bushnell built a one-person, hand-cranked submarine that carried a bomb. The crew of Bushnell's *Turtle* was supposed to nail the bomb onto the bottom of a British ship, but couldn't pierce its copper-covered hull. The first undersea vessel to succeed in destroying another ship was the Confederate army's hand-cranked *Hunley*. Holding a bomb on a long pole, the *Hunley* rammed the explosive into a Federal gunboat's hull. The pilot of the *Hunley* was supposed to back off before detonating the bomb. But it exploded immediately, crippling both ships.

The following years brought several important advances in submarine technology. In 1863, the French inventor Charles Brun used compressed air both to propel his undersea vessel and to expel water from its ballast tanks for surfacing. The French navy built several electric

submarines in the 1880s and 1890s. But they couldn't travel far without recharging their batteries. About the same time, the Swedish inventor Torsten Nordenfelt equipped submarines with torpedo tubes—transforming the underwater craft into a greatly feared weapon.

A new generation of long-distance submarines was born with the USS *Holland*, built by the Irish-born American inventor John Holland in 1900. The *Holland* used an electric motor for underwater travel and a gasoline engine for surface travel. While on the surface, its gas engine could be used to recharge its electric batteries. Undersea vessels similar to the *Holland* played important roles in both world wars. But none could remain underwater for long without surfacing to recharge their batteries and refuel.

The next revolution in submarine technology came with the invention of the NUCLEAR-POWER REACTOR. In 1954, the U.S. Navy launched the first nuclear submarine, the USS *Nautilus*. Though it resembled conventional underwater craft in many ways, the vessel's nuclear engine gave it an unsurpassed range and power. In a sense, it was the first true submarine, designed to travel primarily underwater, where it could remain for several months, and where it moved with more speed and maneuverability than on the surface. In the years since, the United States and the former Soviet Union developed several fleets of advanced nuclear submarines. With the end of the Cold War, disposal of their radioactive engines remains a major concern.

SUNDIAL

First crafted by the Egyptians, more than three thousand years ago, the sundial may be the most ancient of scientific instruments. Then as today, most sundials indicated time with a

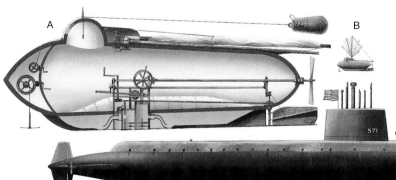

The *Nautilus* built by Robert Fulton in 1800 was among the world's first practical submersibles (A and B). The *Nautilus* launched by the U.S. Navy in 1954 was the first nuclear-powered submarine (C).

shadow cast from a pointer. As the Sun moved across the sky from morning to night, the shadow passed across a dial on which the hours were marked.

From Egypt, the use of sundials spread throughout the Roman Empire. With the increasing accuracy of clocks and the adoption of standard time in the 1800s, sundials lost much of their practical value.

SUPERCONDUCTORS

When certain metals are cooled to temperatures near absolute zero (-460 degrees Fahrenheit, or -273.3 degrees Celsius), they become superconductors, conducting electricity virtually without resistance—that is, without power loss. This phenomenon was discovered in 1911 by the Dutch physicist Heike Kamerlingh Onnes, while he was working with frozen mercury. In 1933, the German physicist Walther Meissner discovered that superconducting materials repel certain magnetic fields. Together, these two discoveries led physicists to dream of creating giant magnetic fields with superconductors—fields that might enable trains and other vehicles to "float" above magnetic tracks, traveling at high speeds with little expenditure of energy. Superconducting wires, in turn, could transmit electricity without any loss of power.

In 1986, the European physicists Georg Bednorz and Alex Müller took a giant step toward the goal of building practical superconductors. They created new CERAMIC materials that became superconductors at temperatures above absolute zero, specifically -396 degrees Fahrenheit (-237.8 degrees Celsius). They made their "high-temperature" superconductors from a ceramic mixture of copper, oxygen, barium, and lanthanum. Bednorz and Müller's breakthrough spurred worldwide efforts to create materials that become superconductors at still higher, more practical temperatures. Among the most promising were materials developed in 1987 by scientists at the University of Houston and the University of Alabama. Their exotic ceramics achieve superconductivity at -283 degrees Fahrenheit, or -175 degrees Celsius, a temperature that can be reached with the affordable refrigerant liquid nitrogen.

In 1995, U.S. researchers announced the development of a superconducting tape that

Current Flow and Resistance

Insulator

In materials with extremely high resistance, such as rubber or glass, electrons are tightly bound to atoms and cannot be jostled loose to sustain a flow of current.

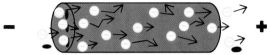

Conductor

In materials with lower resistance, some electrons are loosely bound and form a current when voltage is applied. Resistance is a measure of the energy lost in the form of heat from electron collisions.

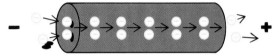

Superconductor

When materials become superconductive, all resistance disappears because electrons are bound into pairs, which move in step with each other, avoiding collisions. Current flows with no energy loss.

could carry more than one hundred times as much current as copper wire of the same thickness. But the goal of putting such materials to use in the first superconducting power lines, levitating trains, and superefficient motors remains to be met in the twenty-first century.

SWORD

As metalworkers learned to forge bronze around 3000 B.C., one of their most frightening creations was a hand weapon featuring a long blade sharpened to a flesh-cutting edge. The sword would remain the preeminent weapon of hand combat for thousands of years.

Early swords, made by pouring molten bronze into a stone mold, included the Viking double-edge sword (top), the Celtic iron blade (middle), and the Bronze Age thrusting sword (bottom).

S

The first reliable swords—resistant to breakage despite heavy blows—appeared around 2000 B.C. in two basic types. One was a cutting sword with a leaf-shaped blade. The other had a longer, narrower thrusting blade. The Vikings revolutionized warfare in the sixth century when they forged stronger, sharper swords by repeated firing and hammering. By the tenth century, the sword had been lengthened into a slashing weapon with a hand guard at the hilt. Sword styles continued to multiply till the late 1800s, when repeating (multiple-shot) firearms ended their use as military weapons.

SYNTHETIC MATERIALS

Humans crafted their first inventions from materials found in nature—basically sticks and stones and plant fibers. Then, some five thousand years ago, people began combining natural materials to produce useful new substances never before seen on Earth. These were the first synthetic materials. Their numbers would swell, slowly at first, until industrialization spurred demand for substances with specific qualities such as extreme strength or heat resistance. Today, our world is filled with such artificial materials. Among the most important are metal alloys, complex ceramics, and synthetic polymers.

The story of their creation begins at the end of the Stone Age, about 4000 B.C., when humans discovered they could shape simple tools out of copper. Though easy to forge, ordinary copper proved too soft to be of much use. Then someone in eastern Europe or western Asia found a way to improve upon nature. About 3500 B.C., that person heated some copper with a small amount of tin to produce an entirely new and more useful metal—BRONZE. Bronze was the world's first synthetic material

The invention of steel, an iron alloy, permitted the erection of skyscrapers. The first was a ten-story structure built in Chicago in the 1870s.

as well as the first alloy—a chemical mixture of different metals. Its invention marked the beginning of what anthropologists call the Bronze Age.

About 1000 B.C., the Iron Age dawned across Europe and Asia. Iron was a natural material slightly stronger than copper. About 400 B.C., Chinese blacksmiths vastly increased iron's strength by heating it to the melting point and introducing some carbon (from charcoal in the fire). This created cast iron, the first iron alloy.

Other early ironworkers introduced less carbon to the iron they melted, and made a still harder and much more flexible metal—STEEL. Produced in large quantities in the 1800s, steel became the world's most commonly used iron alloy. Metallurgists have created other important iron alloys with additional ingredients. Combining iron with both carbon and tungsten, for example, gives us the extremely hard and strong metal used in lamp filaments.

Industry's need for metals with very specific qualities spurred the creation of many non-iron alloys as well. Examples include Monel, a nickel-copper alloy first produced in 1905 and still important for its resistance to corrosion and high temperatures. In more recent times, metallurgists have produced extremely light but strong titanium alloys. Titanium-aluminum-vanadium

The Chinese used bronze, the world's first synthetic material, to create elaborate ceremonial objects such as this wine vessel from the Shang dynasty (1750-1045 B.C.).

S

Reinforced concrete—that is, concrete laced with internal steel beams—made possible the dramatic "sails" of the Opera House in Sydney, Australia.

alloy, for example, is the material of choice for jet air frames and engines.

The history of CERAMICS, like that of metal alloys, begins with a natural substance. Stone Age people made the first ceramic pots from ordinary clay dug out of the ground. As humans become more inventive, they learned to create entirely new kinds of ceramics by mixing different clays with finely crushed particles of substances such as carbon, magnesium, or calcium. Sometime after A.D. 620, the Chinese mixed kaolin, a pure clay, with petuntse, a mineral found in granite. At higher temperatures of about 2400 degrees Fahrenheit (1300 degrees Celsius), the two compounds fused to produce a white, translucent ceramic of great strength and beauty. The new material was PORCELAIN.

Similarly, some two thousand years ago, Roman builders blended and heated a mixture of volcanic ash and limestone, then ground the resulting ceramic into a powder, which they named *caementum*, and which we know as CEMENT. When mixed with water, the substance became an excellent building material, a kind of artificial rock we call concrete. Throughout ancient times and the Middle Ages, craftspeople continued to create new ceramics from various combinations of raw materials such as feldspar, bauxite, talc, and silica.

In the twentieth century, chemists began cooking up more exotic ceramics by mixing together complex chemical compounds and fusing them together at intense temperatures often exceeding 3000 degrees Fahrenheit (1600 degrees Celsius). Combining alumina, silica, and magnesium, for example, produces refractories, materials so resistant to high temperatures that they can be used to line steelmaking furnaces. In the 1980s, physicists invented SUPERCON-DUCTOR ceramics by lacing various metal-oxide ceramics with elements such as yttrium and barium. These ceramics lose nearly all electrical resistance at temperatures of about -280 degrees Fahrenheit (-173.3 degrees Celsius) and so can carry an electrical current with no loss of energy. Used in power lines, superconducting ceramics may someday save trillions of dollars in electricity. Their ability to carry electricity without generating heat may also make possible super-small, super-powerful computers and electromagnets.

A worker at a recycling center sorts plastic discards so they can be ground, melted, and reformed into new products.

A third class of artificial materials—synthetic polymers—is created by chemically combining hundreds or thousands of smaller molecules into long chains. Since the 1950s, products made of synthetic polymers have become the stuff of everyday life.

The very first synthetic polymer was a smelly yellow, moldable substance called pyroxylin, created in 1865 when the British chemist Alexander Parkes combined a chemically treated form of cellulose, or plant fiber, with camphor. Nothing useful was ever made of pyroxylin. But in 1869, the American inventor John Hyatt improved on Parkes's cellulose-camphor recipe to create CELLULOID. The first successful plastic, celluloid quickly became an important manufacturing material used in everything from collar stays and combs to false teeth, billiard balls, and movie film.

Celluloid was followed, in 1884, by the first artificial fiber—later named RAYON, or artificial silk—which was likewise created from chemically treated plant fibers.

Then, in 1909, the Belgian-born American chemist Leo Baekeland produced the first plastic made entirely from artificial ingredients. Cooked up with the chemicals phenol and formaldehyde, syrupy BAKELITE hardened when heated to form an extremely durable, heat-resistant plastic that became extremely useful in the construction of electrical items such as radios.

The U.S. chemist Wallace Hume Carothers, working for the DuPont laboratories, made a huge breakthrough in the late 1930s by creating the first entirely synthetic fiber—NYLON, most familiar in stockings but also used in many other applications. Like the many synthetic fibers that followed, nylon was manufactured out of a gluey mixture of petroleum products forced through machine nozzles to form fine threads. Today, such fibers are sometimes blended with metals or ceramics to produce high-tech composite materials with extreme strength, conductivity, or other desirable properties.

Throughout the second half of the 1900s, the synthetic-polymer industry grew at breakneck speed, with the invention of thousands of useful new plastics, fibers, and rubbers. Among the most fascinating is KEVLAR, a kind of fiber made from liquid crystals that solidify in a way that produces fabric so strong it stops bullets.

Ironically, the extreme durability that makes synthetic polymers so useful eventually became one of their biggest drawbacks. With many billions of tons produced each year, disposal of these long-lasting materials has become an overwhelming task. The challenge ahead includes both greater recycling and the invention of biodegradable polymers, designed to break down when their useful life has ended.

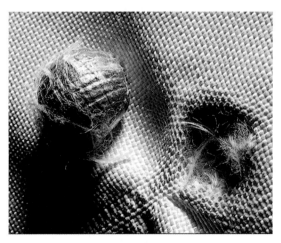

A plastic stronger than steel, Kevlar can be woven into bullet-resistant cloth.

T

TANK (MILITARY)

In the opening years of World War I, military vehicles were often stuck in mud or blocked by trenches. In 1915, the British military assigned its engineers the challenge of designing a new kind of "landship" able to go over or around off-road obstacles, withstand enemy guns, and have guns of its own to fire. The result was a strange, armored, boxy vehicle that moved on long, heavily treaded loops strung over one front and one rear wheel. To hide the true purpose of their experimental fighting machine, the British called them "water tanks," and the name "tank" stuck.

The first tanks moved slowly, barely more than 3 miles (4.8 kilometers) an hour. By World War II, some tanks could move faster than fleeing soldiers could run, and were equipped with cannon and gun turrets. Today's tanks may be supplied with sophisticated missiles as well as guns.

TEFLON

The American chemists Roy Plunkett and Jack Rebok, working in the laboratories at the DuPont Company, invented Teflon in 1938. The two chemists had been searching for a safe refrigerant gas. Instead, they came up with a waxy white plastic that proved to be the slipperiest substance on Earth and one of the toughest.

Teflon was one of the first synthetic polymers, or long-chain molecules. It is composed of carbon atoms surrounded by fluorine atoms. Neither heat nor electricity nor corrosive chemicals can affect it. During World War II, it was classified as a military secret and was used to make virtually indestructible tools necessary in manufacturing the atom bomb. Since then, Teflon has been made into electrical insulators, heat shields for spaceships, and artificial body parts such as hip-joint replacements. Unlike many other substances, Teflon is not rejected

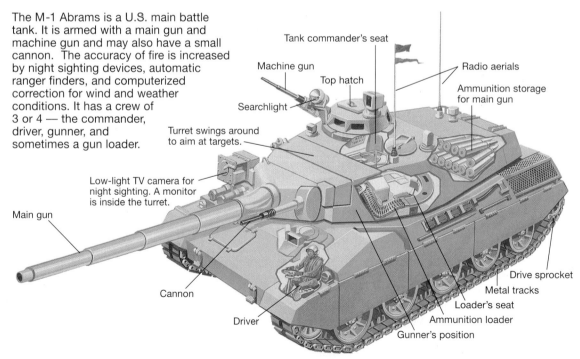

The M-1 Abrams is a U.S. main battle tank. It is armed with a main gun and machine gun and may also have a small cannon. The accuracy of fire is increased by night sighting devices, automatic ranger finders, and computerized correction for wind and weather conditions. It has a crew of 3 or 4 — the commander, driver, gunner, and sometimes a gun loader.

Tank commander's seat

Machine gun

Top hatch

Radio aerials

Searchlight

Ammunition storage for main gun

Turret swings around to aim at targets.

Low-light TV camera for night sighting. A monitor is inside the turret.

Main gun

Drive sprocket

Metal tracks

Cannon

Loader's seat

Driver

Ammunition loader

Gunner's position

The U.S. Army's modern M-1 tank weighs 44 tons and travels up to 45 miles (72 km) an hour.

by the human body and is so tough it can last for decades. But Teflon is most familiar as a non-stick coating for cookware.

TELEGRAPH

For most of human history, the only way to communicate over long distance was to make a very loud noise, as with a tolling bell, or make a visible signal such as a beacon fire on a hill. Then, around 1800, scientists learned that an electric current could travel through metal wires. They wondered if they could use this phenomenon to send messages.

Several inventors built systems for sending short pulses of electricity over wires with a switch connected to a BATTERY. A method for detecting these electric pulses was invented in 1819, when the Danish physicist Hans Oersted found that an electric current could move a magnetic needle. In 1837, the English inventors Sir Charles Wheatstone and Sir William Cooke assembled the first deflected-needle telegraph to send messages along a railway track. The recipient could "read" the message by means of compass needles mounted on dials showing the letters of the alphabet.

Then, in 1844, the American Samuel F.B. Morse completed the first truly practical telegraph system. He devised a code in which short and long electric impulses (dots and dashes) represented the letters of the alphabet. Then he sent a historic message ("What hath God wrought!") along a wire by pressing the switch of an electric circuit and creating impulses that represented his message in MORSE CODE. At the other end of the wire, which ran from Baltimore to Washington, the electric impulses activated an electromagnet, which reproduced the short and long pattern so that the message could be decoded by an operator.

By 1861, telegraph wires had been erected from the Atlantic to the Pacific. And five years later, an underwater cable allowed Americans to send telegrams to Europe. In 1874, THOMAS EDISON invented a device that permitted four telegraph messages to be transmitted along a single wire simultaneously. "Wireless" telegraph became possible after the invention of the RADIO by Guglielmo Marconi in 1894. The early 1900s brought teleprinters—typewriter-like telegraph machines that could transmit and receive printed messages.

Make Your Own Telegraph Set

You and a friend can make a simple telegraph set. You will need two electric buzzers, two 6-volt batteries, a roll of 18-gauge wire, two small blocks of wood, two thin strips of metal, and four round-head screws.

Make two sending keys. For each, use a block of wood as a base and a strip of metal as a sender. Ask an adult to cut the metal from the lid of a can. Bind the sharp edges of the metal with tape so you do not cut yourself. Sandpaper the lacquer off the underside of one end to allow the electric current to pass through. Screw one of the screws into one end of the block. Attach one end of the metal strip to the other end of the block with a second screw so that the unattached end of the strip is over the first screw. Bend the metal upward so that it will not make contact with the screw unless pressed down.

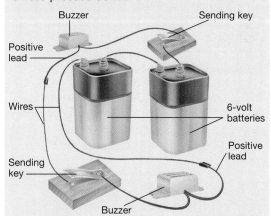

Attach the wires as shown in the diagram. Be sure to connect the positive (+) terminal of one battery with the negative (-) terminal of the other. Scrape off the insulation at the end of each wire so that its connection is made with bare wire. If your buzzers come with lead wires already attached, connect the positive (red) leads as shown. Twist the bare ends of the connecting wires together, and then cover the connection with tape. Now connect the wires to the sending keys by looping the bare wire under the head of each screw and tightening the screw against the wood.

When both keys are pressed to the contact screws, a complete electrical circuit is formed. Electric current flows through the circuit, and the buzzers sound. To send messages, use Morse code, keeping the key down longer for a dash than for a dot. (A table of the alphabet in MORSE CODE can be found on page 90.) Messages can be sent by only one person at a time. When your partner is sending a message, you must hold your key down so that there will be a continuous electric circuit.

153

TELEPHONE

Alexander Graham Bell developed the first successful telephone in 1876, naming it with the Greek words for "far" and "sound." True to its name, the telephone uses electricity to carry the sound of the human voice over once unimaginable distances. Today, telephones connect more than six hundred million people around the globe. In the United States alone, almost two billion phone calls are placed each business day.

Early telephones had three main parts: the transmitter, the receiver, and the wiring that connected them. You spoke into the transmitter, a kind of MICROPHONE that changed the sound waves of your voice into electric signals. A typical telephone transmitter was made of a thin metal disk, or diaphragm, covering a small chamber of carbon granules. As soon as the

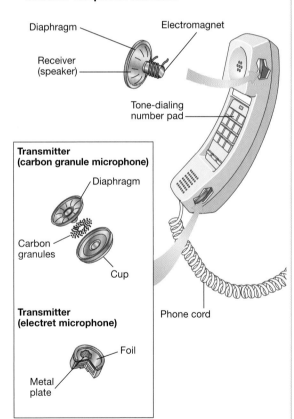

Inside a Telephone Handset

Diaphragm
Electromagnet
Receiver (speaker)
Tone-dialing number pad

Transmitter (carbon granule microphone)
Diaphragm
Carbon granules
Cup

Transmitter (electret microphone)
Foil
Metal plate

Phone cord

When you speak into a telephone, the transmitter changes the sound waves of your voice into an electric current.

telephone was switched on (by lifting the handset or pushing a button), electricity began to flow through the granules. When you spoke, the sound waves of your voice struck the diaphragm, which pressed on the granules, changing the strength of the electric current passing through them. In this way, your voice created a pattern in the electrical current. This pattern traveled over telephone wires. Along the way, it passed through various switching mechanisms that directed your call to the right destination.

If someone answered your call, the electric current reached the receiving device of that person's telephone. Inside the receiver were an ELECTROMAGNET and an ordinary magnet, with a metal diaphragm between them. In the absence of electricity, the ordinary magnet kept the diaphragm close against its surface. When electric current passed into the electromagnet, it pulled the diaphragm away. How far the diaphragm moved depended on the strength of the electric signals. In this way, the receiver translated the pattern in the signal back into sound—the sound of your voice. Today's telephones work on the same principles, but the speaker and receiver use different materials.

Early telephones required operators to place calls, and by 1940 there were tens of thousands of telephone operators in the United States alone. But by the 1970s, automatic devices took over the job of switching calls so that it was possible to dial nearly every other telephone in the country directly.

The telephone's basic functions remain much the same as they were in Bell's time. But modern devices are far more convenient than was Bell's first telephone. For example, in early telephones, the transmitting mechanism also served as the receiver. So the device had to be held first to the mouth and then to the ear. Later designs had a mouthpiece on the main phone body (typically hung on the wall) and a separate earpiece. The handset, with transmitter and receiver on either end, was introduced in 1928. Other modern telephone conveniences include magnetic memory banks for storing and replaying numbers with a push of a button, and speakers for "hand-free" operation. Cordless phones have handsets complete with dialing mechanisms that are linked to a base unit by a two-way radio connection. (*See also* CELLULAR PHONE.)

Profile: Alexander Graham Bell

The date was March 10, 1876. The place: a small laboratory in a Boston boardinghouse. A young man was working with an electrical instrument that was linked by wires to a similar device in another room. Suddenly a voice came from the instrument: "Mr. Watson, come here. I want you." Thomas Watson rushed into the other room, where his employer, Alexander Graham Bell, had spilled some acid on his clothing. Both men forgot the acid in their excitement over Watson's report: Bell's words, spoken near one instrument, had issued clearly from a second instrument in another room. It was the world's first TELEPHONE call.

Bell was born in 1847 in Edinburgh, Scotland. His grandfather and father worked with the hearing-impaired. His mother was an accomplished musician. The Bells schooled their children largely at home. At thirteen, Alexander spent a year in London with his grandfather, in whose library he read extensively about sound and human speech. Later, he read the writings of Hermann von Helmholtz, a German scientist who had used electric vibrations to make vowel sounds. Bell began to study electricity so that he could repeat Helmholtz's experiments.

At age twenty-four, Bell moved to Boston to teach the hearing-impaired. Funded by the wealthy parents of two of his students, he also continued his electrical experiments, hoping to invent a "harmonic" telegraph able to carry several messages over a wire at once. In 1875, Bell and his assistant, Watson, experimented with a telegraph consisting of two devices made of thin steel reeds connected to each other by an electric wire. They found that plucking a reed in a device in one room produced an identical vibration in the reed of a second device in another room. The electric current traveling between the reeds had reproduced the vibrations.

Bell reasoned that if an electric current could be made to vary in this way, then it could be made to carry any sound, even that of a human voice. Another year of experimentation led to Bell's "emergency" telephone call to Watson. By the end of 1877, the first telephones were in public use.

Having invented the telephone before he turned thirty, Bell spent the remaining forty-five years of his life experimenting in many fields of science. He did research on sending sound by light waves, explored problems with early airplane flight, even dabbled in heredity research while breeding sheep. Bell also continued working for the deaf and hearing-impaired.

Bell's spirit of inventiveness was carried on by Bell Laboratories, a prestigious research company in Murray Hill, New Jersey, founded in 1925. Bell Labs has produced thousands of scientific and engineering innovations that have earned researchers several Nobel Prizes. Among the most notable is the 1956 Nobel Prize in physics awarded to Bell researchers John Bardeen, Walter Brattain, and William Shockley for their invention of the TRANSISTOR. The labs are now part of Lucent Technologies.

TELESCOPE

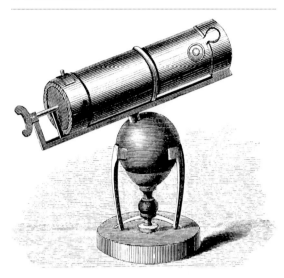

The design of Newton's original reflecting telescope remains the basis of most optical telescopes today.

A telescope is an instrument that produces magnified images of distant objects. It does so by gathering and focusing electromagnetic radiation. The most familiar form of electromagnetic radiation is light, and optical, or light-gathering, telescopes are the oldest and most widely used. Other telescopes scan the skies for radio waves, infrared (heat) waves, or X rays from distant stars, planets, and other celestial objects.

The two main types of optical telescopes are called refracting and reflecting. The refracting telescope consists of a long tube with a set of lenses, called the objective, at the front end, and a second set of lenses, the eyepiece, at the back end. When light strikes the objective, it bends to focus at a point within the tube, and there forms a small image of the object being viewed. This image is magnified by the eyepiece.

In a reflecting telescope, the objective is a concave (inward-curved) mirror at the back of the tube. Coated with a thin layer of silver or aluminum, the mirror faces outward, toward the light source. Light striking the mirror reflects back up the tube to a smaller, flat mirror. This second mirror is angled to direct the light to the eyepiece, typically on the side of the telescope tube.

The first telescopes were simple refractors. The first person known to have made such a device was the Dutch optician Hans Lippershey. In 1608, Lippershey reported fashioning a telescope out of a long, hollow tube with two curved lens positioned a precise distance apart.

The first person to report using a telescope to look at the heavens was the Italian scientist GALILEO GALILEI. In 1609, Galileo heard reports about Lippershey's telescope. Using his knowledge of light and lenses, Galileo made his own without ever having seen one. In 1668, the great English scientist Sir Isaac Newton made the first crude reflecting telescope.

Today, the world's largest telescopes are reflectors. The two enormous Keck telescopes, situated on Mauna Kea in Hawaii, each has a mirror that is more than 32 feet (9.75 meters) across. The mirrors are each composed of

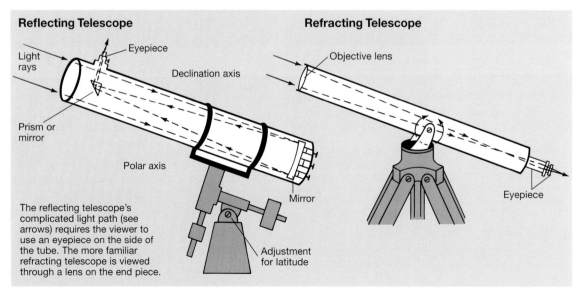

Reflecting Telescope

Light rays
Eyepiece
Declination axis
Prism or mirror
Polar axis

The reflecting telescope's complicated light path (see arrows) requires the viewer to use an eyepiece on the side of the tube. The more familiar refracting telescope is viewed through a lens on the end piece.

Mirror
Adjustment for latitude

Refracting Telescope

Objective lens
Eyepiece

thirty-six six-sided pieces, which adjust the shape of the mirrors as the telescopes turn.

In 1937, the Illinois astronomer Grote Reber built the first radio telescope. A modern radio telescope works somewhat like a reflector. But instead of a mirror, it has an antenna—a metal structure, usually bowl-shaped, that is covered with wire netting or sheets of metal. The antenna detects radio waves given off by objects in space and sends them to a receiver that amplifies them. The amplified waves are changed to electric pulses, or signals, and are recorded by a computer. Radio telescopes, which can receive radio waves from objects too far away to be seen by even the most powerful optical telescopes, have enabled astronomers to discover phenomena such as quasars (special kinds of galaxies) and pulsars (shrunken old stars).

But the thick blanket of atmosphere surrounding the Earth prevents most of the radiation from the stars and galaxies from ever reaching the earth. So the National Aeronautics and

Profile: Galileo Galilei

Galileo Galilei has been called the father of modern physics and telescope astronomy. His insightful understanding of mathematics, motion, and the solar system revolutionized scientific thought in the 1600s, though he was condemned for his ideas at the time.

Galileo was also one of the world's most prolific inventors. He designed and built the first known THERMOMETER. His work with PENDULUMS led to the first accurate clocks. Galileo also built one of the earliest microscopes. (see MICROSCOPE, OPTICAL.) But he is probably best known for building one of the first TELESCOPES and for being the first person to use this invention to study the heavens.

Galileo was born in Pisa, Italy, in 1564. His father, Vincenzo Galilei, was a composer and theorist who wanted his son to be a doctor. When Galileo was a young boy, his family moved to Florence, Italy, and he received his early education in a nearby monastery. Later, he studied medicine at the University of Pisa.

Though bored by medical classes, the young Galileo grew fascinated with mathematics and physics. It was also during this time that Galileo established the practice of "observation followed by experiment" that would guide modern scientific research. Galileo's experiments with pendulums, for example, were inspired by his observation of oil lamps swinging from the ceiling of a cathedral. In working out the laws of gravity, Galileo tested his theories by dropping balls of different weights from the same height.

Then, in 1609, Galileo pointed his newly created telescope to the heavens and discovered what no one had seen before: that the Moon was not perfectly smooth, that the planet Jupiter had moons revolving around it, and that Venus appeared to rotate around the Sun.

Many of Galileo's observations disproved the long-accepted views of the Greek philosopher Aristotle. They also supported the views of Copernicus, who sixty years earlier had claimed that the Earth and other planets revolve around the Sun. The church condemned these views and ordered Galileo to renounce them, which he did. But his theories proved to be correct. In his later years, Galileo quietly continued his work as an inventor. In an age when most scholars still wrote in Latin, Galileo wrote in Italian, which ordinary people could understand. He continued researching, inventing, and writing up to his death in 1642.

Galileo's many discoveries, theories, inventions, and books remain important to this day. But his most important achievement may have been his relentless questioning of untested ideas—a process that we now call the scientific method.

T

In 1993, the crew of the space shuttle *Endeavour* installed a new camera and special lenses to correct flaws in the focus of the $1.5 billion Hubble Space Telescope. Since then, Hubble has enabled astronomers to see deeper into space than ever before possible.

Space Administration (NASA) has built and put into orbit powerful space telescopes. The Hubble Space Telescope (HST), the Compton Gamma Ray Observatory (CGRO), and the Chandra X-Ray Observatory, all launched in the 1990s, are equipped with special instruments that can detect and record various kinds of radiation. The astonishing photographs they have relayed back to Earth have increased our knowledge of the universe immeasurably.

TELEVISION

Television—transmitting pictures by electromagnetic signals—is one of the world's most popular forms of entertainment. It also has many other uses, including the monitoring of hospital patients, stores, and elevators.

A television camera converts light and sound into electronic signals. These signals can be sent through the air as high-frequency radio signals, recorded on MAGNETIC TAPE AND RECORDER, or sent a short distance through "closed-circuit" cables. The receiver separates and amplifies the image and sound signals. The video signals pass into a picture tube, where they are converted back into images matching the one collected by the camera. When you watch television, you are looking at the front end of the picture tube, called the screen. The inside surface of a typical TV screen is coated with substances that emit light when struck by electrons. At the opposite side of the picture tube, electron

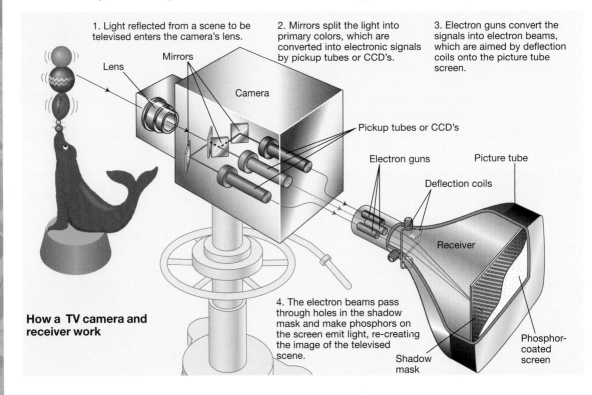

1. Light reflected from a scene to be televised enters the camera's lens.

2. Mirrors split the light into primary colors, which are converted into electronic signals by pickup tubes or CCD's.

3. Electron guns convert the signals into electron beams, which are aimed by deflection coils onto the picture tube screen.

Mirrors

Lens

Camera

Pickup tubes or CCD's

Electron guns

Picture tube

Deflection coils

Receiver

How a TV camera and receiver work

4. The electron beams pass through holes in the shadow mask and make phosphors on the screen emit light, re-creating the image of the televised scene.

Shadow mask

Phosphor-coated screen

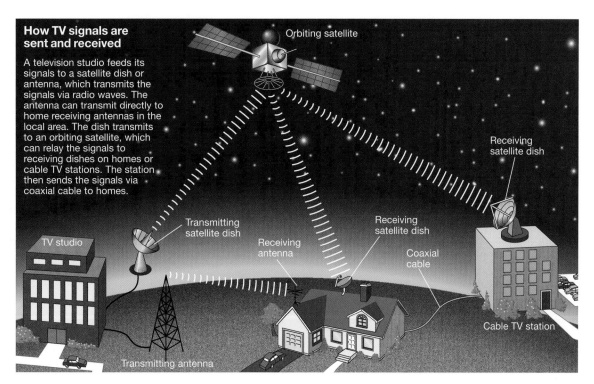

How TV signals are sent and received

A television studio feeds its signals to a satellite dish or antenna, which transmits the signals via radio waves. The antenna can transmit directly to home receiving antennas in the local area. The dish transmits to an orbiting satellite, which can relay the signals to receiving dishes on homes or cable TV stations. The station then sends the signals via coaxial cable to homes.

Orbiting satellite

Receiving satellite dish

Transmitting satellite dish

Receiving antenna

Receiving satellite dish

Coaxial cable

TV studio

Cable TV station

Transmitting antenna

guns shoot beams of electrons at the inner surface of the screen. Bits of the picture are scanned across the screen so fast that the viewer sees them as complete, moving pictures.

The development of television technology began in the late 1800s, as scientists came to realize they could transmit signals through the air with electromagnetic waves. In 1884, Paul Nipkow of Germany invented a crude device that could mechanically scan a scene with light and project a fuzzy "televised" image. Nipkow's system of mechanical scanning was refined by inventors in the United States and Britain, but in the 1920s, scientists found that scanning images with electron beams produced a much sharper image.

In the meantime, others were at work solving the problem of transmitting so much information electromagnetically. Several American scientists and engineers worked to make television practical, among them Allen Dumont, Philo Farnsworth, and Vladimir Zworykin. Zworykin developed one of the first successful television receiver tubes. His work culminated in 1931, when Radio Corporation of America (RCA) began experimental television broadcasts from the Empire State Building in New York City. Development of regular television broadcasting began in the late 1930s, but was delayed by World War II, and did not reach most homes until around 1950. All broadcasts

(and receivers) were for black-and-white images only. Color broadcasts (and the more expensive color receivers) became widespread around 1970.

Early television was broadcast over the airwaves. Today, new technologies enable viewers to receive television pictures via cable, SATELLITE, magnetic tape, and LASER DISC. At the dawn of the twenty-first century, the television industry is developing high-definition television. HDTV produces sharper images by more than doubling the electron-scanning lines delivered to the picture tube.

TEXTILE

Among the most ancient and widespread of inventions, woven cloth—or textile—dates back at least seven thousand years, the age of the oldest known scraps of linen fabric. Indeed, textile making has been an important part of the world's economy ever since Stone Age humans first traded their animal skins for fabric. Then as today, the weaver produced cloth by continually interlacing two sets of yarns or threads. The first major advance in textile making came with the invention of the LOOM around 4400 B.C. All textiles were made from animal hair, plant fiber, or silk

T

(thread "woven" by silkworm larvae) until the late 1800s. Since then, many synthetic fabrics such as NYLON have become widely used.

THERMOMETER

The invention of the thermometer, an instrument for measuring temperature, is usually credited to the great Italian scientist GALILEO. Around 1592, he experimented with a glass tube closed at one end. He half filled it with water, then turned it upside down so that its open end was underwater in a basin. As the air trapped in the top of the tube warmed or cooled, it expanded or contracted, changing the level of the water in the tube.

Galileo's thermometers gave a rough idea of heat or cold, but the water level was also affected by natural fluctuations in air pressure. This was overcome with the first sealed-glass liquid thermometer, developed by the Italian Cardinal Leopoldo de Medici, in 1654. Leopoldo's thermometer used colored wine as its liquid column. Around 1710, the German physicist Daniel Fahrenheit developed a much more accurate thermometer with a column of liquid mercury. He also established an early temperature scale—now called Fahrenheit—which he fixed at 32 degrees (0 degrees Celsius) for the melting point of ice and 96 degrees (35.6 degrees Celsius) for normal body temperature. (We now put normal body temperature at between 98 and 99 degrees Fahrenheit or between 36.7 and 37.2 degrees Celsius.)

Since Fahrenheit's time, inventors have developed many other devices for measuring temperature. The only type to measure heat and cold directly is the radiation thermometer. An example of this type of thermometer is the electronic "ear" thermometer used to detect fevers. A radiation detector inside the device measures the length of infrared (heat) waves emanating from the eardrum.

When a thermometer is used to control another device, such as an oven or heater, it is called a thermostat. When the thermometer in a thermostat reaches a certain temperature, it takes some action. For example, a thermostat may be set to keep the temperature in a house at 68 degrees (20 degrees Celsius). When the temperature falls to 67 (19.4 degrees Celsius), the thermostatic switch turns on the furnace. When the furnace heats the house to 68 once again, the switch turns the furnace off.

Clinical Thermometer

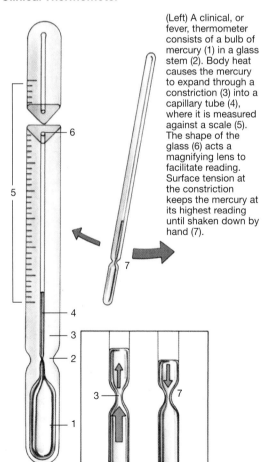

(Left) A clinical, or fever, thermometer consists of a bulb of mercury (1) in a glass stem (2). Body heat causes the mercury to expand through a constriction (3) into a capillary tube (4), where it is measured against a scale (5). The shape of the glass (6) acts a magnifying lens to facilitate reading. Surface tension at the constriction keeps the mercury at its highest reading until shaken down by hand (7).

A bimetallic strip thermometer (A) registers temperature changes based on the difference in expansion rates of two metals. The thermometer's indicator (1) is connected to a coiled metal helix (2) consisting of two lengths of copper and invar, which is a nickel-iron alloy, bonded together. As the temperature rises (B), the copper expands more rapidly than the invar. The helix then unwinds (3), which causes the indicator to move along the scale.

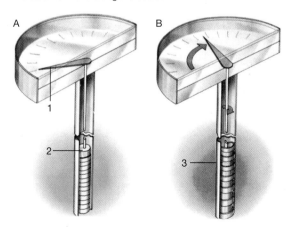

T

THRESHER

Before the development of threshing machines in the 1830s, farm laborers had to separate grain from straw by trampling it underfoot or beating it with sticks. The resulting mixture was then tossed into the air to separate the heavy grain from the light chaff, which was blown away by the wind. Early threshing machines used horses to turn a cylinder with revolving teeth that beat against stationary bars. When unhusked grain was fed into the cylinder, the seed was knocked through the bars into a collecting pan.

In 1837, the American inventors John and Hiram Pitts devised a thresher that was much more efficient than previous designs. Farmers piled their harvests in huge stacks and awaited the machines, which were drawn by teams of horses who moved from farm to farm.

After the Civil War, farmers in North America's Great Plains began using steam-powered threshers. In the 1920s, the steam threshers were gradually replaced by COMBINE HARVESTERS, which were powered by INTERNAL-COMBUSTION ENGINES. A combine harvests the grain and also threshes it.

TIMEKEEPING

For most of human history, the Sun, Moon, and stars were the only aids to timekeeping. But with the growth of civilization, people needed to coordinate their activities more precisely.

The Egyptians were the first to invent time-keeping devices, as well as the twenty-four-hour day, about 1500 B.C. They employed shadow clocks, or SUNDIALS, to divide the period from sunrise to sunset into twelve equal parts. At night, they used water clocks—a series of clay pots, each with a small drain at the bottom and twelve hour lines etched on the inner surface to register the decreasing water level. Because the length of days and nights varies through the seasons, so did the Egyptian "hour," with a night hour being longest in winter and a day hour longest in summer. About 300 B.C., Babylonian astronomers made all twenty-four hours equal in length, regardless of season. But the equal-hour day did not become widespread until well after the invention of reliable mechanical clocks.

By the year A.D. 300, Greeks had invented the sandglass, allowing them to measure time in units smaller than an hour. Working on the same principle as a water clock, sandglasses measured passing minutes and hours by the steady flow of sand from one glass bulb to another. These ancient timepieces had the added advantage of being portable. For centuries, the large sand-glasses known as hour-glasses were the only reliable timekeepers aboard ships; Columbus used a half-hour glass on his voyage to America. The sandglass's disadvantage

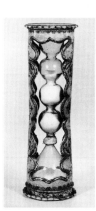
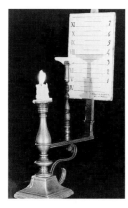

Over the ages, timekeeping devices have progressed from the Greek sandglass and medieval time candle to early mechanical timepieces such as the water clock (center), the ornate revolving globe clock (1710, France), and the American tall clock of the late 1700s (far right).

T

was that someone had to be ready to turn it at the precise moment the sand emptied.

The invention of the mechanical clock has been hailed as one of history's most important technological developments because it enabled people to reliably measure not only time, but also speed (the measure of distance traveled in a stretch of time, such as miles per hour).

All mechanical clocks harness a source of energy—be it a falling weight, a wound spring, or an alternating current. Typically this energy source turns a wheel and a system of GEARS. The speed of the gear is controlled by a mechanism called the ESCAPEMENT, which forces the gear teeth to move forward at a steady, unvaried pace.

Large mechanical clocks appeared in European monasteries after 1300. These crude, weight-driven clocks triggered a bell that sounded the hours, setting the schedules for prayer, work, and sleep. Soon huge versions of these bell-tolling clocks were being hung from cathedrals and other public buildings throughout Europe.

Modern clocks with a dial and hands were developed and powered in a variety of ways. About 1500, the German Peter Henlein began crafting small, spring-driven dial clocks, each with a single hand for the hour. Like other early timepieces, Henlein's dial clocks could gain or lose as much as thirty minutes a day. Accuracy made a great advance with the invention of the pendulum clock by the Dutch scientist Christiaan Huygens in 1656. The swing of the PENDULUM was an effective way to control the clock's movement before other escapement mechanisms were invented. Perfecting Huygens's design, clockmakers continued to improve accuracy. In 1670, they added the minute hand. A few years later, Huygens himself created an accurate pocket watch, introducing an escapement mechanism that relied on a hairspring and a balance wheel.

Clock- and watchmaking remained a painstaking craft until the mid-1800s, when American manufacturers began using precision machines to mass-produce timepieces. When electricity became available in the 1880s, inventors experimented with clocks in which electrical currents replaced a weight or spring as a source of power. In 1916, the American inventor Henry Warren developed a reliable electric clock that ran on household current.

Perhaps the greatest leap in the accuracy of everyday clocks came with the first quartz-crystal clock, built by the Canadian-born American engineer Warren Marrison in 1929. Like the QUARTZ-CRYSTAL TIMEPIECES of today, Marrison's clock kept time according to the vibration of a ring of quartz suspended in a heat-insulated chamber. The quartz crystal is set into motion by the current of a small electric battery. So precise is the frequency of the quartz-crystal's vibration that this type of clock or watch loses less than a minute of accuracy per year.

Surpassing even the quartz timepiece in accuracy is the atomic clock, its motions based on the vibrations of certain atoms such as cesium and rubidium. The U.S. National Bureau of Standards (NBS) built the first atomic clock in 1949. The most recent cesium clock, designed in the 1990s, has a maximum accuracy loss of about one second in every three million years. Atomic clocks are used as the world's master clocks and are vital for certain scientific experiments.

TIRE

A tire is simply a ring that encircles the rim of a wheel. Yet today, this invention can be found in more than thirty-five hundred forms and sizes. They range from 1-½-pound (.7 kilograms) tires used on airplane-tail wheels to 3-ton tires used on earthmoving equipment. They can be solid or inflated with air (pneumatic). Most are made out of some form of rubber.

The inventor of the pneumatic tire, the Scottish engineer Robert Thomson, was far ahead of his time. His 1845 patent went unnoticed in his lifetime and did not result in any products. In 1888, John Dunlop of Belfast, Ireland, reinvented the pneumatic tire while tinkering with his son's tricycle. Dunlop made his tire by placing a vulcanized-rubber tube in a casing of linen fabric, which he laced to the

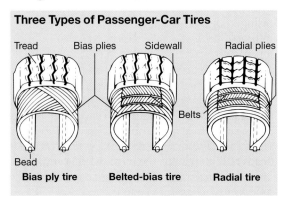

Three Types of Passenger-Car Tires

Tread Bias plies Sidewall Radial plies

Belts

Bead

Bias ply tire **Belted-bias tire** **Radial tire**

There are more than 3,500 kinds and sizes of pneumatic tires. They range from 1½-pound airplane tail wheels to the giant 3-ton tires used on earth-moving equipment.

wheel. When filled with air, the tube cushioned the bumpy ride over Belfast's rough cobblestone streets, making pedaling easier. The time was right for Dunlop's tire, which soon appeared on bicycles around the world.

The age of the automobiles was beginning about the same time. The first cars rolled slowly along on solid rubber tires. But car manufacturers soon adopted the pneumatic tire because it helped smooth out an otherwise bumpy ride, which was better both for the car and its passengers. Treads to prevent sideslip were introduced in 1910, and the 1930s brought tougher tires made of synthetic rubber.

Present-day tires contain both natural and synthetic rubber. Up until the 1950s, pneumatic tires were made in two parts, with a heavy outer casing of rubber meshed with fabric, and a thin, inflatable "inner tube." Tubeless tires, with airtight inner liners, were introduced in 1954. Used on virtually all large vehicles today, the tubeless pneumatic tire consists of four basic parts. The only part visible when the tire is mounted is the tread-and-sidewall unit. Beneath this outer layer are several layers of woven rubber cloth, called plies, which give the tire its strength. Wire rings called beads hold the tire to the metal wheel rim, and an inner liner maintains an airtight seal. (*See also* RUBBER, SYNTHETIC and RUBBER, VULCANIZED.)

TOILET

The inventor of the first toilet, or flush lavatory, installed his curious invention in the palace of England's Queen Elizabeth I in the 1590s. We know he was the queen's godson, Sir John Harington. But Harington left only a brief description of his device, with few mechanical details.

Today's flush toilets trace back to a design pioneered in 1775 by the London watchmaker Alexander Cumming, and improved in 1778 by another Londoner, Joseph Bramah. Cumming's design featured a cast-iron bowl with a flap valve that permitted water to flow in only one direction when opened. The bowl emptied directly into a sewer pipe. Later, a curved section of water-filled pipe, called a trap, was added to prevent sewer gas from backing up into the house. But these toilets were designed to operate without running water.

In the mid-1800s, large cities provided their citizens with running water, making true indoor plumbing possible on a large scale. At the same time, ceramic toilet bowls made for easier cleaning, and traps were made more effective by venting them outside the home. Around 1890, various inventors developed the

The water tank of a modern toilet contains a one-way valve opened by depressing the outside lever. The water empties into the bowl, flushing its contents down the drain. The drop in tank water triggers a second valve that allows incoming water to flow till the tank fills to a preset level.

T

modern "washdown" toilet with an elevated water tank for flushing. The tank was lowered to its present position about 1915.

TRACTOR

The name tractor usually refers to a self-propelled machine for pulling and pushing or powering other machinery. Though similar to the AUTOMOBILE, most tractors are designed for rugged, off-road use. In the early 1900s, tractors revolutionized agriculture, making it possible for farmers to pull PLOWS and COMBINE HARVESTERS through their fields, and greatly reducing the manual labor required.

The term tractor was first used for a steam-powered machine developed in the mid-1800s for pulling plows and other farm equipment. The introduction of the INTERNAL-COMBUSTION ENGINE in the 1890s reduced tractor weight and increased their versatility. In 1904, American Benjamin Holt patented the first successful tractor with long crawler tracks. It resembled the TANK (MILITARY), which was developed around 1915, and led later to the development of the bulldozer. Larger tractors were built in the 1930s, using diesel engines that were more efficient than early gasoline motors.

The basic work tractor is a multipurpose machine that is mounted on either crawler tracks or rubber tires. It provides low-speed, high-power traction and can be harnessed to

A modern tractor serves multiple purposes for this Iowa farmer.

power machines such as front-end loaders and pipe-laying equipment. Today, many tractors are built for specific purposes such as bulldozing, scraping, or digging.

The "truck tractor" is a powerful vehicle used to haul large trailers. It forms the working end of a tractor-trailer rig. Many are diesel-powered, but some of the largest use gas-turbine engines.

TRAFFIC SIGNAL

If you've ever been stuck in a traffic jam, you understand the need for traffic control. The first widely used traffic signals were semaphores, flag-like devices operated by hand to direct cars at intersections. During the daytime, the semaphores had movable panels with the words "stop" or "go." At night, they had red and green lenses illuminated by kerosene lamps. The city of Toledo, Ohio, installed an early system of semaphore signals in 1908.

The first electric traffic signal was used in Cleveland, Ohio, in 1914. In 1923, the American inventor Garrett Morgan invented the three-way traffic light (red, yellow, and green). By 1931, it was in wide use. The first automatic three-way lights were pre-timed. Internal clocks changed the lights at set intervals, regardless of how much traffic was on the road. Many traffic lights still operate in this way. When set in a carefully timed sequence along a stretch of road, they can allow traffic to move at the speed limit without stopping.

Today, traffic lights can also be programmed to change according to the amount of traffic.

The gasoline tractor from 1908 used "caterpillar" treads to ascend steep inclines.

Sensors under the road or electric-eye sensors can provide information that adjusts the timing of a light or series of lights so that traffic on the more heavily traveled street gets longer green signals.

In 1963, Toronto, Canada, installed a computer system to control up to one thousand traffic signals at the city's busiest intersections. Since then, many cities have installed similar computer systems to help prevent massive traffic jams in heavily traveled areas. Traffic lights may also be used to restrict entry to congested freeways and expressways.

TRANSISTOR

A major revolution in electronics took place in the late 1940s when researchers learned that electron flow can be controlled by solid-state devices as well as by ELECTRON TUBES. Made of materials called SEMICONDUCTORS, they would allow or restrict the flow of electrons depending on slight irregularities that could be designed into them.

The finished devices were called transistors. They were much smaller than tubes, required far less power to operate, and generated less heat. And they were far more reliable. Transistors allowed the miniaturization of electronic devices, making possible small radios and televisions, desktop computers, heart pacemakers, handheld calculators, and many other devices we now take for granted.

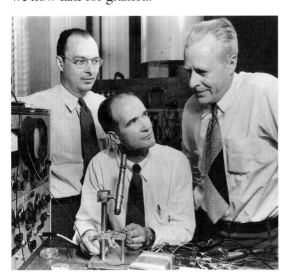

In 1948, Bardeen, Shockley, and Brattain unveiled the transistor developed in their New Jersey lab.

The American physicists John Bardeen, Walter Brattain, and William Shockley built the first transistor in 1948 at Bell Telephone Laboratories. Their first transistors were made out of the semiconducting element germanium laced with dopants such as arsenic, antimony, and phosphorus. Later, scientists would find a way to etch many transistors onto a single tiny wafer of the semiconductor silicon to create the still smaller and more powerful INTEGRATED CIRCUIT.

TRANSPORTATION

Since prehistoric times, people have been devising ingenious ways to move themselves and their belongings. The first means of transportation was no doubt the human back, and it's likely that some of the first inventions included devices for carrying firewood and children.

The first vehicles were probably crude sleds fashioned out of branches covered with skins or sticks and pulled by prehistoric people or their animals. The forerunners of the WHEEL were rollers made of logs, which could help move heavy objects over short distances. The wheel is so familiar today that it's hard to imagine vehicles without it. But before there were level roads, wheeled vehicles would have been nearly useless anyway. The earliest evidence of their use comes from Mesopotamia (modern-day Iraq), where oxen pulled two-wheel carts some thirty-five hundred years ago. Over the next three thousand years, the use of wheeled vehicles—and the building of roads—would spread out across Asia and Europe.

Long before the wheel, humans discovered the ease of traveling across water. South Pacific islanders were already rafting and canoeing

The first known wheels probably developed from logs used as rollers under heavily loaded sleds.

T

The fastest sailing ships ever built, the magnificent "clippers" ruled the seas from 1840 to 1860.

between islands some fifty thousand years ago. At some point before recorded history, people also harnessed the power of the wind, by stretching sails made of animal skins across poles erected in their vessels.

The next great leap in transportation came with the building of galleys—large boats held together by strong wooden frames, or hulls. Galleys first appeared in the Mediterranean some five thousand years ago, powered by square sails and huge crews of up to two hundred oarsmen. Ships such as these enabled the Greeks, Phoenicians, and Romans to extend trade and warfare across the Mediterranean and beyond. Sailing ships improved again about fifteen hundred years ago, with the invention of the triangular lateen sail. Running the length of the ship instead of across it, the lateen sail enabled a skillful sailor to travel not only with the wind but also across or even against it.

Yet with no instruments for navigation, early mariners generally stayed within sight of land, venturing into open ocean only when clear skies allowed them to steer by the Sun and stars. The magnetic COMPASS—devised by the Chinese about 300 B.C.— reached Europe about A.D. 1200. It allowed mariners to determine directions without the aid of Sun, stars, or landmarks, and encouraged further exploration.

Shipbuilders later fashioned more slender and manageable vessels, adding more and bigger sails. Sailing ships continued to rule the seas till the middle of the 1800s, when the STEAM ENGINE began to replace the wind as the mariner's most important source of energy.

American shipbuilders took the lead during the Civil War (1861–65), building the first IRONCLAD WARSHIPS. Propellers replaced paddle wheels, and in the early 1900s, diesel engines replaced steam. Twentieth-century inventors created practical SUBMARINES for traveling underwater, and HOVERCRAFT to glide above the water.

Meanwhile, transportation on land had advanced from animal-drawn carts to the first self-powered vehicle—the steam engine locomotives. By the end of the century, railroads had opened the vast North American continent to development and had connected the East Coast to the West. Horse-drawn carriages and wagons remained important for transporting people and goods over short distances.

The first mode of transportation to challenge the railroad was the AUTOMOBILE, made practical by the development of the INTERNAL-COMBUSTION ENGINE in the 1860s and 1870s. Automobiles found their greatest popularity in the United States, where the first "horseless

Railroad construction crews met at Promontory Summit, Utah, on May 10, 1869, to complete North America's first transcontinental railroad.

T

carriages" appeared in the 1890s. In 1908, Henry Ford introduced his "Model T," and soon mass production made it affordable to millions. By 1930, more than twenty million Americans owned cars. During the same period, buses and large trucks began stealing the railways' business of long-distance transport.

Today, traffic jams and automotive air pollution may be forcing a partial shift back to railways. Already high-speed "bullet" trains have proved their worth in Japan and parts of Europe, traveling smoothly and cleanly at speeds over 180 miles (289.9 kilometers) per hour.

The ultimate mode of transportation—human flight—remained the stuff of dreams and legend until 1783, the year that the Montgolfier brothers of France first carried passengers aloft in a hot-air balloon. More than 130 years later, a German team crossed the Atlantic Ocean in an AIRSHIP, a rigid-framed balloon propelled by gas engines.

By 1900, inventors around the world were trying to harness steam and gas engines to power heavier-than-air craft, or AIRPLANES. The first to do so were the Wright brothers of Ohio, who flew into history on the beach of Kitty Hawk, North Carolina, on December 17, 1903. Little more than a decade later, airplanes dueled in the sky over France during World War I. After the war, mail and passengers traveled regularly by air.

The 1940s and 1950s brought the JET ENGINE, able to power a plane at double the speed and altitude of propellers, at nearly half the cost,

On June 4, 1783, the first Montgolfier balloon carried passengers above the village of Annonay, France.

and making air flight a practical means of travel for tens of millions of passengers each year.

The airplane's hovering cousin, the HELICOPTER, was invented in the 1930s. Driven by horizontal rotors and able to take off and land vertically, the helicopter's main advantage is its ability to land and take off from small landing areas. It is valuable for search-and-rescue missions and for surveillance of ground activity such as traffic.

Humankind moved into the Space Age in the 1960s, when ROCKETS carried the first astronauts beyond our planet's atmosphere and then to the Moon. Since the 1980s, the U.S. National Aeronautics and Space Administration (NASA) has operated a small fleet of SPACE SHUTTLES whose crews perform scientific experiments in space and service orbiting SATELLITES and space stations. Each shuttle is blasted into orbit by a pair of million-pound, solid-fuel rockets before switching over to its own liquid-fuel rocket engine for spaceflight and landing. Inventors in the early years of the

A New York City gas station charged 25 cents a gallon in the 1920s.

T

Transportation systems of the future may resemble the German-designed Maglev (magnetic-levitation) train, which glides ½ inch (1.3 cm) above its track, lifted by powerful magnets in its undercarriage.

2000s hope to build an aerospace plane able to take off from a conventional runway with enough power to escape gravity and shoot into orbit without the aid of rocket boosters.

TURBINE

A turbine is a type of engine powered by the movement of water, steam, or extremely hot gas. Inside a turbine, a series of blades are mounted at an angle on a central shaft. Liquid or gas moving over the blades causes them to turn and the shaft to spin. The spinning shaft provides the power to do work. Turbines are used in hydroelectric- and nuclear-power plants, in rocket fuel pumps, and in the engines of large ships, military TANKS, and many kinds of JET ENGINES.

The ancestors of the turbine are the WATERWHEEL and the WINDMILL. The turbine is much more efficient than these ancient machines because its blades and shaft are completely enclosed. Thus, little of the power of the moving liquid or gas is lost.

The French engineer Benoît Fourneyron invented the first practical turbine in 1827. It consisted of a circular barrel enclosing a vertical shaft with a set of blades at the bottom. Water flowing down along the shaft rushed through the blades to turn them. Water turbines set on waterfalls and rivers became an important source of electricity in the 1880s. They are the ancestors of the huge turbines used today in large hydroelectric-power plants.

Steam turbines are powered by blasts of steam hitting the blades from a set of nozzles. The first steam turbines able to do real work were developed by the Swedish engineer Carl Gustaf de Laval in the 1880s. About the same time, the English engineer Sir Charles Parsons invented a steam turbine that used several circles of blades to produce greater power at lower speeds. Modern Parsons turbines have as many as fifty rows of blades on the same shaft. They are the most common turbine for running steam-powered electric plants and propelling large ships.

The gas turbine is the newest kind of turbine, powered by fuel that's burned inside an engine to produce intensely hot, rapidly expanding

Steam-powered Turbine

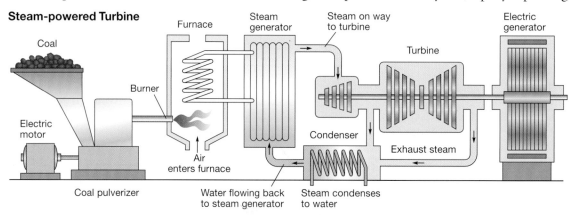

In an electricity-generating steam station, pulverized coal is first burned in a furnace. The heat from the burning coal transforms water passing through the generator into steam; the steam, then superheated, causes the turbine to spin, producing electric current.

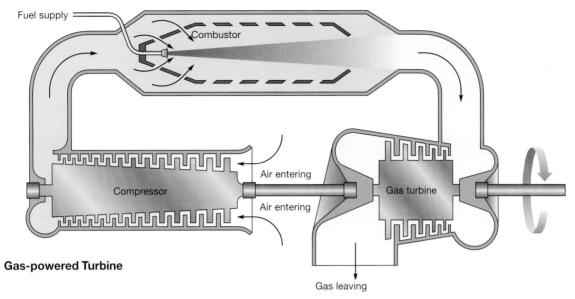

Gas-powered Turbine

Compressed air entering a gas turbine mixes with fuel and burns. The gases produced by the combustion turn the turbine, driving both the air compressor and an electric generator.

gases. The Englishman John Barber patented the first gas turbine in 1791. But the intense heat of gas combustion burned and pitted its blades, which were made of ordinary steel. The problem was solved in the 1930s, when scientists developed new alloys (metal mixtures) able to withstand the intense heat. Today, gas turbines power jet aircraft, military tanks, and ships.

TYPEWRITER

The first machine to write more quickly and legibly than the human hand was invented in 1867 by the Milwaukee journalist Christopher Latham Sholes. Like today's typewriters, it produced printed characters on paper at the stroke of a key. Sholes's simple "literary piano" printed only capital letters, and the typist couldn't see the letters being typed. But within ten years, improved models of the typewriter were being sold by the thousands. They featured the basic keyboard letter arrangement still found on English-language keyboards.

The typewriter revolutionized business and created a new office position—typist. Many early typists were women, who were beginning to appear in offices to do clerical and secretarial work.

Typewriters were improved many times in the 1900s. In the 1950s and 1960s, electric mod-

els replaced the manual machines and provided much better type quality and easier operation. But in the 1980s, computer-based word-processing systems replaced typewriters for most office uses, and by the end of the century, they were becoming antique curiosities.

An early typist used a foot treadle to return the typewriter carriage. She couldn't view her work until after the page was done.

ULTRASOUND IMAGING

During World War II, scientists learned to use high-frequency sound waves for important military purposes. Navy commanders used one type, called SONAR, to detect enemy submarines. Meanwhile, shipbuilders used ultrasound devices to detect flaws in the metal hulls of new ships. It soon occurred to physicians that perhaps an ultrasound device could detect changes in the human body.

The earliest medical ultrasound devices were created in the 1940s and 1950s to detect abnormal objects in the body—gallstones, kidney stones, and tumors. Then, in the late 1950s, Scottish physician Ian Donald saw that ultrasound could safely produce images of human fetuses in the womb. (Use of X-RAY IMAGING to study fetal growth is dangerous because X rays damage human cells.)

Ultrasound created high-frequency sound by applying electric current to a piezoelectric crystal (*see* QUARTZ-CRYSTAL TIMEPIECE). The crystal lies inside a device called the transducer, which is placed against the skin and is moved over the area being studied. The waves penetrate the body, strike structures within, and bounce back through the skin to the transducer, where they cause another crystal to vibrate. The vibrations produce an electric current that is converted electronically into still or moving pictures on a computer screen.

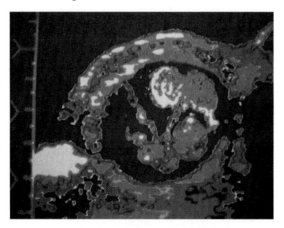

Safe and noninvasive, an ultrasound image reveals healthy twins developing inside the womb.

UMBRELLA

Today we associate umbrellas with rain. But for most of its history, this portable, hand-held device was used primarily to protect people from sun. (The name itself derives from the Roman *umbra*, meaning "shade.") Umbrellas first appeared in the Orient, probably China, from which they spread throughout the world. Most umbrellas consist of a round canopy made of fabric, paper, or plastic that is opened or collapsed by means of hinged ribs that radiate from a central shaft, which in turn extends down to a handle. With the advent of mass production in the late 1800s, the making of steel-wire umbrellas became a major industry.

The beautiful paper-and-bamboo umbrellas of the Orient were designed to protect people from sun rather than rain.

U
V

VACCINES

Vaccines are substances that can prevent people from getting serious infectious diseases. Early vaccines were discovered rather than invented. In 1796, the English physician Edward Jenner observed that milkmaids who contracted a mild disease called cowpox seemed to be protected from the far deadlier disease, smallpox. He reasoned that perhaps others who were exposed to cowpox would be immune to smallpox. He took material from a cowpox sore and put it in a scratch on the arm of a young boy. This was the first known successful vaccination—the boy proved immune to smallpox.

Scientists learned that vaccines like Jenner's give disease protection by "alerting" the patient's immune system to be on the lookout for future infections from the same or similar microbes. Today, vaccines contain a killed or weakened version of a disease-causing microbe. In some cases, live disease-causing organisms are killed with heat or chemicals, but still cause the body to develop an immunity. Some vaccines are made from organisms that have been weakened by chemical treatment. Still other vaccines contain only certain proteins from the disease-causing organism. These proteins do not cause illness, but still stimulate a patient's immune system.

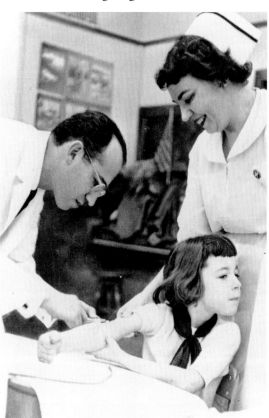

American physician Jonas Salk vaccinates a young girl during the 1954 test trials of the vaccine he developed to prevent polio.

VACUUM CLEANER

Second only to the WASHING MACHINE as the most popular household appliance, the vacuum cleaner has greatly reduced the drudgery of housecleaning in the twentieth century.

The American James Murray Spangler invented the first portable vacuum for home use in 1907. Spangler's device was manufactured by William Hoover, whose company was the first to

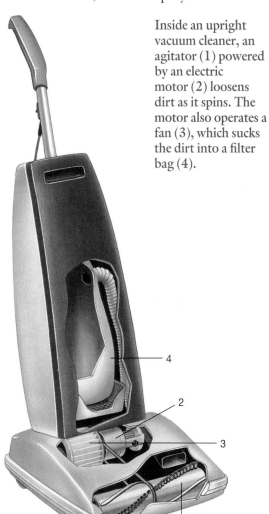

Inside an upright vacuum cleaner, an agitator (1) powered by an electric motor (2) loosens dirt as it spins. The motor also operates a fan (3), which sucks the dirt into a filter bag (4).

mass-produce vacuum cleaners and remains a leading name in the industry. Since then, vacuums have become steadily smaller and more powerful. But their basic design remains largely unchanged.

Inside the vacuum cleaner, a small electric motor turns a high-speed fan that creates a vacuum (an area of low air pressure). This draws a current of air into the machine through a suction nozzle. In some machines, rotating brushes attached to the nozzle loosen and sweep dirt from the surface being cleaned. The dirt is drawn into a bag or canister that allows air, but not dirt, to escape.

Before Spangler's invention, vacuum cleaners were huge machines. The first electric vacuum, invented by the English engineer Hubert Booth in 1901, was transported by horse-drawn carriage from house to house, where its 800-foot (243.8-meter) hose was used for spring cleaning.

VACUUM TUBE

See ELECTRON TUBE

VELCRO

In 1941, the Swiss engineer George de Mestral returned from a walk in the country to find his socks covered with burrs. Intrigued by the stubborn grip of the seed heads, he examined one under a microscope. He saw that it was covered with tiny hooks, perfect for snagging fur or fabric. After several years of tinkering, Mestral invented Velcro, a fabric that emerges from the loom covered with tiny NYLON loops. Clipping some of the loops creates a tiny forest of stiff hooks that, when pressed against a strip of unclipped loops, take hold with an amazing grip. In fact, it takes ten to fifteen pounds of force per square inch to separate standard Velcro when the pieces are pulled in directly opposite directions. Yet even a child can separate Velcro fasteners by peeling them at an angle.

Mestral's clever invention became popular in the late 1960s, and since then has become a universal fastener. It is used on everything from clothes to artificial hearts, and has become standard equipment on SPACE SHUTTLES and space stations, where it's used to keep things in place in a weightless environment—including, in some instances, the astronauts themselves.

VENDING MACHINE

Be it midnight or 3 A.M., a mountaintop rest station or the hallway of a college dormitory, chances are a vending machine stands ready to dispense snacks, drinks, maps, and other goods whenever someone inserts enough coins or paper money into its slots. Since the 1940s, automatic selling machines have sold billions of dollars of goods and services each year. But the idea behind these "silent salesmen" with their built-in cash registers traces back to antiquity.

The first known vending machine was described by Hero, the Greek mathematician. It was an automatic device for dispensing holy water in temples around 200 B.C. Inserting a five-drachma coin through a slot set the machine in motion. The dropped coin tipped a small scale, which in turn lifted a LEVER that allowed a brief flow of water before the coin slipped off the scale, lowering the lever and stopping the flow. The next recorded use of a vending machine comes some eighteen hundred years later, when English tobacco makers sold their products in taverns by way of a brass box whose lid popped open when a coin was inserted into a slot.

In the 1900s, vending machines reached a height of popularity with the success of "Automats." These fully automated restaurants supplied customers with entire menus of prepared food and drinks through banks of coin-triggered glass compartments. (The last Automat closed, in New York City, in 1991.)

Up until the 1990s, banks of vending machines dispensed sandwiches, side dishes, and desserts at Automat cafeterias in New York City.

Most modern vending machines operate by mechanical triggers that check the precise diameter, thickness, and weight of different coins and then total their worth. More recent designs also accept paper money—discerning different denominations with light scanners. Vending machines remain a major convenience today, with their ability to dispense food, goods, and services around the clock with only occasional attention from service people.

VIDEOCASSETTE AND RECORDER

See MAGNETIC TAPE AND RECORDER

UV

The Changing World 1957

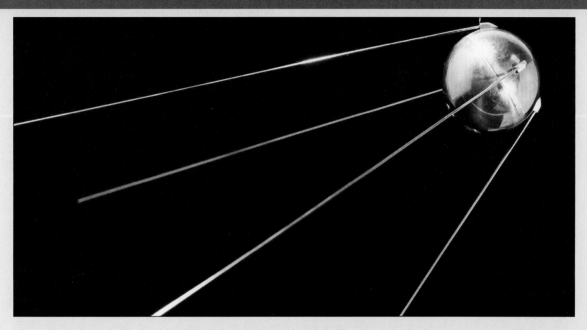

The spherical *Sputnik 1* is only slightly larger than a beach ball and carries little more than a radio beacon and thermometer. The name means "traveling companion" in Russian.

"Russia Launches a Moon" proclaims the front page of the October 4 *London Daily Mail*. The Soviets shock the West and open the space race with the launch of the world's first SATELLITE. *Sputnik 1* is still beaming radio signals back to Earth on November 3, when the Soviets launch *Sputnik 2*. This one carries a dog, Laika, in a pressurized compartment to test whether living things can survive in space.

The frenzied attempt by the United States to match the Soviets ends with a thud on December 6, when a Vanguard rocket carrying a 4-pound (1.8-kilogram) satellite fails to get farther than 4 feet (1.2 meters) off the launching pad at Cape Canaveral, Florida.

But the United States still excels in other fields. The world's first atomic SUBMARINE, the USS *Nautilus*, can circumnavigate the world without surfacing, thanks to its own NUCLEAR-POWER REACTOR. And on December 18, the nation's first fully operational nuclear-power plant opens at Shippingport, Pennsylvania.

Although many local residents remain apprehensive, the plant will operate safely for decades.

As humankind flexes its new technological powers, philosophers and scientists alike are warning that Mother Earth may not be able to withstand the strain. The latest warnings concern PESTICIDES such as DDT, which biologists say are poisoning birds and other wild animals. New evidence suggests that pesticide residues may be accumulating in humans as well.

WASHING MACHINE

Washing clothes was hard physical labor for thousands of years. Finally, in the 1800s, machines were created to help with the work. In 1858, the Pittsburgh inventor Hamilton Smith patented one of the first home washers. It was operated by turning a crank that rotated paddles on a shaft inside a tube filled with water and clothes. But Smith's machine, like other early washers, was still hard work to operate, and it often damaged clothes. So most families continued to wash their laundry by hand with a tub and corrugated washboard.

The Chicago inventor Alva Fisher devised the first electric washer in 1910. It featured a small electric motor for churning the washing blades and for turning a set of rubber rollers, called a wringer, that squeezed water from the sopping-wet clothes. But someone still had to lift the clothes from the water and feed them through the rollers by hand. In 1937, the first fully automatic washer was introduced. It rinsed and then spun water out of the clothes after washing—all in the same tub. The 1950s brought automatic washers with preset programs for selecting water temperature, water-level control, and gentle or heavy-duty agitation.

Even with the luxury of the new hand-cranked wringer washer, most 19th-century homemakers needed a full day to wash the week's laundry.

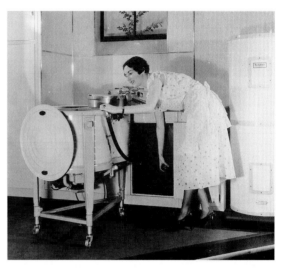

In 1937, "all the modern conveniences" included an automatic washer you could hook up to the kitchen sink.

WATERWHEEL

Invented just over two thousand years ago, the waterwheel was the first device to harness a power source other than animals. Specifically, the waterwheel taps the force of flowing water with paddles mounted around its rim. The water pushes the wheel, turning it on its axle. The resulting energy can be used to drive machinery. For many centuries, waterwheels remained the world's primary source of mechanical power, used to grind grain, raise irrigation water, and saw wood.

The earliest waterwheels were of the undershot type: water passed beneath the upright wheel, to strike its curved or flat paddles from below. The later overshot wheel was more efficient, designed to catch water flowing from above, typically in bucketlike paddles. A third type was the horizontal wheel, in which water flowing through a chute was directed against the side of a sideways waterwheel to turn an upright shaft.

In Europe, the era of waterwheels lasted from early medieval times to the 1800s, when some twenty thousand of these devices powered early industries. By the mid-1800s, steam

Waterwheels

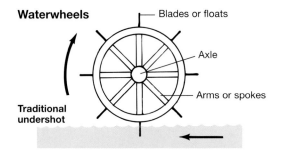

Over the centuries, mills and factories employed many different kinds of waterwheels. Yet the overshot wheel remained unsurpassed in efficiency.

engines were replacing the waterwheel. A modern version of the waterwheel is the highly efficient water turbine, invented in the 1820s by the French engineer Benoît Fourneyron. Instead of paddles, water TURBINES have curved blades resembling those of a ship propeller.

WEAPONS

Humankind's earliest tools, sticks and rocks, were also its earliest weapons. It probably didn't take long for early humans to realize they could improve on nature's weaponry by sharpening sticks into spears and splitting rocks into crude knives and ax blades. The oldest known spear, found in Europe, dates back some five

Bows, arrows, and spears figure prominently in the 2,700-year-old stone carvings of the warlike Assyrians of the Middle East.

hundred thousand years; the oldest stone ax with a handle, 230,000 years. Such primitive weapons were used in both hunting game and in hand-to-hand combat.

Early warriors and hunters extended the reach of their attack with the invention of the BOW AND ARROW, which seems to have been used in Africa, North America, and Europe in prehistoric times. The bow and arrow remained the chief weapon of many cultures until the end of the 1500s. Greatly increasing the arrow's power was the European CROSSBOW, invented in the tenth or eleventh century. With it, an archer could pierce chain-mail ARMOR from a thousand feet away.

The first metal weapons—copper AXES and BRONZE swords—were forged by the early blacksmiths of the Bronze Age, between 3000 and 4000 B.C. Their invention, in turn, spurred the development of metal shields and armor. About the same time, the invention of the WHEEL (3500 B.C.) revolutionized warfare, enabling Egyptian, Assyrian, and other Middle Eastern armies to launch swift chariot attacks on each other's cities.

In response, cultures began building massive fortifications around their cities. To breach city walls, the Greeks and Romans introduced giant crossbow-like devices called ballistae, and missile throwers such as the CATAPULT. Meanwhile, on the open seas, Mediterranean nations

The ancient Romans used the engine of war called the catapult to hurl boulders and flaming javelins at enemy fortifications.

W

were waging battle with small, agile galleys designed to ram and destroy other vessels.

The greatest advance in weaponry may have been the invention of GUNPOWDER by the Chinese in A.D. 1000. The first explosive, gunpowder was initially used for amusement—as fireworks. But by 1304, Arabs were using charges of gunpowder to shoot arrows out of the first crude GUN—a bamboo-and-iron tube. Within a few years, the Italians had developed metal handguns that sprayed iron bullets. In the early 1500s, French bell casters produced the first accurate cannon. These early firearms were heavy, clumsy, slow-firing, and useless in rain.

Sweden's King Gustav II (Gustavus Adolphus), who reigned in the early 1600s, has been called the father of modern warfare. His many innovations in weaponry included light, mobile field cannon, and the paper cartridge, which contained both gunpowder and shot and so enabled soldiers to load their guns on the run.

Until the 1800s, personal firearms had to be reloaded after every shot. Then Samuel Colt produced a practical REVOLVER, a handgun able to fire off six bullets in succession. In the later 1800s, warfare took new strides with the invention of Richard Gatling's MACHINE GUN and the development of powerful explosives such as TNT. Naval warfare likewise grew deadlier during the Civil War, as guns grew more powerful, STEEL hulls replaced wooden ones, and STEAM ENGINES replaced sails.

The invention of nuclear weapons brought World War II to an abrupt end. Here, the mushroom cloud over Nagasaki, Japan, signals the destruction of half the city and the death of some 75,000 people on August 9, 1945.

SUBMARINE warfare debuted in World War I, spurring the development of effective sea mines and torpedoes. On land, the automatic machine gun drove armies into trenches and forced troops to abandon direct attacks.

The most decorated pilot of World War I, American flying ace Eddie Rickenbacker shot down 22 enemy planes and 4 spy balloons from his propeller-driven biplane.

U.S. cruise missiles and laser-guided "smart" bombs and Iraqi antimissile fire light up the night sky over Baghdad during the 1991 Persian Gulf War.

Military science reached new levels of sophistication and deadliness in World War II, beginning with the development of RADAR, SONAR, and GUIDED MISSILES and climaxing with the creation and use of NUCLEAR WEAPONS. After the war, nuclear weapons became so powerful and numerous that they threatened the future of all humanity.

The 1980s brought the testing of a new generation of space-based weapons using LASERS, particle beams, and other sophisticated technologies. The bombing of Iraq during the Gulf War of 1991 employed the first laser-guided "smart" bombs—able to adjust their own course to follow moving targets. That war also saw the first use of such advanced weapon systems as the ocean-launched Tomahawk cruise missile and the Patriot antimissile. At the end of the twentieth century, the newest generation of missiles employed Global Positioning System (GPS) satellite signals to find their targets.

WELDING TORCH

The beginning of the Industrial Age, with its huge factories, machines, steel ships, and automobiles, brought the need for a device that could join together large metal plates or wires. Bolting or riveting metal together didn't create the unbroken seal needed for watertight joints or reliable electric connections. The answer was the welding torch, which melts metal edges and surfaces to fuse parts together. Today, virtually all heavy-manufacturing processes use some form of welding.

The American inventor Robert Hare developed the first gas-welding torch in 1801. It burned a mixture of oxygen and hydrogen to produce a flame hot enough to melt steel. Nearly a century later, the French chemist Henri Le Châtelier showed that a mixture of acetylene and oxygen produce a far hotter flame. Oxyacetylene torches remain widely used today, especially in the repair of cars, appliance, and other metal machinery.

Even more widely used is the arc-welding torch, first devised by the Russians Nikolas von Bernardos and Stanislav Olczewski in 1885. This type of torch uses heat from an electric arc to melt metals. To use the torch, the operator connects one terminal of an electric circuit to the parts that need welding. A handheld rod called an electrode is connected to the other terminal. When the electric current is turned on, the welder briefly touches the electrode to the parts to be welded, then pulls back slightly, creating a bright, hot arc between them. The arc is then drawn along the workpieces, melting their edges. The electrode also melts, producing molten metal that helps fill the joint. Welders must wear special masks that shield their eyes from the intense light of the arc. In automated welding machines, electronic controls take the place of a human welder.

A third type of welding—using electrical resistance—was invented by the British-born American electrical engineer Elihu Thomson in 1877. In resistance welding, two sheets of metal are pressed together between two electrodes. As the current flows from one electrode to the other, it meets resistance at the interface between the two sheets. The resulting heat causes the metals to melt and fuse. The process is used for both spot and seam welding.

More recently, several high-tech forms of welding have become important for special purposes. LASERS have been used for welding since their invention in 1960. Laser welding is especially important when heat must be focused

Virtually every modern manufacturing endeavor uses or produces some type of welded product—from the welded vats used to process foods and chemicals to the assembly-line welding of an automobile.

W

below the surface of a material. Electron-beam welding is another high-tech method, used mostly with certain highly reactive metals such as zirconium alloys.

WHEEL AND WHEELED VEHICLE

The wheel is one of civilization's greatest inventions. The earliest known wheels were made in ancient Mesopotamia (modern Iraq) between 3500 and 3000 B.C. They were of two kinds— the cart wheel and the potter's wheel. The potter's wheel was the ancestor of the PULLEY, WATER-WHEEL, GEAR, ESCAPEMENT (clock mechanism), and other wheeled machinery.

The earliest known cart wheel was made of three planks, held together by crosspieces. A strap of leather or copper around the rim acted as a crude TIRE. The first wheeled vehicles included farm carts, war chariots, and royal hearses. All were pulled by animals. Some had two wheels, others four. But early four-wheeled vehicles were awkward affairs. They couldn't make even wide turns until, some two thousand years ago, someone mounted the front wheels on an axle that could pivot back and forth beneath the vehicle.

Solid wheels were practical for slow, heavy loads. But a much lighter wheel was needed for swift movement. To meet this need, the spoked wheel was invented in southwestern Asia about 2000 B.C. To make such a wheel required great skill, for it had to be assembled from a number of parts, including hub, spokes, and rim. By 1000 B.C., Egyptian wheelwrights were making beautiful chariot wheels. There was little improvement in wheel design until modern times, when stamped-metal parts and rubber tires were introduced.

WINDMILL

Windmills, or wind machines, are designed to capture the power of the wind. They usually consist of two or more blades or sails to catch the wind. The sails turn a shaft, which can then be used to perform work.

The first known windmills were used in Persia about A.D. 500 to pump water for irrigating crops. By the 1100s, their use had spread throughout Europe. Early European windmills also turned stone mills to grind grain into meal or flour. The Dutch used windmills to drain wetlands after building their famous dikes. The largest of their time, Dutch windmills were made of wooden frames over which canvas was stretched to form sails that turned in the wind. Windmills became, and remain, a symbol of the Netherlands.

During the late 1800s, thousands of windmills were in operation throughout Europe and the rural United States, for pumping irrigation water. Many were gradually replaced by STEAM ENGINES and ELECTRIC GENERATORS, but others continued to supply power in isolated locations. In the 1970s, a sharp rise in petroleum costs revived interest in using machines to harness the free energy of the wind. By the

Windy Altamont Pass near Livermore, Calif., contains the world's largest concentration of electricity-generating windmills, 7,500 in all. Together, the valley's propeller-driven turbines generate about 1 billion kilowatt-hours of electricity each year.

1980s, more than thirty U.S. companies were manufacturing wind machines. "Wind farms" with one hundred or more machines can generate several hundred megawatts of electric power.

Although many types of windmills have been built, most modern machines fall into one of two classes. The traditional windmill is a horizontal-axis machine. So, too, are the familiar multibladed windmills of the American prairies, which are equipped with pitch-and-pivot devices that keep them turned into the wind.

Newer, vertical-axis machines can resemble eggbeaters, spinning drums, or airplane propellers. Though they are somewhat less efficient than traditional windmills in generating power or work, they cost less to build and don't need to be turned to face the wind.

WORLD WIDE WEB

See INTERNET

The Changing World 1978

The big electronics manufacturers scoff at the idea of home computers. But the new Apple II is being snapped up by students and families so fast that neighborhood electronics stores can't keep it in stock. Shrunk down to desktop size, such microcomputers are being dubbed PCs, or personal computers.

Computer hobbyists are not surprised by the new fad. For the past three years, they have been assembling their own Altair PCs, using a $400 do-it-yourself kit sold by the small electronics firm MITS. But now even computer dummies can join in the fun. You don't need to know computer programming to use the Apple PC. Also making its debut this year is the Commodore, a PC that plugs into your television set.

Meanwhile, computers many times the size of PCs have begun to rev-

Students from kindergarten to college hurry home after class to power up the newest computer games. Some of the most computer-adventurous are even learning to write their own programs.

olutionize medicine with computed tomography, or CAT, scanning (*see* X-RAY IMAGING). Using one of a handful of CAT scanners in operation, a radiologist can X-ray a patient's brain or other organ from several angles, while feeding the information into a powerful computer that assembles the views into a detailed cross section of the body part.

Several large supermarkets are now using optical scanners to ring

up purchases. The clerk has nothing more to do than "swipe" each grocery item across a window on the surface of the checkout stand. In an instant, a LASER beam "reads" a coded bar pattern on the package and relays the information to a computer that both registers the price and tracks the store's inventory.

Though computers are dominating the news, the boldest headlines are being reserved for reports coming out of the new fields of genetic engineering and in-vitro fertilization. The American biotechnology company Genentech has announced the first GENETICALLY ENGINEERED DRUG, using a transgenic strain of bacteria to produce human insulin. This year's biggest birth announcement is that of the first "test-tube baby" (from an egg fertilized in a laboratory dish).

X-Z

X-RAY IMAGING

In 1895, the German physicist Wilhelm Roentgen was experimenting with a cathode-ray tube whose surface would glow when electric current flowed through the tube. Roentgen noticed that every time he turned on the electricity, a chemically treated piece of paper lying on his workbench began to glow. He knew that cathode rays could not travel more than an inch or two outside the tube. So he theorized that some other, previously undiscovered rays must be traveling through the air to the treated paper. Since X stands for something unknown, Roentgen called the new rays X rays, a name that we still use.

Roentgen soon learned how to produce the new rays on purpose, and studied their characteristics. When he put his hand between the X-ray source and the treated paper, he saw the image of the bones of his hand, and concluded that X rays pass more easily through soft body parts such as skin and muscles than through more solid parts such as bones.

In 1913, the American scientist William Coolidge built the X-ray tube, a more efficient electronic device for producing these rays. Inside the tube's vacuum chamber, the cathode emits electrons that accelerate across the tube toward a positively charged piece of metal, the anode. When some of the speeding electrons directly hit atoms in the anode, they produce X rays. These are beamed through the body part being studied and are picked up by a sheet of photographic film on the other side.

X rays penetrate different materials in different amounts. This difference shows up on the film, revealing the inner structure of the object. Bones and lungs show up especially clearly on X rays. The stomach and intestines can be seen clearly when a patient drinks a barium mixture that X rays cannot easily penetrate. Other kinds of solutions can be injected into blood vessels to produce images of other organs.

In the 1970s, Sir Godfrey Hounsfield of Britain and Allen Cormack of the United States developed an extraordinary new X-ray machine called the computed tomography (CAT or CT) scanner. The machine combines X-ray technology with sophisticated computer programs that produce cross-sectional views of the body. The CAT scan enables doctors to distinguish much smaller differences in soft tissues than can be seen in ordinary X-ray films.

Photographic plate

Object to be X-rayed

Polarizing screen

X rays

X-ray source

Electrons

X rays pass through soft tissue to blacken areas of the photographic plate. Hard tissue such as bone stops the rays, leaving other areas light.

ZIPPER

Not until the twentieth century did any mother order her child to "zip up" before going out in the cold. The idea of a slide fastener is credited to the American inventor Whitcomb Judson,

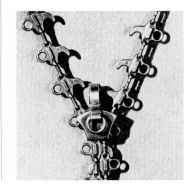

Judson's "clasp locker" proved to be the forerunner of the modern zipper.

who in 1893 exhibited his "clasp locker," a series of hooks and eyes with a sliding device for closing and opening them. In 1923, the B.F. Goodrich Company introduced a hookless version of Judson's invention for closing its new line of overshoes, dubbing it the "zipper." Within five years, such interlocking slide fasteners were widely used on garments and bags.

X Y Z

The Changing World 1995

Whirling through space, two huge spaceships gently make contact on June 29, in a maneuver that thrills millions of earthbound TV viewers. The docking of the U.S. SPACE SHUTTLE *Atlantis* and the Russian space station *Mir* marks a new era in cooperation between the superpowers. The first docking of a U.S. shuttle with a Russian craft, the rendezvous forms the heaviest SATELLITE ever to orbit the Earth.

Also this year, the recently repaired Hubble Space TELESCOPE helps answer the question Where do baby stars come from? From its supreme vantage point outside Earth's distorting atmosphere, Hubble is sending back clear pictures of the Eagle Nebula, some seven thousand light-years away. The nebula's monstrous towers of hydrogen gas and space dust resemble nothing so much as sea serpents. But their tips reveal a glowing nursery of new stars being born.

Meanwhile, back on Earth, TV viewers captivated by the O.J. Simpson murder trial are learning how today's scientists can identify someone by a single strand of hair or drop of blood. The sensational trial has focused world attention on POLYMERASE CHAIN REACTION, a genetic tool used in so-called DNA fingerprinting.

On a more practical matter, the United States is rapidly running out of TELEPHONE numbers, because of an explosion in the number of COMPUTER modems, FACSIMILE (FAX) MACHINES, CELLULAR PHONES, and pagers. To meet the demand, the telecommunications industry is introducing an array of new area codes this year.

The big hit of this year's holiday season is the world's first fully computer-animated, full-length MOTION PICTURE. *Toy Story* has amazed audiences with the three-dimensional, realistic appearance of its characters, including a pull-string cowboy doll named Woody and a plastic space hero named Buzz.

During their historic space rendezvous, the crew of the space shuttle *Atlantis* maneuver the *Mir* Space Station's Kristall module into the shuttle's open cargo bay.

Chronology of Inventions

Invention	World History	
Egyptians use **LOOMS** to weave cloth (c. 4400 B.C.) **WHEELS** are made in Mesopotamia (c. 3500 B.C.) **BRONZE** is invented in Southwestern Asia (c. 3500 B.C.)	5000 to 3500 B.C.	Egyptian and Mesopotamian civilizations develop, characterized by first written records and first city life
AXES with metal blades are forged by Europeans Egyptians make **INK** for writing on papyrus	3000 B.C.	
First reliable metal **SWORDS** are made in Middle East **ARMOR** is worn by warriors in Greece and Sumer	2000 B.C.	Indus civilization flourishes in region of modern Pakistan and northwestern India
Chinese invent the **ABACUS**, the first calculating machine	800 B.C.	
	500 B.C.	Athens becomes leading Greek city-state
Greeks invent the **CATAPULT** for use in warfare	400 B.C.	
	350 B.C.	Alexander the Great extends his Empire from Greece to India
PUMPS are used by Greeks and Persians to remove water from the holds of ships	200 B.C.	Mayan civilization emerges in Mesoamerica
Chinese mix wood pulp and cloth to make **PAPER** **WATER WHEEL** is the first device to harness a power source other than animals **SPINNING WHEELS** are used in Asia	Around the Year 0	Augustus rules Roman Empire
Chinese devise a magnetic **COMPASS**	A.D. 200	
Persians use **WINDMILLS** to pump water for crop irrigation **HARNESS**, or horse-collar, is invented in China	500	Justinian rules Byzantine Empire
Chinese develop **GUNPOWDER**	C. 1000	
	1066	William of Normandy conquers England
First practical **EYEGLASSES** made in Italy (c.1270)	1200s	Genghis Khan founds Mongol Empire
Blacksmiths make the first **GUNS** (c. 1350)	1300s	Ming Dynasty established in China (1368)
Johann Gutenberg invents the **PRINTING PRESS** (1440s) in Germany	1400s	Joan of Arc executed in France (1431) Aztec and Inca empires established in Western Hemisphere Columbus sails to New World (1492)
Galileo invents **THERMOMETER** (1592)	1500s	Arts and literature flourish during European Renaissance Elizabeth I rules England (1558-1603)
	1607	English establish Jamestown colony in Virginia
Galileo builds first astronomical **TELESCOPE**	1609	
Dutch engineer Cornelius Drebbel builds first **SUBMARINE**	1620	
Evangelista Torricelli, an Italian, invents **BAROMETER** to measure atmospheric pressure	1643	
Dutchman Anton von Leeuwenhoek creates one-lens optical **MICROSCOPE**	C. 1660	France, under Louis XIV, is the leading power in Europe
Thomas Newcomen develops early **STEAM ENGINE** in England to pump water from mines	1712	

Invention		World History
Scottish inventor James Watt patents practical, all-purpose **STEAM ENGINE**	1769	
	1776	U.S. Declaration of Independence written
	1789	French Revolution begins George Washington becomes first U.S. President
Eli Whitney's **COTTON GIN** mechanizes removal of seeds from cotton in America	1793	
English doctor Edward Jenner develops **VACCINE** to prevent smallpox Alessandro Volta invents **BATTERY** in Italy	1796	
	1803	Thomas Jefferson purchases Louisiana Territory from France
Development of an early photographic process called the daguerreotype (*see* **CAMERA**)	1829	
First **ELECTRIC MOTORS** are developed in England and Americas	1830s	
McCormick's **REAPER** speeds farm harvests in U.S.	1834	
American Charles Goodyear invents process for **VULCANIZED RUBBER**	1839	
	1848	U.S. wins Mexican War and extends its borders to the Pacific
Bessemer converter permits increased **STEEL** production	1856	
First crude **INTERNAL-COMBUSTION ENGINE** is produced in France	1857	
	1861	U.S. Civil War begins
First **MACHINE GUNS**, developed in U.S., fire 700 rounds a minute	1862	
	1865	Lincoln assassinated; Civil War ends
Alexander Graham Bell invents **TELEPHONE**	1876	Native Americans defeat Custer at Battle of Little Big Horn U.S. celebrates 100th birthday
Thomas Edison invents **PHONOGRAPH**	1877	
Edison develops long-lasting **INCANDESCENT LAMP**	1879	
Improvements lead to wide popularity of **BICYCLES**	1880s	
MOTION PICTURE camera is developed in U.S. and France	1890s	
Gasoline-powered **AUTOMOBILE** is first manufactured in U.S. Wilhelm Roentgen discovers **X RAY** in Germany	1895	
	1898	U.S. fights in Spanish-American War
RADIO signals are transmitted between England and Canada	1901	
Wright Brothers launch the first powered, controllable, heavier-than-air **AIRPLANE**	1903	
	1914	World War I begins
	1917	Russian Revolution begins
	1920	Women win right to vote in U.S.
Robert Goddard launches first liquid-fuel **ROCKET** in U.S.	1926	

Invention		World History
Penicillin, an **ANTIBIOTIC**, is discovered by Sir Alexander Fleming when mold in a laboratory dish kills surrounding bacteria	1928	
Synthetic fabric **NYLON** is made from chemicals by an American, Wallace Carothers Regular **TELEVISION** broadcasts begin **GUIDED MISSILES** are developed in Germany and U.S.	1930s	Great Depression grips U.S.; Franklin D. Roosevelt launches New Deal to stimulate economic recovery World War II begins in Europe
Artificial kidney, or dialysis machine, first used in Netherlands, opening era of **ARTIFICIAL ORGANS**	1940s	
	1941	Japan attacks Pearl Harbor; U.S. enters World War II
First **COMPUTER** performs sequences of operations without human help First **PHOTOCOPIER** is introduced by American Chester Carlson	1944	
The atomic bomb, a **NUCLEAR WEAPON**, is tested in the New Mexico desert	1945	Germany surrenders in Europe U.S. drops atomic bombs on Japan, ending World War II
TRANSISTOR is built by three Americans	1947	
	1950	Korean War begins
First **NUCLEAR REACTOR** generates electric power in Idaho	1951	
Russians launch *Sputnik 1*, a **SATELLITE**, into space First **INTEGRATED CIRCUIT** is produced	1957	
AUTOMATED TELLER MACHINES are introduced in Britain First **LASER** beams are produced by American Theodore Maiman	1960s	
	1964	U.S. involvement in Vietnam War increases
	1969	U.S. astronauts walk on Moon
FIBER OPTICS technology is developed in New York	1970s	
	1973	Last U.S. troops leave Vietnam
First **GENETICALLY ENGINEERED DRUGS** are produced in U.S.	1978	
America's reusable **SPACE SHUTTLE** goes into service **MAGNETIC RESONANCE IMAGING (MRI)** introduced for medical diagnoses by British scientists	1981	Iran releases U.S. hostages held for more than a year
First **CELLULAR PHONES** are test-marketed in Chicago	1983	
Information-retrieval system called World Wide Web is developed (*see* **INTERNET**)	1991	U.S. and allies expel Iraq from Kuwait Communism ends in Russia
U.S. biochemist Kary Mullis wins Nobel Prize for inventing **POLYMERASE CHAIN REACTION**, a process that multiplies DNA fragments for medical tests	1993	
	1995	Car bomb explodes outside federal office building in Oklahoma City, killing 168 people
Mars Pathfinder lands on Mars and deploys robotic rover *Sojourner* to gather data	1997	
	1999	Senate acquits President Bill Clinton of impeachment charges
Scientists announce mapping of human genome, the sequence of chromosomes and genes that determine all human traits	2000	

INDEX

Page numbers that appear in boldface type indicate the main entry on a topic or a feature box on that subject. Those page numbers set in italics indicate the presence of a photograph or diagram.